Vocabulary Workshop

Introductory Course

Norbert Elliot

HOLT, RINEHART AND WINSTON

Austin • *New York* • *Orlando* • *Chicago* • *Atlanta* • *San Francisco* • *Boston* • *Dallas* • *Toronto* • *London*

Author

Norbert Elliot, the author and general editor of this new edition of *Vocabulary Workshop*, has a Ph.D. in English from The University of Tennessee. He is an associate professor of English at New Jersey Institute of Technology. A former site director for the National Writing Project, he has directed summer language arts institutes for kindergarten through twelfth-grade teachers in the public schools. A specialist in test development and evaluation of writing, Norbert Elliot has written books and articles on writing assessment, communication, and critical thinking. Dr. Elliot is the father of five children and is married to Lorna Jean Elliot, under whose care, he says, "everything thrives."

Contributing Writers

Raymond and Sylvia Teague collaborated on the writing of *Making New Words Your Own* and *Reading New Words in Context* for this edition of *Vocabulary Workshop*. The Teagues have been writing educational materials for eight years. After graduating from Texas Christian University, Raymond worked for the *Fort Worth Star-Telegram* as a writer and editor of news and features. He is now the newspaper's children's book editor. Sylvia earned her bachelor's and master's degrees from the University of Texas at Arlington, where she taught economics. Raymond and Sylvia have a daughter, Alexandra, who now attends college. The Teagues live on a mountaintop outside Eureka Springs, Arkansas, where they share a wonderful view, a crowded office, two cats, and an aging goldfish.

Lorna Jean Elliot wrote the *Connecting New Words and Patterns* sections for this edition of *Vocabulary Workshop*. She is a graduate of Susquehanna University, where she taught composition for several years. She earned her Masters of Arts degree in English literature from the Bread Loaf School of English in Middlebury, Vermont. The author of an award-winning novella, Mrs. Elliot currently has her hands full as a freelance writer and as the mother of five thriving children.

Printed in the United States of America

ISBN 0-03-043013-5

2 3 4 5 6 164 95 94

CONTENTS

The Natural World

MAKING NEW WORDS YOUR OWN 1

UNDERSTANDING NEW WORDS AND THEIR USES 123

CONTEXT: Amazing Nature

CONTEXT: People and Places

CONTEXT: Ecology and Environment

CONNECTING NEW WORDS AND PATTERNS 155

READING NEW WORDS IN CONTEXT **173**

CONTEXT: Amazing Nature

CONTEXT: People and Places

CONTEXT: Ecology and Environment

MAKING NEW WORDS YOUR OWN

How We Make New Words Our Own

There are several steps you can take to improve your vocabulary, to make new words your own. Trying to figure out what a word means by looking at the words around it, at its context, is one step. Looking up the word in a dictionary and studying its different definitions is another step. The best way to learn new words is to combine these steps. The exercises that follow will show you how to go about making new words your own.

EXERCISE 1   *Mapping*

In these exercises you will read a new word in a sentence. First, you will be asked to take a guess at its meaning. Next, you will be asked to check your guess against the dictionary and to write the definition of the new word. Finally, you will be asked to find other forms of the word.

Here's an example of a Mapping exercise.

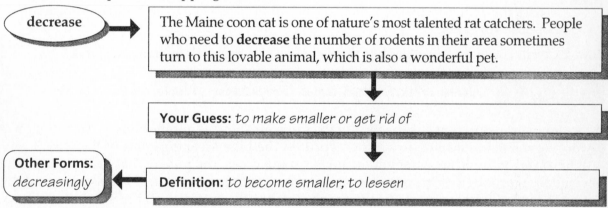

decrease → The Maine coon cat is one of nature's most talented rat catchers. People who need to **decrease** the number of rodents in their area sometimes turn to this lovable animal, which is also a wonderful pet.

Your Guess: *to make smaller or get rid of*

Other Forms: *decreasingly*

Definition: *to become smaller; to lessen*

Hint #1 Look for clues to the meaning of the word in the sentences. The first sentence tells us that Maine coon cats catch rats. The second sentence tells us that the Maine coon is used to **decrease** rodent populations. Catching rats could cause the rodent population to become smaller or to disappear.

Hint #2 Base your guess on a good hunch. In the example, the student guessed **decrease** meant to make smaller or to get rid of.

Hint #3 Be sure to read all the definitions and to choose the one that best fits the given sentence. In this case, the student found definitions for **decrease** both as a verb and as a noun. The student correctly chose the verb's definition. The student also discovered that the second part of the guess was incorrect.

Hint #4 Are there any other forms of the word? In the dictionary, the student found that the adverb form of the word is **decreasingly.**

EXERCISE 2 *Context Clues* ✍

In this exercise you will again see the new word used in a sentence. This exercise gives you the word's definition, and you must match the word in the sentence with its meaning. The word may be used in the same way as it was used in Mapping, or it may be used in a new way.

Here's an example of a Context Clue exercise:

COLUMN A	**COLUMN B**

__D__ **1.** word: _____*decrease*_____ :

v. to become smaller; to lessen;
n. a lessening

(D) Recent years have seen a steady rise in the number of cat owners. On the other hand, there has been a **decrease** in the number of dog owners.

Hint #1 First, scan the definitions in Column A. Then, read Column B and look for clues to the meaning of the word. Here, the words "on the other hand" tell us that the sentence containing the word **decrease** contrasts with the sentence containing the words "a steady rise." Thus, the correct definition is probably the opposite of "a steady rise."

Hint #2 Read column A and look for a likely definition of the word. In the example, the student chose the definition that contained the meaning "a lessening," which is most nearly the opposite of "a rise."

Hint #3 Write the word in the blank so that later you can find its definition at a glance.

EXERCISE 3 *Like Meanings and Opposite Meanings* ✍

A synonym is a word that has practically the same meaning as another word. An antonym is a word opposite in meaning to another word. In the Like Meanings part of Exercise 3, you will be asked to find the synonym for (or, in some cases, the phrase that best defines) the vocabulary word. In the Opposite Meanings part of Exercise 3, you will be asked to find the antonym for (or, in some cases, the phrase that means the opposite of) the vocabulary word.

Here's an example of a Like Meanings item:

21. **decrease** the shedding of fur
   (A) remove
   (B) make comfortable
   (C) add to
   (D) lessen

Hint #1 Don't be fooled by choices that are closely related to the vocabulary word. Choice A may be tempting, but the removal of shedding is more extreme than a **decrease** in shedding.

Hint #2 Don't be fooled by distantly related choices. An animal may be more comfortable when it sheds, but there is no direct link between **decrease** and choice B.

Hint #3 Don't be fooled by the opposite of the vocabulary word. Choice C would be the correct choice if this were an Opposite Meanings exercise, but here you are looking for a similar meaning.

MAKING NEW WORDS YOUR OWN

| Lesson 1 | **CONTEXT: Amazing Nature**

The Humpback: A Whale of a Singer

Last winter, my family and I went on a whale watch near Hawaii. The small boat we were in moved slowly across the water while we looked for whales. Suddenly, a huge humpback whale sprang from the water, curved its back, and disappeared into the waves. When it was underwater, we could hear it singing. How? The boat had an underwater microphone called a hydrophone, which picked up sounds from deep in the water. We were amazed to hear the whale's complex tune. I decided that I had to learn more about these wonderful creatures.

In the following exercises, you will have the opportunity to expand your vocabulary by reading about humpback whales. Below are ten vocabulary words that will be used in these exercises.

| definite | descendant | majority | reliable | twilight |
| deny | doubtful | navigator | symbol | vivid |

| EXERCISE 1 | *Mapping* ✍️

Introduction. In the item below, a vocabulary word is provided and used in a sentence. Take a guess at the word's meaning and write it in the box labeled **Your Guess**. Then look the word up in your dictionary and write the definition in the box labeled **Definition**. Finally, use your dictionary to find other forms of the word, such as adjective, noun, or verb forms. Write these words in the box labeled **Other Forms**.

Then, on a separate sheet of paper, draw your own map and follow the same instructions for each of the nine remaining vocabulary words.

1.

```
( definite ) ──▶ Only male humpbacks sing, and all that are in a group sing the
                 same definite tune. The complicated arrangement of certain tones
                 and sounds is the same for one year, and then a different song is
                 sung the next year.
                                    │
                                    ▼
                 Your Guess:

                                    │
                                    ▼
Other Forms:  ◀── Definition:
```

2.

deny → Whale experts do not **deny** that it is still a mystery why humpbacks compose and sing these songs. There are many theories, but no one has proven whether the songs are to attract females, to establish territory, or to communicate socially.

3.

descendant → Humpbacks spend their summers in polar waters and their winters in warm seas where their calves are born. As the older humpbacks die off, their **descendants** continue to return to the same areas year after year.

4.

doubtful → After I heard the humpback sing, I was not at all **doubtful** of what the guide told us. I believed her when she said that humpbacks are able to make about one thousand different sounds, which include clicks, groans, whistles, screams, and moans.

5.

majority → More than half—that is, the **majority**—of the species of whales have teeth. Out of about eighty species of whales, only eleven species, including the humpback, are baleen (toothless) whales.

6.

navigator → The **navigator** of our boat talked to us as he directed our course to keep us within sight of the humpback. He told us that baleen whales are the largest whales in the world.

7.

reliable → We knew that the people in charge of the whale watch were **reliable**. So we knew we could depend on them for accurate information, such as the fact that adult humpbacks are about fifty feet long and weigh thirty to fifty tons.

8.

symbol → Many people see the whale as a **symbol** of the need for humans to protect the oceans' environment. Once, whales represented only economic gain; now they stand for the beauty and wonder of all ocean life.

9.

twilight → Just after sunset, we headed back to shore. In the **twilight** I looked back over the water for one last sight of the magnificent whale we had been watching.

10.

vivid → Seeing and hearing the humpback is one of the most **vivid** experiences of my life. It remains a bright memory that encourages me to do all that I can to protect whales from extinction.

EXERCISE 2 *Context Clues* ✍

Introduction. Scan the definitions in Column A. Then think about how the boldface words are used in the sentences in Column B. To complete the exercise, match each definition in Column A with the correct vocabulary word from Column B. Write the letter of your choice on the line provided. Finally, write the vocabulary word on the line before the definition.

COLUMN A

_____ **11.** word: _____:
n. more than half the total; the greater part

_____ **12.** word: _____:
adj. having limits; certain

_____ **13.** word: _____:
n. something that stands for or represents something else

_____ **14.** word: _____:
adj. not clear or definite; uncertain

_____ **15.** word: _____:
n. a person who steers or directs a ship or an aircraft

_____ **16.** word: _____:
adj. lively; bright; clearly perceived by the mind

_____ **17.** word: _____:
v. to refuse to give; to reject as untrue

_____ **18.** word: _____:
n. the period from sunset to dark; *adj.* pertaining to the period from sunset to dark

_____ **19.** word: _____:
n. something that comes from an earlier form; offspring

_____ **20.** word: _____:
adj. dependable; trustworthy

COLUMN B

(A) Whales are warmblooded marine mammals. They are the **descendants** of land mammals that adapted to the sea millions of years ago.

(B) Many governments believe the reports of **reliable,** or trustworthy, people who say that whaling has lowered the numbers of whales, including the humpback, to dangerous levels.

(C) It is still **doubtful,** even with bans on most whaling, whether some species will survive—no one knows for sure.

(D) Laws protect whales from whale watchers by setting a **definite** distance the watchers must stay from the whales. Whale watchers must not cross over the set boundary.

(E) In polar waters each humpback eats over four thousand pounds of food a day. The **majority** of this food is made up of tiny sea creatures, but some larger fish are also eaten.

(F) When people observe the humpbacks, they carry away **vivid** impressions clearly locked in their memories.

(G) I had hoped that while the sun was still bright, before **twilight,** I would see a mother humpback and a calf, but none were visible.

(H) When our class formed an environmental club, I didn't want to **deny** them the use of my pamphlets and books about humpbacks. Now everyone in the club uses them.

(I) Because of the club members' interest in humpbacks, they voted to use the humpback as a **symbol** that would represent the club's support of endangered wildlife.

(J) One of our members has decided to become a **navigator** and to spend her life on a ship tracking whales for a wildlife-protection organization.

EXERCISE 3 *Like Meanings and Opposite Meanings* ✍

Introduction. For each item below, circle the letter of the choice that means the same, or about the same, as the boldface word.

21. a **vivid** ocean sunset
(A) light
(B) bright
(C) dark
(D) dull

22. the **navigator** looking for the whales
(A) person who steers a ship
(B) anyone who goes on a ship
(C) whale-watching guide
(D) person who is lost

23. the **majority** of the whale watchers
(A) exactly half
(B) less than half
(C) every one
(D) more than half

24. the **symbol** of ocean life
(A) reality
(B) interest
(C) representative
(D) character

25. a **definite** sign
(A) unlimited
(B) certain
(C) invisible
(D) uncertain

Directions. For each item below, circle the letter of the choice that means the opposite, or about the opposite, of the boldface word.

26. the **twilight** cruise
(A) between sunset and dark
(B) the middle of the night
(C) between sunrise and noon
(D) rainy season

27. **denied** bothering the whales
(A) rejected as untrue
(B) admitted
(C) continued
(D) stopped

28. the **reliable** guide
(A) trustworthy
(B) honest
(C) undependable
(D) independent

29. the **descendants** of the humpbacks
(A) ancestors
(B) children
(C) cousins
(D) region

30. **doubtful** that whales could sing
(A) amazed
(B) suspicious
(C) undecided
(D) certain

MAKING NEW WORDS YOUR OWN

Lesson 2 CONTEXT: Amazing Nature

Fire-breathing Myths: Chinese Dragons

Introduction. What do you think of when you picture a dragon? A scary, cruel monster? An enormous fire-breathing lizard with a long, scaly tail? This is how many people think of dragons. But in China and much of Asia, the dragon is considered to be a friendly, even a lucky, creature. There are many myths about Chinese dragons. In these stories, dragons are described as animals ridden by the gods. Two popular dragon festivals are still held in China. One is the dragon dance, held during the Chinese New Year celebrations. The other is the dragon boat festival, which may have originally been a rainmaking festival.

In the following exercises, you will have the opportunity to expand your vocabulary by reading about Chinese dragons. Below are ten vocabulary words that will be used in these exercises.

astonish	innumerable	journalism	quote	summarize
conference	interview	legend	session	unexpectedly

EXERCISE 1 *Mapping*

Directions. In the item below, a vocabulary word is provided and used in a sentence. Take a guess at the word's meaning and write it in the box labeled **Your Guess**. Then look the word up in your dictionary and write the definition in the box labeled **Definition**. Finally, use your dictionary to find other forms of the word, such as adjective, noun, or verb forms. Write these words in the box labeled **Other Forms**.

Then, on a separate sheet of paper, draw your own map and follow the same instructions for each of the nine remaining vocabulary words.

1.

(**astonish**) ➡ Does it **astonish** you to learn that in Chinese tradition the dragon is a sign of good luck? It sure surprises me.

⬇

Your Guess:

⬇

Other Forms: ⬅ **Definition:**

2.

conference ➤ In some of the dragon myths, rulers would hold **conferences**. At these meetings, they would discuss how they could honor the dragons.

3.

innumerable ➤ Every year **innumerable** people—too many to count—attend the dragon dance in San Francisco.

4.

interview ➤ Would you like to **interview** a dragon? What kinds of questions would you ask if you could meet one face to face?

5.

journalism ➤ Some reporters in the field of **journalism** are interested in collecting and publishing news about Chinese cultural events.

6.

legend ➤ Have you ever heard the **legend** of the dragon of the Gaoliang Bridge? It's one of China's oldest and most popular stories.

7.

quote ➤ The storyteller **quoted** a statement made by an ancient Chinese emperor and then translated the words for us.

8.

session ➤ In the story "Liu Yi and the Dragon King," Liu meets with the dragon king. In this **session**, they discuss the king's daughter.

9.

summarize ➤ I will briefly **summarize** the story of "The Dragon's Pearl." First, a young boy finds a pearl that belongs to a dragon. The pearl makes everything—grass, money, and rice—multiply. By accident, the boy swallows the pearl and turns into a dragon.

10.

unexpectedly ➤ The Chinese believed that angry dragons could cause a lot of trouble **unexpectedly**. For instance, a flood or storm might suddenly occur without warning.

EXERCISE 2 *Context Clues* ✍

Directions. Scan the definitions in Column A. Then think about how the boldface words are used in the sentences in Column B. To complete the exercise, match each definition in Column A with the correct vocabulary word from Column B. Write the letter of your choice on the line provided. Finally, write the vocabulary word on the line before the definition.

COLUMN A

_____ **11.** word: _____:

v. to amaze; to surprise

_____ **12.** word: _____:

n. a popular story or myth handed down for generations; a person whose deeds are remembered as stories; a note on an illustration or map

_____ **13.** word: _____:

n. a face-to-face meeting for evaluating or questioning; *v.* to meet with for the purpose of evaluating or asking questions

_____ **14.** word: _____:

adv. suddenly; in an unannounced way; in a way that was not known before

_____ **15.** word: _____:

v. to reproduce word for word; to refer to as an example; to state, as a price; *n.* words repeated exactly

_____ **16.** word: _____:

adj. too many to be counted; countless

_____ **17.** word: _____:

n. a formal meeting for discussion

_____ **18.** word: _____:

n. the work of collecting, writing, and publishing news

_____ **19.** word: _____:

n. a meeting of a group; a continuous series of such meetings; a period of activity; a school semester or term

_____ **20.** word: _____:

v. to give a brief account of; to say briefly

COLUMN B

(A) St. George, who is said to have fought a dragon in fourteenth-century England, has become a **legend**. His deeds are still remembered.

(B) Like the European dragon, the Chinese dragon is believed to guard **innumerable** priceless treasures. These countless items are hidden in the dragon's lair.

(C) It is difficult to **summarize** Chinese beliefs about dragons. There are just too many to describe briefly.

(D) In an **interview,** the Chinese storyteller Li Cho discussed Chinese dragons. This face-to-face discussion was videotaped.

(E) To **quote** a famous Chinese emperor, "The dragon is the symbol of the throne."

(F) **Journalism** cannot capture the excitement of the dragon boat race. Reading the news is just not the same as being there!

(G) The colorful costumes worn during the dragon-boat festival will **astonish**, or amaze, you.

(H) Storytelling **sessions** in China have always been popular group activities.

(I) Can you imagine a **conference** of dragons? It's funny to think of dragons holding a formal meeting.

(J) Just when we thought he was finished, our teacher **unexpectedly** added a dragon myth to the list of readings for tomorrow.

EXERCISE 3 *Like Meanings and Opposite Meanings* 👉

Directions. For each item below, circle the letter of the choice that means the same, or about the same, as the boldface word.

21. to **astonish** with a roar
 (A) respond
 (B) surprise
 (C) call
 (D) yell at

22. an **interview** with a king
 (A) meeting
 (B) audition
 (C) dance
 (D) argument

23. **journalism** in San Francisco
 (A) storytelling
 (B) celebration
 (C) myth-making
 (D) news-writing

24. to **quote** the price of
 (A) state
 (B) misunderstand
 (C) pay
 (D) hear

25. an afternoon **session**
 (A) nap
 (B) meal
 (C) meeting
 (D) fight

Directions. For each item below, circle the letter of the choice that means the opposite, or about the opposite, of the boldface word.

26. a **conference** of Chinese scholars
 (A) family
 (B) competition
 (C) informal meeting
 (D) interview

27. **innumerable** scales on the dragon's back
 (A) slimy
 (B) few
 (C) hard
 (D) countless

28. a **legend** in Chinese culture
 (A) scholar
 (B) well-known reporter
 (C) little-known figure
 (D) mythical emperor

29. to **summarize** a dragon's actions
 (A) describe in full detail
 (B) predict
 (C) understand fully
 (D) give a brief account of

30. dragons flying overhead **unexpectedly**
 (A) as predicted
 (B) in formation
 (C) angrily
 (D) at a low altitude

MAKING NEW WORDS YOUR OWN

| Lesson 3 | **CONTEXT:** Amazing Nature

Earthquakes: Rocking and Rolling

Imagine that you are sitting on the couch reading a book when the ground begins to tremble. You hold your breath until the shaking stops. You have just experienced an earthquake! What causes earthquakes? An earthquake occurs when pressure builds underground, often along a fault where two large pieces of rock meet. The rock shifts or breaks to relieve the pressure. When this happens, the surface of the earth vibrates for miles around. Not all earthquakes can be felt above ground. Sometimes the only way scientists know there has been an earthquake is if they record it on a special machine called a seismograph.

In the following exercises, you will have the opportunity to expand your vocabulary by reading about earthquakes. Below are ten vocabulary words that will be used in these exercises.

| collapse | disastrous | foundation | incident | nuisance |
| collide | fatal | ignore | mischievous | predict |

EXERCISE 1   *Mapping* ✍

Directions. In the item below, a vocabulary word is provided and used in a sentence. Take a guess at the word's meaning and write it in the box labeled **Your Guess**. Then look the word up in your dictionary and write the definition in the box labeled **Definition**. Finally, use your dictionary to find other forms of the word, such as adjective, noun, or verb forms. Write these words in the box labeled **Other Forms**.

Then, on a separate sheet of paper, draw your own map and follow the same instructions for each of the nine remaining vocabulary words.

1.

collapse → Recent efforts to make earthquake insurance available to all Californians have **collapsed**. Talks between insurance companies and members of Congress have broken down.

Your Guess:

Other Forms:

Definition:

2.

collide ➤ Tsunamis are tidal waves caused by earthquakes. Great walls of water, sometimes two hundred feet high, **collide** with the shore at incredible speeds. If they crash into populated areas, they can cause much damage and loss of life.

3.

disastrous ➤ San Francisco has been the site of two **disastrous** earthquakes—in 1906 and 1989. Both earthquakes caused great damage.

4.

fatal ➤ Earthquakes can be **fatal**. More than 230,000 people died in 1976 in a quake in northern China.

5.

foundation ➤ The **foundation** of the Transamerica Pyramid in San Francisco is designed to be earthquake-proof. When the earth shakes, the base of the building rolls back and forth.

6.

ignore ➤ Although it is tempting to **ignore** the facts, any region that has had earthquakes in the past may expect them in the future. People who live in these places should not disregard the danger.

7.

incident ➤ Sometimes earthquakes cause changes in the level of the earth's surface. A major shock hit Alaska in 1899. After the **incident**, some parts of the sea floor were fifty feet higher.

8.

mischievous ➤ Many tall tales are told about earthquakes. One story is that the earth opens up during a quake, swallows people and houses, and then closes. This tale is told by **mischievous** people who like to tease others.

9.

nuisance ➤ Planning ahead for earthquakes can seem like a bother. But in spite of the **nuisance**, it is wise to think ahead.

10.

predict ➤ Some people believe that weather and animal behavior can help **predict** earthquakes and can warn people when the earthquakes might happen.

EXERCISE 2   Context Clues

Directions. Scan the definitions in Column A. Then think about how the boldface words are used in the sentences in Column B. To complete the exercise, match the definition in Column A with the correct vocabulary word from Column B. Write the letter of your choice on the line provided. Finally, write the vocabulary word on the line before the definition.

COLUMN A	COLUMN B

_____ **11.** word: _____:
adj. teasing; full of tricks that annoy; naughty

_____ **12.** word: _____:
n. the base on which something is built; an establishment or fund; a basic principle; basis

_____ **13.** word: _____:
adj. seriously harmful; damaging

_____ **14.** word: _____:
n. something or somebody causing annoyance or inconvenience

_____ **15.** word: _____:
v. to crash; to come together with a violent impact; to come into conflict

_____ **16.** word: _____:
v. to foretell events; to tell what will happen at some future time

_____ **17.** word: _____:
n. something that happens; an event

_____ **18.** word: _____:
v. to fall down or fall apart; to break down or fail suddenly; *n.* the act of falling down

_____ **19.** word: _____:
adj. destructive; resulting in death; important to the outcome of something; decisive; having to do with fate

_____ **20.** word: _____:
v. to disregard; to pay no attention to

(A) After the Mexico City earthquake of 1985, a special **foundation,** or organization, was set up to help the survivors.

(B) People who live in earthquake-prone regions should be careful. It is dangerous to **ignore** warnings about earthquakes.

(C) The earth experiences about fifty thousand earthquakes each year. Luckily, however, a **disastrous** earthquake only occurs about once every two years. The rest do little damage.

(D) Most quakes are light shocks. They might be a **nuisance,** but they do not cause serious harm.

(E) Computers help scientists **predict** earthquakes. But it is still hard to tell for certain where and when an earthquake will strike.

(F) In fact, an earthquake may be occurring nearby at this very moment, but it may be so slight that you are unaware of the **incident**.

(G) Earthquakes usually don't harm people directly. Many injuries are caused when objects **collide** or crash into each other or when buildings fall down or catch fire.

(H) One of the earliest recorded **fatal** earthquakes took place in Corinth, Greece, in A.D. 856. About forty-five thousand people were killed.

(I) Most one- and two-story buildings survive serious earthquakes. They do not **collapse** unless their roofs are too heavy.

(J) My **mischievous,** troublemaking brother once played a trick on me. When I was asleep, he rocked my bed back and forth. I woke up sure there was an earthquake!

EXERCISE 3 *Like Meanings and Opposite Meanings*

Directions. For each item below, circle the letter of the choice that means the same, or about the same, as the boldface word.

21. to **collide** with great force
(A) bend
(B) divide
(C) rise
(D) crash

22. a **foundation** of self-respect
(A) basis
(B) high expectation
(C) definition
(D) certain kind

23. an earthshaking **incident**
(A) party
(B) event
(C) story
(D) visit

24. a great **nuisance**
(A) explanation
(B) belief
(C) annoyance
(D) picture

25. to **predict** an earthquake
(A) analyze
(B) live through
(C) describe
(D) foretell

Directions. For each item below, circle the letter of the choice that means the opposite, or about the opposite, of the boldface word.

26. the **collapse** of homes
(A) expansion
(B) building
(C) selling
(D) painting

27. a **disastrous** tidal wave
(A) helpful
(B) harmful
(C) surprising
(D) enormous

28. a **fatal** event
(A) important
(B) boring
(C) free
(D) life-giving

29. to **ignore** warnings
(A) pay attention to
(B) issue
(C) disregard completely
(D) suggest

30. a **mischievous** child
(A) well-behaved
(B) troublesome
(C) highly entertaining
(D) exciting

MAKING NEW WORDS YOUR OWN

Lesson 4 | CONTEXT: Amazing Nature

There They Go Again: Animal Migrations

All animals must have food and a safe place to raise their young. Twice a year, in the spring and fall, certain animals travel hundreds and sometimes thousands of miles. They migrate between two home areas that are often far apart. These animals include birds, whales, bats, caribou, butterflies, fish, and other animals. Scientists are still trying to understand how animals find their way around the globe. Some birds, for instance, fly thousands of miles. Often, they return in the spring to the same nests they left in the fall. How do you think they find their way back?

In the following exercises, you will have the opportunity to expand your vocabulary by reading about animal migrations. Below are ten vocabulary words that will be used in these exercises.

aviation	declare	departure	disturb	locally
bombard	demonstration	detect	exception	miraculous

EXERCISE 1 | Mapping ✍

Directions. In the item below, a vocabulary word is provided and used in a sentence. Take a guess at the word's meaning and write it in the box labeled **Your Guess**. Then look the word up in your dictionary and write the definition in the box labeled **Definition**. Finally, use your dictionary to find other forms of the word, such as adjective, noun, or verb forms. Write these words in the box labeled **Other Forms**.

Then, on a separate sheet of paper, draw your own map and follow the same instructions for each of the nine remaining vocabulary words.

1.

aviation → The Arctic Tern is a miracle of **aviation**. It flies about twenty-two thousand miles each year—as much as some airplanes!

Your Guess:

Other Forms:

Definition:

2.

bombard → Baby turtles find the ocean soon after they hatch. They crawl toward the shore and **bombard** the water as they dive in with a great splash.

3.

declare → Rosie **declared** in her science class, "I saw a flock of geese flying south this morning." She made the announcement so other students could look for geese, too.

4.

demonstration → A **demonstration** was held at the university last Friday. Students wanted to show their support for blue whales, which are hunted when they migrate.

5.

departure → The **departure** of the Pacific salmon from the rivers marks the beginning of a long journey. Four years after leaving the rivers for the sea, the salmon will return and swim upstream against a fierce current to breed.

6.

detect → Birds that travel at night **detect** the positions of the stars. Seeing the stars helps them travel in the right direction.

7.

disturb → The destruction of the rain forest and other nesting places means that fewer songbirds breed each year. This problem **disturbs** many scientists and lovers of nature.

8.

exception → Most mammals cannot fly. The bat is an **exception**: With its wings it can fly quite well.

9.

locally → Whooping cranes are rare, endangered birds. **Locally** popular in Texas, where they spend the winter, they are eagerly welcomed every year.

10.

miraculous → Hummingbirds, which weigh only one eighth of an ounce, do a **miraculous** thing every year. They fly about five hundred miles across the Gulf of Mexico. Amazingly, they make the trip in about ten hours!

EXERCISE 2 *Context Clues*

Directions. Scan the definitions in Column A. Then think about how the boldface words are used in the sentences in Column B. To complete the exercise, match each definition in Column A with the correct vocabulary word from Column B. Write the letter of your choice on the line provided. Finally, write the vocabulary word on the line before the definition.

COLUMN A

_____ **11.** word: _____:
n. the art or science of flying airplanes

_____ **12.** word: _____:
v. to break up order or quiet; to upset someone emotionally; to bother

_____ **13.** word: _____:
adj. like a miracle; wonderful; able to work a miracle

_____ **14.** word: _____:
adv. within a given area; in a local way

_____ **15.** word: _____:
v. to attack physically or verbally without stopping

_____ **16.** word: _____:
v. to announce; to make clearly known

_____ **17.** word: _____:
n. a person to whom or a case to which something does not apply; something left out

_____ **18.** word: _____:
n. the act of proving something through example; the act of showing something through example; an outward display of, or a gathering to express, an opinion or protest

_____ **19.** word: _____:
v. to discover; to notice something not obvious

_____ **20.** word: _____:
n. the act of going away or leaving

COLUMN B

(A) When monarch butterflies migrate to and from Mexico, wind and other obstacles do not **disturb**, or bother, them.

(B) According to Africans who share the forest with elephants, the enormous creatures stay **locally** for the summer. They only move to the open country when it rains.

(C) If you look carefully, you may **detect** bands attached to the legs of some migrating birds. These bands are placed there by scientists and are used to track the birds' movements.

(D) If you ask a bird-watcher to explain migration to you, be careful. He or she will probably **bombard** you with so much information that you may feel as if you are under fire.

(E) People who practice **aviation** tell interesting stories. These pilots sometimes see thousands of migrating birds that fly too high to be seen from the ground.

(F) The whalebone whale is an **exception** to many migrating animals. Unlike them, it travels to colder regions to find food.

(G) After the **departure** of singing warblers in the fall, the empty trees they leave behind are silent.

(H) The amazing penguin performs a **miraculous** trick—it never lets its eggs touch the ice after they have been laid.

(I) At the nature center, the ranger held a **demonstration** to show hikers how to avoid dangerous wildlife on the trails.

(J) First, the senator **declared** that Grove State Park would be a sanctuary for migrating birds. Then she made some other announcements.

EXERCISE 3 | *Like Meanings and Opposite Meanings* ✍

Directions. For each item below, circle the letter of the choice that means the same, or about the same, as the boldface word.

21. the science of **aviation**
(A) diving
(B) migration
(C) biology
(D) flying

22. to **bombard** from the air
(A) attack
(B) fall
(C) float
(D) drive

23. a **demonstration** of the facts
(A) simplifying
(B) fight
(C) showing
(D) division

24. to **detect** migrating whales
(A) hunt
(B) follow
(C) assist
(D) discover

25. an **exception**, the flying bat
(A) identical situation
(B) special case
(C) warmblooded mammal
(D) rejection

Directions. For each item below, circle the letter of the choice that means the opposite, or about the opposite, of the boldface word.

26. to **declare** an opinion
(A) form
(B) make known publicly
(C) understand
(D) keep hidden

27. the **departure** of the caribou
(A) arrival
(B) death
(C) absence
(D) leaving

28. to **disturb** a gathering of birds
(A) restore calm to
(B) openly observe
(C) greatly annoy
(D) track down

29. birds found nesting **locally**
(A) nearby
(B) along the coast
(C) within an area
(D) far away

30. **miraculous** migrating animals
(A) unhealthy
(B) amazing
(C) ordinary
(D) wonderful

MAKING NEW WORDS YOUR OWN

| Lesson 5 | **CONTEXT: Amazing Nature**

Lava Alert at Hawaii's Kilauea Volcano

How would you like to visit an active volcano? Kilauea is one of the most active volcanoes in the world. It lies on the eastern slopes of the Mauna Loa volcano in Hawaii Volcanoes National Park. The park is located on the big island of Hawaii. Kilauea's crater is two and a half miles long, two miles wide, and four hundred feet deep. At one point, a smaller crater within this large one held a lake of molten lava. Kilauea erupts regularly, and visitors to the park often see these eruptions.

In the following exercises, you will have the opportunity to expand your vocabulary by reading about Hawaii's Kilauea volcano. Below are ten vocabulary words that will be used in these exercises.

caution	dread	generation	heroic	previous
congratulate	error	gratitude	involve	separation

EXERCISE 1   *Mapping*

Directions. In the item below, a vocabulary word is provided and used in a sentence. Take a guess at the word's meaning and write it in the box labeled **Your Guess**. Then look the word up in your dictionary and write the definition in the box labeled **Definition**. Finally, use your dictionary to find other forms of the word, such as adjective, noun, or verb forms. Write these words in the box labeled **Other Forms**.

Then, on a separate sheet of paper, draw your own map and follow the same instructions for each of the nine remaining vocabulary words.

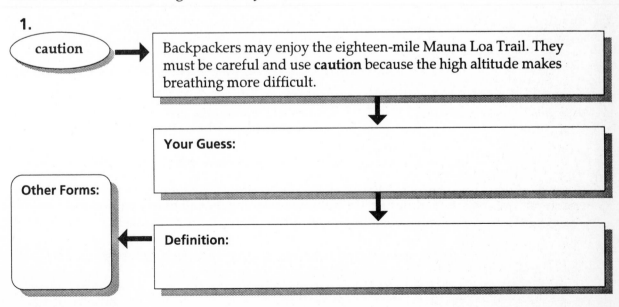

1.

caution → Backpackers may enjoy the eighteen-mile Mauna Loa Trail. They must be careful and use **caution** because the high altitude makes breathing more difficult.

Your Guess:

Other Forms:

Definition:

2.

The Volcano House, a famous hotel, is located on the rim of Kilauea's Halemaumau crater. Anyone spending the night there should be **congratulated,** or praised, for their good fortune.

3.

Many visitors to Kilauea feel **dread**. They are afraid the volcano might erupt and hurt them.

4.

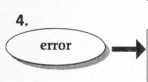

It would be an **error** to say that no one has been injured by Kilauea. In 1924, a photographer was killed by a falling rock from the Halemaumau crater.

5.

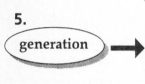

Devastation Trail leads through a forest that was burned by cinder and lava in 1959. An entire **generation** of trees, all from the same time period, were killed.

6.

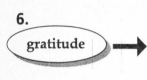

We thanked the Kilauea park ranger for showing us the Thurston Lava Tube. We walked through the tube, which is more than 450 feet long, and we felt **gratitude** for the special experience.

7.

Some Hawaiians believe that the goddess Pele lives in the steaming Halemaumau crater. They think that anyone brave enough to walk near the crater must be truly **heroic**!

8.

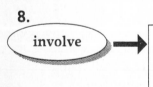

A visit to the Volcano House should **involve** many activities. A typical visit, for example, may include watching a film of the 1959 eruption.

9.

From 1823 to 1924, Kilauea's Halemaumau crater was full of bubbling molten lava. **Previous** visitors had a thrill that today's tourists can only imagine.

10.

Separation on the trails is something that all hikers on Kilauea should avoid. It is important for hikers to stay together.

EXERCISE 2 *Context Clues*

Directions. Scan the definitions in Column A. Then think about how the boldface words are used in the sentences in Column B. To complete the exercise, match each definition in Column A with the correct vocabulary word from Column B. Write the letter of your choice on the line provided. Finally, write the vocabulary word on the line before the definition.

COLUMN A	COLUMN B
_____ **11.** word: _____: *n.* a feeling of grateful appreciation for something received or something done	(A) Some fearful people **dread** walking into the Kilauea Iki crater. Although it is cool today, twenty-five years ago it was a boiling—and frightening—lake of lava.
_____ **12.** word: _____: *n.* a warning; carefulness; *v.* to warn	(B) Ruins in the national park show where people who lived many **generations** ago practiced ancient rituals.
_____ **13.** word: _____: *v.* to include; to relate to; to associate	(C) Our **previous** visit to Kilauea was not as interesting as the trip this time.
_____ **14.** word: _____: *n.* a wrong belief or opinion; a wrongdoing; a mistake	(D) I **congratulate** and applaud you for back-packing to the top of the volcano. Good for you!
_____ **15.** word: _____: *v.* to express pleasure for general good fortune or success	(E) You will feel **gratitude** after you have walked through Sulfur Banks. I always feel thankful after I have passed by that foul-smelling area.
_____ **16.** word: _____: *adj.* brave; strong and noble; like a hero	(F) The government is eager to get **involved**, or to associate, with people who want to preserve Hawaii Volcanoes National Park.
_____ **17.** word: _____: *n.* all the people born and living at about the same time and having similar experiences; the average period of time between the births of parent and child; the act or process of bringing into being; production	(G) A **heroic** Hawaiian queen once bravely and nobly walked right up to the edge of the crater while Kilauea was erupting.
	(H) The national park creates a **separation** between Hilo, a region of Hawaii, and southern Hawaii. The two parts of the island are divided by volcanoes.
_____ **18.** word: _____: *n.* a setting or putting apart; a division	(I) To believe that Kilauea will stop erupting is an **error**. Scientists can tell you correctly that Kilauea is still active.
_____ **19.** word: _____: *v.* to look forward to with fear; *n.* great fear; *adj.* inspiring awe or fear	(J) I **caution** all visitors to Kilauea to avoid wandering off the trails. I warn them that it is easy to get lost, and it is very dangerous!
_____ **20.** word: _____: *adj.* occurring before something or someone else in time or order	

EXERCISE 3 *Like Meanings and Opposite Meanings* ☞

Directions. For each item below, circle the letter of the choice that means the same, or about the same, as the boldface word.

21. to **caution** about bubbling lava
- (A) warn
- (B) inform
- (C) excite
- (D) write

22. the **dreaded** Devastation Trail
- (A) steep
- (B) isolated
- (C) awe-inspiring
- (D) fun

23. the **generation** of steam from the volcano
- (A) relation
- (B) bringing forth
- (C) slowing down
- (D) explosion

24. to **involve** the Hawaiian government
- (A) inform
- (B) invade
- (C) insult
- (D) include

25. the **separation** from populated areas
- (A) tourists
- (B) pollution
- (C) setting apart
- (D) lack of help

Directions. For each item below, circle the letter of the choice that means the opposite, or about the opposite, of the boldface word.

26. to **congratulate** about success
- (A) show interest
- (B) show feelings
- (C) show sorrow
- (D) show pleasure

27. an **error** about Kilauea's elevation
- (A) correction
- (B) guideline
- (C) mistake
- (D) description

28. with **gratitude** for the wonders of the earth
- (A) too much concern
- (B) complete confusion
- (C) total respect
- (D) lack of thankfulness

29. the **heroic** mountain climber
- (A) timid
- (B) tired
- (C) brave
- (D) experienced

30. the **previous** volcanic eruptions
- (A) ancient
- (B) dangerous
- (C) following
- (D) minor

MAKING NEW WORDS YOUR OWN

Lesson 6 | CONTEXT: Amazing Nature
Going Batty: A Look at the Only True Flying Mammal

Have you ever heard the expressions "blind as a bat" and "he's got bats in his belfry"? Have you been afraid of being bitten by a vampire bat when you've been outside at night? Well, you'll be glad to know that bats have been getting a bad rap. Most bats eat insects, though some eat fish and fruit. The vampire bat does eat blood, but it does not cause serious harm unless it has rabies. In fact, most bats are helpful to human beings. They eat tons of insects every night. And bat guano, or manure, is a valuable fertilizer. In Asia, bats are considered signs of good luck, happiness, and long life.

In the following exercises, you will have the opportunity to expand your vocabulary by reading about bats. Below are ten vocabulary words that will be used in these exercises.

abdomen	competition	flexible	hoist	mobile
commotion	escort	foe	maximum	paralysis

EXERCISE 1 *Mapping*

Directions. In the item below, a vocabulary word is provided and used in a sentence. Take a guess at the word's meaning and write it in the box labeled **Your Guess**. Then look the word up in your dictionary and write the definition in the box labeled **Definition**. Finally, use your dictionary to find other forms of the word, such as adjective, noun, or verb forms. Write these words in the box labeled **Other Forms**.

Then, on a separate sheet of paper, draw your own map and follow the same instructions for each of the nine remaining vocabulary words.

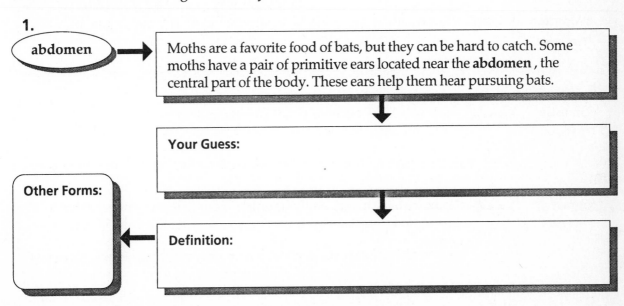

1.

abdomen → Moths are a favorite food of bats, but they can be hard to catch. Some moths have a pair of primitive ears located near the **abdomen**, the central part of the body. These ears help them hear pursuing bats.

Your Guess:

Other Forms:

Definition:

2.

commotion → Bat colonies are extremely noisy places. Yet, in spite of the **commotion**, mothers are able to locate their young by sound.

3.

competition → Roosting areas are often very crowded. There is a lot of **competition** for space as each bat struggles to claim its own territory.

4.

escort → When young bats begin to fly, they are often **escorted** by their mothers, who fly along next to them.

5.

flexible → Unlike the vampire bat, which eats only blood, most insect-eating bats have a **flexible** diet. They can eat a wide variety of insects, from moths to mosquitoes.

6.

foe → Bats do not have many enemies, since they hang from high, hard-to-get-at places. But snakes, owls, and hawks are **foes** of bats.

7.

hoist → Some bats eat fish. They swoop down on the water, snatch the fish, and **hoist** the fish into the air with their powerful hind claws.

8.
maximum → How many different kinds of bats are there? The **maximum**, or greatest, number is about nine hundred.

9.
mobile → Most bats have extremely **mobile** ears and noses. By moving them back and forth, bats are able to hear and smell obstacles and food.

10.
paralysis → Vampire bats are generally harmless. People used to believe that a bite would cause **paralysis**, making it impossible for the victim to move.

EXERCISE 2 *Context Clues* 🖎

Directions. Scan the definitions in Column A. Then think about how the boldface words are used in the sentences in Column B. To complete the exercise, match each definition in Column A with the correct vocabulary word from Column B. Write the letter of your choice on the line provided. Finally, write the vocabulary word on the line before the definition.

COLUMN A	COLUMN B
_____ **11.** word: _____: *n.* the middle part of the body, containing the stomach and other organs; the belly	(A) Dr. Lyons used a **hoist** to lift me into the cave. Then he moved the equipment aside so we wouldn't trip over it.
_____ **12.** word: _____: *v.* to lift or pull up; *n.* a tool or piece of equipment used to pull things up	(B) A bat's fingers support the **flexible** skin of its wings. When the fingers bend, the wings can bend also.
_____ **13.** word: _____: *n.* one or more persons who accompany another; *v.* to go with someone	(C) My science class had a **competition** to see how many kinds of bats we could name. I won the contest!
_____ **14.** word: _____: *adj.* able to move or change easily; movable	(D) As with most mammals, a bat's legs and tail are located below its **abdomen**, or stomach area.
_____ **15.** word: _____: *n.* confusion; noisy rushing around; disturbance; violent motion	(E) Bats eat insects that are the **foes** of farmers. Farmers hate these insects because of the damage the insects do to crops.
_____ **16.** word: _____: *n.* an enemy	(F) Our class visited a bat cave last year. A park ranger was our **escort**, leading us through the cave.
_____ **17.** word: _____: *adj.* able to bend without breaking; easily influenced; easily changed	(G) The first time I saw a bat, I couldn't move. The **paralysis** caused by fear struck my entire body.
_____ **18.** word: _____: *n.* partial or complete loss of a function; a condition in which one cannot act	(H) When tracking down fish, fish-eating bats look for **commotion** in the water. Where violent splashing can be seen, a bat's dinner may be nearby.
_____ **19.** word: _____: *n.* the greatest amount or number possible or reached; *adj.* greatest possible or reached	(I) Bat experts estimate that about 750,000 bats live under the Congress Avenue bridge in Austin, Texas. This is the **maximum**, or greatest number, of bats ever found living in an urban area.
_____ **20.** word: _____: *n.* rivalry; contest	(J) Bats are extremely **mobile**. They move easily around obstacles, even when flying very fast.

EXERCISE 3 *Like Meanings and Opposite Meanings* ✍

Directions. For each item below, circle the letter of the choice that means the same, or about the same, as the boldface word.

21. a furry **abdomen**
(A) head
(B) foot
(C) tail
(D) belly

22. a **competition** for the best flyer
(A) fight
(B) contest
(C) hunt
(D) reward

23. an experienced **escort**
(A) guide
(B) expert
(C) scientist
(D) worker

24. to **hoist** into a cave
(A) push off
(B) fall down
(C) pull up
(D) fly over

25. **paralysis** caused by fear
(A) total panic
(B) loss of function
(C) extreme worry
(D) confusion

Directions. For each item below, circle the letter of the choice that means the opposite, or about the opposite, of the boldface word.

26. a busy **commotion**
(A) confusion
(B) peacefulness
(C) movement
(D) mess

27. **flexible** in its diet
(A) movable
(B) unchangeable
(C) inventive
(D) interested

28. an imaginary **foe**
(A) enemy
(B) insect
(C) farmer
(D) friend

29. the **maximum** wingspan
(A) least possible
(B) measurable
(C) greatest possible
(D) fastest

30. **mobile** ears and head
(A) brown
(B) still
(C) furry
(D) movable

MAKING NEW WORDS YOUR OWN

Lesson 7 CONTEXT: Amazing Nature

Horses: Galloping Through History

The horse probably would not agree with the old saying that a dog is a human's best friend. After all, horses have been around as long as humans. Fossil records show that the first horses appeared about fifty million years ago. About six thousand years ago, people began taming horses. That was the start of a long, productive, and friendly relationship. Over the years, horses have carried people in battle, worked their fields, provided transportation, run races, inspired art, and given friendship.

In the following exercises, you will have the opportunity to expand your vocabulary by reading about horses and their relationship to people throughout history. Below are ten vocabulary words that will be used in these exercises.

dainty	discourage	inhale	regulate	vacuum
discomfort	earnest	linger	requirement	vault

EXERCISE 1 *Mapping* ✍

Directions. In the item below, a vocabulary word is provided and used in a sentence. Take a guess at the word's meaning and write it in the box labeled **Your Guess**. Then look the word up in your dictionary and write the definition in the box labeled **Definition**. Finally, use your dictionary to find other forms of the word, such as adjective, noun, or verb forms. Write these words in the box labeled **Other Forms**.

Then, on a separate sheet of paper, draw your own map and follow the same instructions for each of the nine remaining vocabulary words.

1.

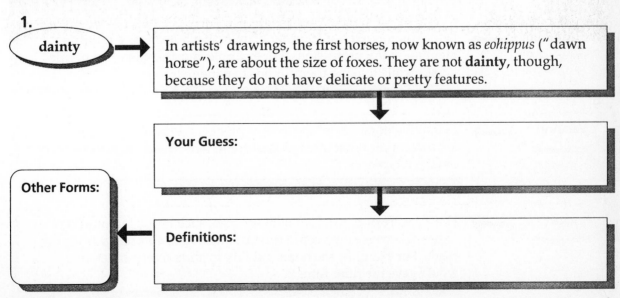

dainty → In artists' drawings, the first horses, now known as *eohippus* ("dawn horse"), are about the size of foxes. They are not **dainty**, though, because they do not have delicate or pretty features.

Your Guess:

Other Forms:

Definitions:

2.

(discomfort) ➤ Greek warriors around 1500 B.C. may have experienced some **discomfort** while riding in horse-drawn chariots. Bumping along on rough roads must have been painful at times.

3.

(discourage) ➤ Apparently, Christopher Columbus's advisors did not **discourage** him from bringing horses to the New World on his second voyage in 1493. Such negative advice might have delayed the horse's introduction into the Americas.

4.

(earnest) ➤ When Native Americans first saw European horses in the 1400s, their surprise was no doubt **earnest**. Their response was so sincere because horses had not been seen in the Americas since 9000 B.C.

5.

(inhale) ➤ In King Louis XIV's enormous stables at Versailles, a visitor could **inhale** without breathing in unpleasant fumes. The horses were so well cared for that a German prince once said they lived better than he did.

6.

(linger) ➤ Even the bravest fighters would not **linger** when they saw a war horse charging at them. Ancient stone carvings show soldiers fleeing from archers atop fierce-looking horses.

7.

(regulate) ➤ The golden age of horse travel was from 1700 to 1900 in Europe and North America. During that time, companies were formed to **regulate** stagecoach systems. In the 1800s, there were also companies that controlled the iron horses, or trains.

8.

(requirement) ➤ Before motorized transportation, owning a horse was a **requirement** for many professions. For example, most doctors had to ride horses while making their rounds to patients.

9.

(vacuum) ➤ Removing horses from the lives of pioneers certainly would have left a **vacuum**. What other animal could have filled the horse's space or taken its place?

10.

(vault) ➤ Horses were once used for mail services, such as the famous Pony Express, because they could run fast and even **vault** obstacles in the roads. For example, the horse's ability to jump over a fallen tree would save the rider time.

EXERCISE 2   Context Clues ✍

Directions. Scan the definitions in Column A. Then think about how the boldface words are used in the sentences in Column B. To complete the exercise, match each definition in Column A with the correct vocabulary word from Column B. Write the letter of your choice on the line provided. Finally, write the vocabulary word on the line before the definition.

COLUMN A	COLUMN B

_____ **11.** word: _____:
v. to continue to stay; to delay or loiter

(A) Knowledge of horses in art is a **requirement** in this class. Also necessary is a knowledge of horses in sports.

_____ **12.** word: _____:
n. uneasiness; minor pain; lack of comfort

(B) Throughout history, horses have been popular subjects of artists. Some paintings portray **dainty** show horses, and others show large workhorses that are not very handsome.

_____ **13.** word: _____:
n. an arched ceiling; a secure room for storing valuables; a burial chamber; a jump; *v.* to jump over

(C) On the arched ceiling is a beautiful painting of horses. The artist used a very tall ladder to reach the **vault** to paint it.

_____ **14.** word: _____:
v. to draw into the lungs; to breathe in

(D) At the museum, I **lingered** to look at the bronze horses created by Frederic Remington. I wanted to stay to see his paintings, too, but I ran out of time.

_____ **15.** word: _____:
adj. serious; not joking; sincere

(E) The **earnest** guide pointed to the painting by Velásquez called *The Lances (Las Lanzas).* "Look at how the artist uses the horses to create depth," the guide said seriously.

_____ **16.** word: _____:
v. to take away courage or confidence; to advise (a person) against something

(F) President Andrew Jackson loved racing horses. Not being able to race horses would have left a **vacuum** in his life—a space that politics alone could not have filled.

_____ **17.** word: _____:
n. something that is necessary or demanded; a necessity

(G) The best jockeys are confident of their abilities. They are not **discouraged** when they ride horses that have never before won.

_____ **18.** word: _____:
adj. delicate and pretty

(H) I wouldn't want to be a jockey because of the **discomfort** of bouncing on a racing horse—it seems very uncomfortable.

_____ **19.** word: _____:
n. a completely empty space; a space left empty by the removal of something usually in it; *v.* to clean with a machine that works by suction

(I) Most horses used in polo matches tire after fifteen minutes of play. You can see them **inhale** deeply in frantic attempts to draw air into their lungs.

_____ **20.** word: _____:
v. to control, govern, or direct according to rule or system; to adjust to a certain standard

(J) The temperature must be **regulated** in some stables for the comfort of the horses. Adjusting the temperature is also important for their health.

EXERCISE 3 *Like Meanings and Opposite Meanings* ✍

Directions. For each item below, circle the letter of the choice that means the same, or about the same, as the boldface word.

21. **vaulted** the hurdle
    (A) jumped over
    (B) stood on
    (C) looked over
    (D) sat on

22. a **vacuum** left by a retired racehorse
    (A) filled space
    (B) deep space
    (C) last place
    (D) empty space

23. **regulated** the American quarter horse show
    (A) neglected
    (B) approved
    (C) controlled
    (D) helped

24. to **discourage** the young jockey
    (A) discover
    (B) praise
    (C) make changes in
    (D) advise against

25. a **requirement** for horse ownership
    (A) suggestion
    (B) necessity
    (C) plan
    (D) luxury

Directions. For each item below, circle the letter of the choice that means the opposite, or about the opposite, of the boldface word.

26. the circus pony's **dainty** costume
    (A) new and costly
    (B) delicate and pretty
    (C) heavy and ugly
    (D) old and cheap

27. **linger** by the Clydesdales
    (A) hurry
    (B) live
    (C) hang around
    (D) sing

28. the harnessed horse's **discomfort**
    (A) uneasiness
    (B) dance
    (C) ease
    (D) expression

29. **inhaled** the dust from the racetrack
    (A) breathed in
    (B) breathed out
    (C) chewed up
    (D) blinded by

30. an **earnest** knight's stallion
    (A) serious
    (B) concerned
    (C) joking
    (D) happy

MAKING NEW WORDS YOUR OWN

Lesson 8   CONTEXT: Amazing Nature

Texas Dinosaurs

You would expect Texas-sized dinosaurs to have roamed the land that became the Lone Star State. In fact, sixteen different species of dinosaurs, or "terrible lizards," once lived in Texas. Some were small; others were gigantic. Some were quiet plant eaters; others were fierce meat eaters. They lived a long time ago—65 to 135 million years ago. Their fossils and footprints have been found in three areas of Texas: the Panhandle, North Central to West Texas, and the Big Bend area.

In the following exercises, you will have the opportunity to expand your vocabulary by reading about the dinosaurs of Texas. Below are ten vocabulary words that will be used in these exercises.

assault	disguise	hibernate	impostor	reference
conceal	gasp	imitate	portion	terminal

EXERCISE 1   *Mapping*

Directions. In the item below, a vocabulary word is provided and used in a sentence. Take a guess at the word's meaning and write it in the box labeled **Your Guess**. Then look the word up in your dictionary and write the definition in the box labeled **Definition**. Finally, use your dictionary to find other forms of the word, such as adjective, noun, or verb forms. Write these words in the box labeled **Other Forms**.

Then, on a separate sheet of paper, draw your own map and follow the same instructions for each of the nine remaining vocabulary words.

1.

assault → The mighty tyrannosaurus, which lived in the Big Bend area, would **assault** other dinosaurs. Its attacks must have been frightening because the tyrannosaurus weighed six to seven tons, was forty feet long, stood eighteen feet high, and had three-foot jaws with sixty sharp teeth.

Your Guess:

Other Forms:

Definition:

2.

conceal

It would have been difficult for the pleurocoelus to **conceal** itself because it weighed thirty-five tons and was fifty feet long. It would be almost impossible for a pleurocoelus herd to hide in the wide, open plains of Central Texas today!

3.

disguise

If a chasmosaurus walked into your yard today, would you be able to **disguise** it and keep it a secret? How could you make a seventeen-foot-long creature with a big, bony plate and horns on its head look like anything but a dinosaur?

4.

gasp

One can imagine the last **gasp** of an animal torn apart by deinonychus, the "terrible claw" dinosaur. With difficulty the animal would try to breathe while the deinonychus attacked with its big, sharp, curved claws.

5.

hibernate

When dinosaurs lived, Texas was a hot and humid marshland. There would have been no need for dinosaurs to **hibernate,** or go into an inactive state, as some animals do in winter.

6.

imitate

The acrocanthosaurus, or "high-spined reptile," found in North Central to West Texas **imitated** the tyrannosaurus by walking and using its claws and teeth in similar ways.

7.

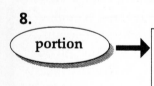
impostor

Don't be fooled by any person who says he or she is a dinosaur expert and can take you to see a live acrocanthosaurus or tyrannosaurus in a secret place in West Texas. That person is really an **impostor**.

8.

portion

What **portion** of the body of a tenontosaurus was its tail? More than half of this fifteen-foot-long dinosaur, which once lived in North Central to West Texas, was tail.

9.

reference

Do you need my **reference** material for the information that technosaurus was named for Texas Tech University in Lubbock? If you do, that source is an interesting book titled *Dinosaur Days in Texas.*

10.

terminal

The **terminal** days for Texas dinosaurs, as for all other dinosaurs and giant reptiles, came about sixty-five million years ago at the end of the Cretaceous Period. No one is certain what caused the end of the dinosaurs.

EXERCISE 2 · *Context Clues* ✍

Directions. Scan the definitions in Column A. Then think about how the boldface words are used in the sentences in Column B. To complete the exercise, match each definition in Column A with the correct vocabulary word from Column B. Write the letter of your choice on the line provided. Finally, write the vocabulary word on the line before the definition.

COLUMN A

_____ **11.** word: _____:
v. to inhale suddenly with surprise; to breathe with difficulty; *n.* a difficult inhalation of breath

_____ **12.** word: _____:
v. to attack violently; *n.* an attack

_____ **13.** word: _____:
v. to give out in parts; *n.* an amount, share, or serving of something

_____ **14.** word: _____:
n. a person who deceives others by pretending to be something he or she isn't

_____ **15.** word: _____:
adj. at the end of something; final; *n.* the ending point; a limit; either end of a transportation line

_____ **16.** word: _____:
v. to hide something by changing its usual appearence; *n.* a costume

_____ **17.** word: _____:
v. to spend the winter in an inactive state

_____ **18.** word: _____:
v. to hide; to keep secret

_____ **19.** word: _____:
n. the directing to a source for information; a mention of something or somebody; the naming of a person who can offer recommendation; *v.* to mention a source; *adj.* used or usable for reference

_____ **20.** word: _____:
v. to copy exactly; to act the same as

COLUMN B

(A) Some books about dinosaurs include **references** to Texas dinosaur finds, but others do not mention them.

(B) If you take a tour of Texas to see dinosaur footprints, make Dinosaur Valley State Park your first stop. The **terminal** for your trip, on the other hand, might be the Big Bend area.

(C) My little sister could get in one of the gigantic footprints, pull a tan blanket over herself, and thus **conceal** herself from view.

(D) Artists have **imitated** the tracks at the park in North Central Texas, but seeing the copies can't compare with seeing the real tracks.

(E) You can imagine a giant dinosaur making an **assault** on a small plant-eating dinosaur. The attack was probably frightening.

(F) The scientist responsible for preserving the tracks is R. T. Bird. No one thought he was an **impostor** because it was plain to see that he was a true authority on dinosaur fossils.

(G) Children often **gasp** when they see the big statues of dinosaurs at the park. After their deep breath of surprise, the children run to see the dinosaurs up close.

(H) While we were picnicking at the park, my mother **portioned** out a box of dinosaur-shaped cookies to us children. It didn't take her long to give each of us our share.

(I) As a child, I thought it would be fun to dress up in a dinosaur **disguise**, run out, and scare visitors at the park.

(J) I asked my mother if I could **hibernate** at the park and curl up in a cave like a bear in winter, but she said the dinosaurs might come back and get me.

EXERCISE 3 *Like Meanings and Opposite Meanings* ✍🏻

Directions. For each item below, circle the letter of the choice that means the same, or about the same, as the boldface word.

21. **gasped** on seeing the dinosaur
    (A) exhaled slowly
    (B) smiled broadly
    (C) inhaled suddenly
    (D) laughed loudly

22. **hibernate** like some mammals
    (A) spend winter in an inactive state
    (B) spend summer in an active state
    (C) spend winter in a southern state
    (D) spend fall in a restless state

23. **assaulted** the reptile
    (A) defended
    (B) supported
    (C) viewed
    (D) attacked

24. your **reference** to a dinosaur egg
    (A) decision about
    (B) mention of
    (C) discovery of
    (D) talk of

25. a good Tyrannosaurus **disguise**
    (A) drawing
    (B) statue
    (C) body
    (D) costume

Directions. For each item below, circle the letter of the choice that means the opposite, or about the opposite, of the boldface word.

26. a **portion** of a dinosaur fossil
    (A) whole
    (B) picture
    (C) part
    (D) likeness

27. **conceals** the fossil
    (A) keeps
    (B) hides
    (C) shows
    (D) takes

28. fossils found by an **impostor**
    (A) deceiving, pretending person
    (B) doubting, sly person
    (C) honest, real person
    (D) wild, dishonest person

29. the **terminal** footprint
    (A) first
    (B) final
    (C) second
    (D) greatest

30. **imitated** a flying reptile
    (A) followed the example of
    (B) pretended to be
    (C) searched for
    (D) acted differently from

MAKING NEW WORDS YOUR OWN

Lesson 9 | **CONTEXT:** Amazing Nature

Weird Weather: El Niño

Climate is not the same everywhere. Even in one place, no two years are exactly the same. Snow may pile high one year and not fall at all the next. One summer may be hotter than most others. Some rainy seasons aren't very rainy. One important factor in global weather variation is the phenomenon known as El Niño. El Niño is a warm water current that occurs every few years in the Pacific Ocean. This warm current is very powerful. It causes dramatic changes in weather around the world.

In the following exercises, you will have the opportunity to expand your vocabulary by reading about El Niño and other mysterious weather phenomena. Below are ten vocabulary words that will be used in the exercises.

bureau	particle	pierce	resign	surgery
lunar	pharmacy	receipt	static	unmanned

EXERCISE 1 *Mapping* ✍

Directions. In the item below, a vocabulary word is provided and used in a sentence. Take a guess at the word's meaning and write it in the box labeled **Your Guess**. Then look the word up in your dictionary and write the definition in the box labeled **Definition**. Finally, use your dictionary to find other forms of the word, such as adjective, noun, or verb forms. Write these words in the box labeled **Other Forms**.

Then, on a separate sheet of paper, draw your own map and follow the same instructions for each of the nine remaining vocabulary words.

1.

bureau → Our weather **bureau,** the National Weather Service, is a government department that predicts and studies the weather. Scientists at the weather **bureau** do not yet understand what causes El Niño. For this reason, they cannot always predict when the next El Niño will occur.

Your Guess:

Other Forms:

Definition:

2.

lunar ➤ **Lunar** attraction, or the gravitational pull of the moon, causes ocean tides. But the moon does not have much effect on ocean currents such as El Niño.

3.

particle ➤ For example, a water **particle** that is caught up in an ocean tide will be carried either towards or away from the shore as the moon pulls the tide. But if that same small molecule of water is caught in a current, it will be carried along in the current's flow.

4.

pharmacy ➤ Plants and animals in the sea are affected by El Niño. Some of these organisms are of value to students of **pharmacy**. Pharmacists use some sea organisms to prepare drugs and medicines.

5.

pierce ➤ When El Niño **pierces** the normally cool waters of South America's Pacific coast, disasterous changes occur. The effect of the warm current passing into cold waters damages the ocean life.

6.

receipt ➤ The disruption of the jet stream has a major effect on world climates. For this reason, scientists are always eager for **receipt** of news about El Niño. Getting such news at the right time can help them predict weather trends.

7.

resign ➤ El Niño affects rainfall around the world. In 1991, the current caused severe flooding in parts of Texas. As the rains continued without letup, many Texans had to **resign** themselves to, or accept, the fact that their homes were gone forever.

8.

 static ➤ The 1991 flooding in Texas occurred because El Niño caused weather systems to become trapped. When a weather system is **static**, the weather in an area remains unchanged for a long time.

9.

 surgery ➤ The Texas floods caused many injuries. As a result, doctors spent more time than usual in **surgery**, performing operations.

10.

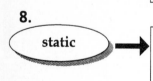 unmanned ➤ Someday, scientists may be able to track El Niño with satellites, devices placed in orbit around the earth. **Unmanned** satellites operated by remote control can tell us a lot about weather on earth.

EXERCISE 2 Context Clues ✍

Directions. Scan the definitions in Column A. Then think about how the boldface words are used in the sentences in Column B. To complete the exercise, match each definition in Column A with the correct vocabulary word from Column B. Write the letter of your choice on the line provided. Finally, write the vocabulary word on the line before the definition.

COLUMN A	COLUMN B

COLUMN A

_____ **11.** word: _____:
v. to pass into or through; to stab; to sharply affect the senses or feelings

_____ **12.** word: _____:
n. the treatment of disease or injury with operations performed by hand; an operation; the operating room

_____ **13.** word: _____:
n. a chest of drawers; an agency, usually one that gives and collects information; a government department

_____ **14.** word: _____:
n. a receiving; proof of receiving

_____ **15.** word: _____:
v. to leave or offer to leave one's job or office; to accept something passively

_____ **16.** word: _____:
n. a very small piece; a slight trace

_____ **17.** word: _____:
adj. not manned; without people aboard and operating automatically

_____ **18.** word: _____:
n. electrical discharges in the atmosphere that produce radio or television interference; *adj.* not moving; still

_____ **19.** word: _____:
n. the profession of preparing and dispensing medicines; a drugstore

_____ **20.** word: _____:
adj. of or on the moon; like the moon: pale, round, or crescent-shaped

COLUMN B

(A) My Uncle Ramon is a fisherman who lives in Arica, Chile. He suffers from arthritis. The pain is severe, but it cannot be helped by **surgery** or other medical treatments.

(B) A friend of his owned a **pharmacy**, so Uncle Ramon decided to go to her drugstore to ask her to recommend a medicine for his pain.

(C) When he arrived at the drugstore, no one was there. Hearing **static** coming from a radio, he followed the crackling sound to the back room. The clerk there told Uncle Ramon that news of El Niño had just arrived.

(D) Uncle Ramon bought some arthritis medicine, and the clerk handed Uncle Ramon a sales slip. Sadly walking outside, Uncle Ramon stuffed the **receipt** for his medicine in his pocket.

(E) He felt the first raindrops **pierce** through his shirt. "I should have known," he thought, feeling the cold water on his skin. "My hands always hurt before a storm."

(F) "Now we must **resign** ourselves to a poor fishing season. We must accept that El Niño will warm the ocean and kill many fish."

(G) "The fishing boats will remain **unmanned** because most fishers will stay home. Crops will fail, prices will rise, and many will suffer."

(H) Arriving home, he placed his medicine in one of the drawers of his **bureau,** or dresser.

(I) Through a window, he stared grimly at the gloomy, **lunar** paleness of the day outside. The gray landscape was veiled with rain.

(J) Rain was washing away nearly every **particle** of his hope for a happy new year. But one small, bright spot cheered him greatly: I would be coming to visit him soon!

EXERCISE 3 *Like Meanings and Opposite Meanings* ✍

Directions. For each item below, circle the letter of the choice that means the same, or about the same, as the boldface word.

21. to study **pharmacy**
(A) business finance
(B) medicines
(C) the rulers of ancient Egypt
(D) crop growing

22. an old **bureau**
(A) tunnel
(B) chest of drawers
(C) den
(D) company

23. emergency **surgery**
(A) vehicle for transporting injured people
(B) strong tidal wave
(C) attack
(D) operation

24. **lunar** timetable
(A) of the ocean
(B) of the sun
(C) of the moon
(D) impossible

25. **pierce** their defenses
(A) penetrate
(B) repair
(C) arise
(D) calm

Directions. For each item below, circle the letter of the choice that means the opposite, or about the opposite, of the boldface word.

26. **particles** of glass
(A) large, whole pieces
(B) thin layers
(C) tiny bits
(D) cups and pitchers

27. **resign** his position
(A) accept
(B) change
(C) formally place a signature
(D) improve

28. an **unmanned** craft
(A) drifting
(B) damaged
(C) out of control
(D) piloted by a person

29. a **static** situation
(A) active
(B) hopeless
(C) a measure of performance
(D) statewide

30. due on **receipt**
(A) rise
(B) sending
(C) cooked
(D) a specific day

MAKING NEW WORDS YOUR OWN

Lesson 10 | CONTEXT: Amazing Nature
Mark Twain's Mighty Mississippi

The Adventures of Huckleberry Finn by Mark Twain (1835–1910) tells the story of Huck Finn. Huck is a boy living near the Mississippi River about one hundred thirty years ago. In the story, Huck and an escaped slave, Jim, travel for miles down the river. Like Huck, Mark Twain, whose real name was Samuel Clemens, grew up along the Mississippi. He worked for a time as a riverboat pilot, but he is most famous for his writing. Although Twain traveled to Europe and lived in San Francisco and other cities, his fondest memories were of the Mississippi River and his days as a riverboat pilot.

In the following exercises, you will have the opportunity to expand your vocabulary by reading about Mark Twain's Mississippi. Below are ten vocabulary words that will be used in these exercises.

automation	gossip	nephew	ransom	suspicion
flammable	license	pry	stray	toll

EXERCISE 1   *Mapping*

Directions. In the item below, a vocabulary word is provided and used in a sentence. Take a guess at the word's meaning and write it in the box labeled **Your Guess.** Then look the word up in your dictionary and write the definition in the box labeled **Definition.** Finally, use your dictionary to find other forms of the word, such as adjective, noun, or verb forms. Write these words in the box labeled **Other Forms.**

Then, on a separate sheet of paper, draw your own map and follow the same instructions for each of the nine remaining vocabulary words.

1.

automation ⟶ Mark Twain grew up during a time before **automation**. The boats that traveled down the Mississippi River were steered by hand, not by machines.

Your Guess:

Other Forms:

Definition:

2.

 → Mississippi steamboats were powered by boilers. **Flammable** materials, such as wood or coal, were burned in the boilers.

3.

 → When he was a boy, Twain loved to hear people **gossip**. He especially enjoyed rumors and tall tales told by people who had traveled on the Mississippi.

4.

 → Twain longed to work on a steamboat. He felt that working on the river would give him the **license** to be free and independent.

5.

 → In *The Adventures of Huckleberry Finn,* Huck pretends to be Tom Sawyer. He convinces Tom's aunt that he is her **nephew**.

6.

 → While traveling down the Mississippi River, Twain managed to convince a pilot to teach him how to steer a steamboat. He had to **pry** the knowledge out of the pilot with difficulty.

7.

 → Twain lost a lot of money when his publishing company failed in 1894. The debt Twain was left with seemed as high as the **ransom** for the release of a king.

8.

 → When he was eighteen, Mark Twain decided that he wanted to wander for a while. He **strayed** from Missouri to New York and Philadelphia, and then finally returned to the Mississippi River.

9.

 → Toward the end of his life, Twain developed a strong **suspicion** of people. He seemed to believe that people in general were greedy and untrustworthy.

10.

toll → After the Civil War, steamboats were replaced by the railroad. This took a **toll** on the small riverside towns, which lost money because they depended on the steamboats for trade.

EXERCISE 2 *Context Clues* ✍

Directions. Scan the definitions in Column A. Then think about how the boldface words are used in the sentences in Column B. To complete the exercise, match each definition in Column A with the correct vocabulary word from Column B. Write the letter of your choice on the line provided. Finally, write the vocabulary word on the line before the definition.

COLUMN A	COLUMN B

COLUMN A

_____ **11.** word: _____:
v. to wander from a place; to fail to concentrate; *adj.* wandering; lost; lone; *n.* person or thing that wanders or is lost

_____ **12.** word: _____:
n. any system that is self-operating

_____ **13.** word: _____:
n. a charge for; a fare; an amount lost or taken; *v.* to ring a bell slowly

_____ **14.** word: _____:
n. formal permission; a legal document giving formal permission; *v.* to give permission formally

_____ **15.** word: _____:
v. to raise or move by force; to obtain with difficulty; to peer or snoop; *n.* a tool for raising or moving something

_____ **16.** word: _____:
n. the act of suspecting guilt; tending to cause others to believe or suspect guilt

_____ **17.** word: _____:
n. the son of one's brother or sister

_____ **18.** word: _____:
n. a person who spreads rumors; idle talk or rumors; *v.* to spread rumors

_____ **19.** word: _____:
n. the price paid for the release of a hostage; *v.* to pay money for such a release

_____ **20.** word: _____:
adj. easily set on fire

COLUMN B

(A) Twain received his pilot's **license** in 1859. This paper gave him permission to operate steamboats.

(B) Steamboats were made out of wood. This means that they were **flammable** and burned easily.

(C) The **toll** for traveling on the river was low when Twain was alive. Today it costs much more.

(D) To make river travel less dangerous, the government sent boats to **pry** and remove obstacles from the water.

(E) **Automation** has changed shipping on the Mississippi River. Today, computers and other machinery make some ships self-operating and therefore much safer.

(F) The Mississippi River is badly polluted today. Many people have a **suspicion** that some industries are dumping dangerous materials in the river, but no one knows for sure.

(G) Twain became a **stray** again after the Civil War began in 1861. He wandered all over the United States and Europe.

(H) Twain was a humorous **gossip** who loved to tell stories about his years on the Mississippi.

(I) The pilot who trained Mark Twain treated him like a young relative, but more like a **nephew** than a son.

(J) In *The Adventures of Tom Sawyer*, Tom and Huck discover a treasure. They find enough money to **ransom**, or pay for the release of, a dozen hostages.

EXERCISE 3 *Like Meanings and Opposite Meanings* ✍

Directions. For each item below, circle the letter of the choice that means the same, or about the same, as the boldface word.

21. the **automation** of river travel
(A) arrival
(B) comfort
(C) beginning
(D) self-operation

22. **license** to operate a boat
(A) permission
(B) training
(C) desire
(D) request

23. Mark Twain's **nephew**
(A) son of a brother or sister
(B) next-door neighbor
(C) editor
(D) sister's husband

24. to **ransom** the captives
(A) kidnap
(B) injure seriously
(C) pay to release
(D) frighten terribly

25. to **toll** a bell
(A) study
(B) ring
(C) cast out
(D) repair

Directions. For each item below, circle the letter of the choice that means the opposite, or about the opposite, of the boldface word.

26. a **flammable** fuel
(A) expensive
(B) fireproof
(C) smelly
(D) hot

27. the **gossip** about life on the river
(A) serious discussion
(B) bad news
(C) rumors
(D) idle talk

28. **pry** into personal affairs
(A) ask about
(B) stay out of
(C) fall
(D) snoop

29. the **stray** cat that begs for food
(A) lost
(B) beautiful
(C) unhappy
(D) homebound

30. **suspicion** that it will rain
(A) knowledge
(B) guess
(C) worry
(D) bet

MAKING NEW WORDS YOUR OWN

Lesson 11 | CONTEXT: People and Places
Checking Out the Chimps with Jane Goodall

From the time she was a little girl, Jane Goodall (b. 1934) wanted to work with animals. When she grew up, she became an ethologist—someone who studies animal behavior. She worked with Louis Leakey (1903–1972), an anthropologist and paleontologist who was interested in animals and early humans. In 1960, Jane Goodall began studying chimpanzees in Gombe, Tanzania. She became very close to several individual chimpanzees. Today, she still spends much of her time in Africa, though she also travels widely, speaking and raising money for research and for efforts to preserve the chimpanzees' habitat.

In the following exercises, you will have the opportunity to expand your vocabulary by reading about Jane Goodall. Below are ten vocabulary words that will be used in these exercises.

analyze	debate	essential	offspring	reaction
career	document	identical	publicity	thorough

EXERCISE 1   *Mapping* ✍

Directions. In the item below, a vocabulary word is provided and used in a sentence. Take a guess at the word's meaning and write it in the box labeled **Your Guess**. Then look the word up in your dictionary and write the definition in the box labeled **Definition**. Finally, use your dictionary to find other forms of the word, such as adjective, noun, or verb forms. Write these words in the box labeled **Other Forms**.

Then, on a separate sheet of paper, draw your own map and follow the same instructions for each of the nine remaining vocabulary words.

1.

(analyze) ⟶ To **analyze** the behavior of chimpanzees, Jane Goodall decided to live with them. This was the best way to examine their actions in detail.

⟶ **Your Guess:**

Other Forms:

Definition:

2.

career → Jane Goodall began her **career** working as a secretary. Soon, she was able to begin working with animals, something she had always wanted to do.

3.

debate → Jane Goodall **debated** with scientists who did not believe that chimps would eat meat. She argued her case by showing them evidence.

4.

document → Every night, Jane Goodall wrote in her journal about her experiences with the chimpanzees. She wanted to **document** everything she had seen during the day.

5.

essential → An **essential** for Jane Goodall was a good pair of binoculars. Without them, she would have had trouble with her research.

6.

identical → Humans and chimpanzees have some **identical** features. For instance, chimpanzees have thumbs that are almost exactly like human thumbs.

7.

offspring → Jane Goodall realized that most chimps travel in small groups. She also noticed that mothers usually carry their **offspring** under their bodies.

8.

publicity → Jane Goodall has received a lot of **publicity** because of her work with chimpanzees. This public attention has helped her find money for her research.

9.

reaction → When Jane Goodall first began to study chimpanzees, they were afraid of her. She was not concerned about their **reaction** because she believed they would soon respond with trust.

10.

thorough → Louis Leakey wanted Jane Goodall to study chimpanzees because he knew she was **thorough**. He believed that only someone who was very exact and who paid close attention to details should do the study.

EXERCISE 2 *Context Clues* ✍️

Directions. Scan the definitions in Column A. Then think about how the boldface words are used in the sentences in Column B. To complete the exercise, match each definition in Column A with the correct vocabulary word from Column B. Write the letter of your choice on the line provided. Finally, write the vocabulary word on the line before the definition.

COLUMN A	COLUMN B

COLUMN A

_____ **11.** word: _____:
adj. necessary; *n.* something that is necessary; a necessary element

_____ **12.** word: _____:
adj. done from beginning to end; complete; painstakingly accurate

_____ **13.** word: _____:
n. any material which makes something known to the public; public attention

_____ **14.** word: _____:
v. to argue; to take part in a formal discussion; *n.* the discussion of a question

_____ **15.** word: _____:
adj. exactly alike; duplicate

_____ **16.** word: _____:
n. a response to something

_____ **17.** word: _____:
n. a written record; *v.* to provide as proof or support; to provide with supporting references

_____ **18.** word: _____:
n. the work one does all one's life; a job; rapid progress; *v.* to move at full speed; to rush; *adj.* pursuing a temporary activity as a life's work

_____ **19.** word: _____:
n. a child or a young animal; a result

_____ **20.** word: _____:
v. to examine in detail; to study the nature of something

COLUMN B

(A) Money is **essential** to Goodall's research. Without funding, she would not be able to travel to Africa.

(B) Although most people think that all chimps are **identical**, individual chimps are quite different in their appearances and actions.

(C) Jane Goodall discovered that female chimps only have one baby, or **offspring**, every five or six years.

(D) Jane Goodall often speaks in the United States. Advance **publicity** lets people know when and where she will speak.

(E) Jane Goodall is **thorough** when she studies the chimpanzees. She records every detail about them.

(F) Written **documents** by Jane Goodall and her assistants in Africa are studied by students of animal behavior.

(G) Jane Goodall was interested in **analyzing**, or studying, the relationships between male and female chimpanzees.

(H) Once, Goodall was startled by three chimpanzees **careering** through the forest. As they moved at top speed, they bared their teeth at her.

(I) How did the chimps respond when Jane Goodall's son was born? Their **reaction** was one of curiosity.

(J) The **debate** about how to protect the chimpanzees continues. It is a good sign, though, that people care enough to discuss the question.

EXERCISE 3 *Like Meanings and Opposite Meanings* ✍

Directions. For each item below, circle the letter of the choice that means the same, or about the same, as the boldface word.

21. to **analyze** animal communication
   (A) listen to
   (B) examine
   (C) understand
   (D) be a part of

22. Louis Leakey's **document**
   (A) degree
   (B) written record
   (C) life story
   (D) spoken word

23. the **offspring** of a discussion
   (A) parents
   (B) answer to
   (C) result
   (D) wish

24. **publicity** about Jane Goodall's research
   (A) public attention
   (B) funding for
   (C) magazines
   (D) tough questions

25. the chimp's **reaction**
   (A) call
   (B) curiosity
   (C) fear
   (D) response

Directions. For each item below, circle the letter of the choice that means the opposite, or about the opposite, of the boldface word.

26. a **career** animal lover
   (A) angry
   (B) lonely
   (C) occasional
   (D) responsible

27. to **debate** environmental issues
   (A) agree about
   (B) refuse
   (C) outline
   (D) explain

28. **identical** child-rearing behavior
   (A) the same
   (B) unusual
   (C) opposite
   (D) poor

29. **essential** for Goodall's health
   (A) required
   (B) unnecessary
   (C) sure
   (D) prescribed

30. a **thorough** study
   (A) expensive
   (B) correct
   (C) humorous
   (D) incomplete

MAKING NEW WORDS YOUR OWN

Lesson 12 **CONTEXT: People and Places**

Looking for Green Gables: Anne's Prince Edward Island

Anne Shirley is the title character of the novel *Anne of Green Gables* by Lucy Maud Montgomery (1874–1942). Although Anne is not real, she is like her creator in many ways. Perhaps most importantly, both lived on and loved Prince Edward Island, Canada's smallest province. As in Anne's and Montgomery's time, Prince Edward Island is mostly farmland. However, many tourists come to the island to see its beauty and to visit the house that Montgomery used as the model for Anne's house, Green Gables.

In the following exercises, you will have the opportunity to expand your vocabulary by reading about Anne of Green Gables and Prince Edward Island. Below are ten vocabulary words that will be used in these exercises.

| biography | determination | notion | respectable | scholar |
| destination | generous | profession | routine | self-confidence |

EXERCISE 1   *Mapping* ☞

Directions. In the item below, a vocabulary word is provided and used in a sentence. Take a guess at the word's meaning and write it in the box labeled **Your Guess**. Then look the word up in your dictionary and write the definition in the box labeled **Definition**. Finally, use your dictionary to find other forms of the word, such as adjective, noun, or verb forms. Write these words in the box labeled **Other Forms**.

Then, on a separate sheet of paper, draw your own map and follow the same instructions for each of the nine remaining vocabulary words.

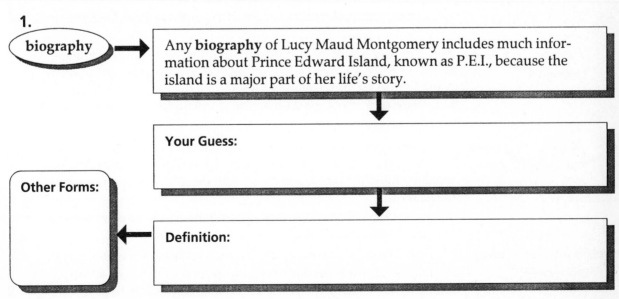

1.

biography → Any **biography** of Lucy Maud Montgomery includes much information about Prince Edward Island, known as P.E.I., because the island is a major part of her life's story.

Your Guess:

Other Forms:

Definition:

2.

destination ➤ I had long wanted to go to P. E. I. because I had read all eight of the Anne books and the story of Montgomery's life. When I set out on my vacation last summer, the island was my **destination**.

3.

determination ➤ My **determination** to go to P. E. I., which is located in the Gulf of St. Lawrence, was great. I also had a firm intention to visit all the places described in the Anne novels.

4.

generous ➤ A **generous** aunt who was willing and eager to share an unexpected inheritance with me, gave me money to go to P. E. I. She showed me pictures that she had taken of Prince Edward Island National Park, where Green Gables is located.

5.

notion ➤ Once actually on P.E.I., I had the **notion** to drive around and look at the farms. It was a good idea, because many farmers were out harvesting the potatoes for which the island is famous.

6.

profession ➤ Farming is one of the main **professions** on the island, which has extremely rich red soil. Another popular occupation is fishing, especially fishing for lobsters and oysters.

7.

respectable ➤ You can take my word for it that the Prince Edward Island lobster is a **respectable** meal. I went to a community lobster dinner where I had oysters that were also of good quality—and more-than-sufficient quantity!

8.

routine ➤ At the dinner, some local children put on an entertaining **routine** based on *Anne of Green Gables*. Of course, a red-haired girl played Anne in the skit and pretended not to like the color of her hair.

9.

scholar ➤ It was my good fortune to meet a woman who was born and raised on P. E. I. and who was a real *Anne of Green Gables* **scholar**. She offered to share her vast knowledge with me and to show me around the island.

10.

self-confidence ➤ My new friend said she admired Anne's **self-confidence** because she herself once suffered from a low opinion of her own abilities. She said that reading the Anne books had helped her to become more sure of herself.

EXERCISE 2 Context Clues ✍

Directions. Scan the definitions in Column A. Then think about how the boldface words are used in the sentences in Column B. To complete the exercise, match each definition in Column A with the correct vocabulary word from Column B. Write the letter of your choice on the line provided. Finally, write the vocabulary word on the line before the definition.

COLUMN A	COLUMN B
_____ **11.** word: _____: *n.* a whim; an idea; a vague thought	(A) When I was in college, a fellow **scholar** once told me that the Micmacs, a Native American people, settled Prince Edward Island.
_____ **12.** word: _____: *n.* a belief in oneself and one's abilities	(B) I later read a **biography** of the French explorer Jacques Cartier, who came to the island in 1534. The story of his life is fascinating.
_____ **13.** word: _____: *n.* a firm intention; firmness of purpose	(C) I didn't plan my activities on P.E.I. but acted on whim. A sudden **notion** to see Charlottetown, the island's capital, resulted in lots of fun.
_____ **14.** word: _____: *adj.* worthy of esteem; proper; fairly good in quality or quantity	(D) I had a firm intention, a **determination**, to see the village of Cavendish because it is the place called Avonlea in Montgomery's books.
_____ **15.** word: _____: *n.* the story of a person's life	(E) The house called Green Gables once belonged to Montgomery's cousins, a **respectable** brother and sister who ran an equally proper farm.
_____ **16.** word: _____: *adj.* willing to give or share; unselfish; ample	(F) I wonder if they were as **generous** as the unselfish brother and sister, Matthew and Marilla, who welcomed Anne.
_____ **17.** word: _____: *n.* the place toward which someone or something is going	(G) When touring the house, I could imagine Anne's summer **routine** as a child. Each day she helped in the kitchen, wrote, and day-dreamed.
_____ **18.** word: _____: *n.* an occupation; a declaration	(H) I think working at Green Gables for the Canadian park service would be a wonderful **profession**. All my reading should be good background for such a career.
_____ **19.** word: _____: *n.* a learned or knowledgeable person; a student	(I) After I went through Green Gables, Anne's Haunted Woods nearby was my next **destination**.
_____ **20.** word: _____: *n.* a regular procedure; a custom; a theatrical skit; *adj.* occurring on a regular basis	(J) P. E. I. is where Montgomery and Anne learned to believe in themselves; I could feel their **self-confidence** there.

EXERCISE 3   *Like Meanings and Opposite Meanings*

Directions. For each item below, circle the letter of the choice that means the same, or about the same, as the boldface word.

21. a **respectable** Canadian author
  (A) favorite
  (B) disliked
  (C) well-known
  (D) esteemed

22. the farming **profession**
  (A) equipment
  (B) community
  (C) occupation
  (D) work force

23. a Canadian **scholar**
  (A) student
  (B) coach
  (C) janitor
  (D) dropout

24. a **notion** to paint a landscape
  (A) hope
  (B) chance
  (C) order
  (D) idea

25. reading a **biography**
  (A) story about the history of Canada
  (B) story of a person's life
  (C) map
  (D) list of a writer's books

Directions. For each item below, circle the letter of the choice that means the opposite, or about the opposite, of the boldface word.

26. **routine** tours of Green Gables
  (A) not regular
  (B) regular
  (C) hourly
  (D) enjoyable

27. a **generous** donation to Parks Canada
  (A) welcome
  (B) unwelcome
  (C) selfish
  (D) unselfish

28. a feeling of **determination**
  (A) purposelessness
  (B) firmness
  (C) unusualness
  (D) originality

29. an island **destination**
  (A) view
  (B) starting point
  (C) end point
  (D) summer storm

30. a writer's **self-confidence**
  (A) belief in oneself and one's abilities
  (B) concern over finishing a book
  (C) lack of faith in oneself and one's abilities
  (D) hope in the ability to create

MAKING NEW WORDS YOUR OWN

Lesson 13 | **CONTEXT: People and Places**

If You Like Peanut Butter, Thank George Washington Carver

Imagine life without peanut butter! Without George Washington Carver (1864–1943), peanut butter might never have been invented. Carver was a scientist who developed more than three hundred products from the peanut. Carver was born into slavery. At an early age he became fascinated with nature. He eventually went to college and later joined the faculty of Tuskegee Institute in 1896. His interest in the peanut eventually made it a major part of agriculture in the South.

In the following exercises, you will have the opportunity to expand your vocabulary by reading about George Washington Carver and peanut butter. Below are ten vocabulary words that will be used in these exercises.

ceremony	consent	ignite	management	quarantine
conduct	fragrant	interrupt	plead	scheme

EXERCISE 1   *Mapping*

Directions. In the item below, a vocabulary word is provided and used in a sentence. Take a guess at the word's meaning and write it in the box labeled **Your Guess**. Then look the word up in your dictionary and write the definition in the box labeled **Definition**. Finally, use your dictionary to find other forms of the word, such as adjective, noun, or verb forms. Write these words in the box labeled **Other Forms**.

Then, on a separate sheet of paper, draw your own map and follow the same instructions for each of the nine remaining vocabulary words.

1.

ceremony → George Washington Carver's funeral service was well attended. At the **ceremony**, people were reminded of his contributions.

Your Guess:

Other Forms:

Definition:

2.

conduct → Carver **conducted** hundreds of experiments in his lab. Under his direction, many products were developed.

3.

consent → Carver invented many uses for the peanut, including peanut massage oil. After being asked, he **consented** to allow the oil to be used to massage some polio victims.

4.

fragrant → Peanut milk was one of Carver's first widely used inventions. The **fragrant**, sweet-smelling liquid was a substitute for cow's milk.

5.

ignite → Carver's laboratory equipment included burners for heating. It was important to **ignite** the burners carefully to avoid setting a fire.

6.

interrupt → Carver testified before a committee of Congress in 1921. The committee was so interested in his unusual peanut products that they frequently **interrupted** his talk to ask questions.

7.

management → Carver helped the peanut industry in the South. The **management** of various companies asked for his help with a variety of problems. These business directors appreciated Carver's knowledge.

8.

plead → One can imagine that if Carver had ever threatened to leave Tuskegee Institute, its directors would have **pleaded** with him, begging him to stay.

9.

quarantine → Carver worked with some plants that were diseased. He had to **quarantine** these plants by setting them apart from the others so that other plants would not catch the diseases.

10.

scheme → Carver's **scheme** was for southern farmers to be more productive. He planned to provide them with useful products.

EXERCISE 2 — Context Clues ✍

Directions. Scan the definitions in Column A. Then think about how the boldface words are used in the sentences in Column B. To complete the exercise, match each definition in Column A with the correct vocabulary word from Column B. Write the letter of your choice on the line provided. Finally, write the vocabulary word on the line before the definition.

COLUMN A

_____ **11.** word: _____:
n. behavior; *v.* to lead; to direct

_____ **12.** word: _____:
n. a carefully arranged plan; a plot; an orderly combination of things; *v.* to construct a plan; to plot

_____ **13.** word: _____:
n. an isolation or restriction of movement to keep disease from spreading; *v.* to isolate

_____ **14.** word: _____:
v. to set on fire; to start burning

_____ **15.** word: _____:
n. a formal act or ritual; the service at which such an act is performed

_____ **16.** word: _____:
v. to break in upon; to stop or obstruct

_____ **17.** word: _____:
v. to agree with; to give approval or permission for something; *n.* an agreement; permission

_____ **18.** word: _____:
adj. having a pleasant smell; sweet-smelling

_____ **19.** word: _____:
v. to offer as an excuse; to declare oneself in court to be guilty or not guilty; to beg

_____ **20.** word: _____:
n. the act of controlling; one or more persons who direct a group or business

COLUMN B

(A) George Washington Carver was sick when he was a boy. He was often **quarantined**, or kept apart, from other children.

(B) When he traveled, Carver often left the **management**, or control, of his experiments with other scientists.

(C) Carver was well known for his polite **conduct**. This behavior was imitated by many of his students.

(D) Carver **schemed** to make crop rotation, the planting of different crops in different seasons, a common practice among farmers. Those who followed Carver's plan found that all their crops improved.

(E) A popular speaker, Carver was in great demand. Organizations such as schools and the YMCA **pleaded** with him to speak to them.

(F) Carver was a champion of the rights of African Americans. He often **ignited** passions and made people burn for justice.

(G) Carver would sometimes **interrupt** his work in the lab to stop and research new ideas.

(H) One of Carver's inventions was a kind of soap made from peanuts. The soap had a pleasant, **fragrant** smell.

(I) Carver asked some of his students to write to him after they left Tuskegee Institute. Most of them were glad to **consent**: They readily agreed to write.

(J) Without **ceremony**, Carver often led informal nature tours.

EXERCISE 3 *Like Meanings and Opposite Meanings*

Directions. For each item below, circle the letter of the choice that means the same, or about the same, as the boldface word.

21. a formal **ceremony**
  (A) ritual
  (B) classroom
  (C) trophy
  (D) suit

22. to suddenly **interrupt**
  (A) finish
  (B) break in
  (C) inform
  (D) find

23. to **plead** ignorance
  (A) declare
  (B) overcome
  (C) find the cause of
  (D) make an excuse for

24. to **conduct** an experiment
  (A) ruin
  (B) follow
  (C) design
  (D) direct

25. a **scheme** to find more uses for peanuts
  (A) grant
  (B) plan
  (C) lab
  (D) reason

Directions. For each item below, circle the letter of the choice that means the opposite, or about the opposite, of the boldface word.

26. **quarantined** for a short time
  (A) in public
  (B) kept apart
  (C) ill
  (D) healthy

27. **consent** to do more research
  (A) hope
  (B) plan
  (C) dream
  (D) refuse

28. a **fragrant** flower
  (A) stinking
  (B) yellow
  (C) sweet
  (D) blooming

29. to **ignite** a match
  (A) light
  (B) put out
  (C) freeze
  (D) steam

30. the peanut industry's **management**
  (A) workers
  (B) scientists
  (C) bosses
  (D) teachers

MAKING NEW WORDS YOUR OWN

Lesson 14 | **CONTEXT: People and Places**

Just Where Did *the Red Fern Grow? Appalachia . . .*

Wilson Rawls's (1913–1984) *Where the Red Fern Grows* is a story of love and triumph. A boy forms a deep friendship with two dogs who give up their lives to save him from danger. The young-adult novel is set in Appalachia, a region in the southeastern mountains of the United States. This area has some of the country's most beautiful scenery and some of its poorest people. Every year, thousands of hikers walk along all or part of the Appalachian Trail, which runs for more than two thousand miles from Georgia to Maine. And hundreds of species of birds live in or visit the region annually.

In the following exercises, you will have the opportunity to expand your vocabulary by reading about Appalachia. Below are ten vocabulary words that will be used in these exercises.

| architect | desperate | eternal | realm | victim |
| betray | district | glimpse | sacrifice | victorious |

EXERCISE 1 *Mapping* 👉

Directions. In the item below, a vocabulary word is provided and used in a sentence. Take a guess at the word's meaning and write it in the box labeled **Your Guess**. Then look the word up in your dictionary and write the definition in the box labeled **Definition**. Finally, use your dictionary to find other forms of the word, such as adjective, noun, or verb forms. Write these words in the box labeled **Other Forms**.

Then, on a separate sheet of paper, draw your own map and follow the same instructions for each of the nine remaining vocabulary words.

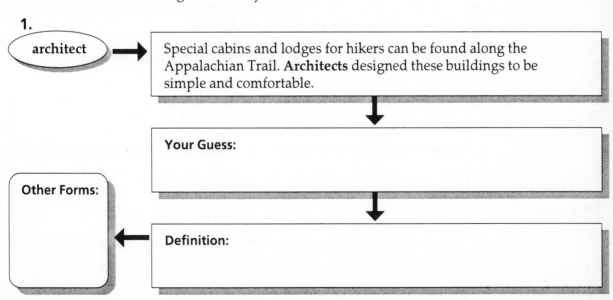

1.

architect → Special cabins and lodges for hikers can be found along the Appalachian Trail. **Architects** designed these buildings to be simple and comfortable.

Your Guess:

Other Forms:

Definition:

2.

betray

The hounds Old Dan and Little Ann would never turn against their owner in *Where the Red Fern Grows.* They were too faithful to **betray** him.

3.

desperate

Many miners and farmers in Appalachia are **desperate** about the economy. They are losing their hope that things will get better.

4.

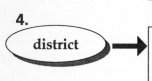
district

The Appalachian Trail is over two thousand miles long. It passes through many **districts**, running through county after county and state after state from Maine to Georgia.

5.

eternal

The Appalachians are the oldest mountains in North America. Some people think of them as **eternal,** as if they have always existed.

6.

glimpse

Driving on the Blue Ridge Parkway, one can **glimpse** a number of secluded villages. A driver should not be tempted to take a longer look, though, because the road is high and winding!

7.

realm

The Appalachians are a **realm** for wildlife. Bears and bobcats are the rulers of this animal kingdom.

8.

sacrifice

In Rawls's book, Old Dan and Little Ann make a **sacrifice** for their owner: They give up their lives to save him.

9.

victim

The narrator of *Where the Red Fern Grows* is seriously injured when he becomes the **victim** of a mountain lion attack.

10.

victorious

People concerned about the environment have been at least partially **victorious** in Appalachia. They have won protection for several endangered species.

EXERCISE 2 *Context Clues* ✍

Directions. Scan the definitions in Column A. Then think about how the boldface words are used in the sentences in Column B. To complete the exercise, match each definition in Column A with the correct vocabulary word from Column B. Write the letter of your choice on the line provided. Finally, write the vocabulary word on the line before the definition.

COLUMN A	**COLUMN B**

COLUMN A

_____ **11.** word: _____:
n. a person who designs plans for the construction of buildings or other structures

_____ **12.** word: _____:
adj. in a state resulting from a loss of hope; having a great need

_____ **13.** word: _____:
v. to glance at; to see briefly; *n.* a brief, quick view

_____ **14.** word: _____:
n. something offered to the gods; something given up for something of greater value; *v.* to offer something; to give up something of value for something else

_____ **15.** word: _____:
v. to deceive; to turn against someone

_____ **16.** word: _____:
adj. existing forever; everlasting

_____ **17.** word: _____:
n. a person who is injured; one who suffers from some loss

_____ **18.** word: _____:
n. a kingdom; an area

_____ **19.** word: _____:
n. a defined area or region; a geographical or political division

_____ **20.** word: _____:
adj. having gained a victory; winning

COLUMN B

(A) In *Where the Red Fern Grows,* the red fern was planted on the hounds' grave as an **eternal,** or everlasting, symbol of their love.

(B) Most **architects** in Appalachia live in the cities, where they can find work designing buildings.

(C) Some people who live in Appalachia give up high salaries when they move there. They are willing to make this **sacrifice** to live in such a beautiful place.

(D) **Victorious** hikers celebrate the achievement of their goal when they reach the end of the Appalachian Trail.

(E) If you look carefully, you can sometimes **glimpse** a deer as it leaps swiftly through the woods.

(F) Some of the Appalachian school **districts** are very large in area but small in population. Such large geographical divisions can cause problems for families with school-age children.

(G) Out in the woods, the main character in *Where the Red Fern Grows* felt like a king with his own small **realm.**

(H) In some parts of Appalachia, birds and animals, **victims** of development, have lost much of their home territory.

(I) Poverty is a serious problem in Appalachia. Many people are **desperate** in their need for food and medical care.

(J) The boy's grandfather in *Where the Red Fern Grows* would never **betray** his grandson. He always tells the boy the truth.

EXERCISE 3 *Like Meanings and Opposite Meanings*

Directions. For each item below, circle the letter of the choice that means the same, or about the same, as the boldface word.

21. the best **architect**
- (A) high school teacher
- (B) building designer
- (C) shipbuilder
- (D) miner

22. a **district** of West Virginia
- (A) region
- (B) writer
- (C) school
- (D) trail

23. a mountain **realm**
- (A) lion
- (B) stream
- (C) path
- (D) kingdom

24. a **sacrifice** for love
- (A) proof
- (B) offering
- (C) prayer
- (D) hope

25. the **victim** of a fierce attack
- (A) injured person
- (B) mugger
- (C) eyewitness
- (D) root cause

Directions. For each item below, circle the letter of the choice that means the opposite, or about the opposite, of the boldface word.

26. to **betray** a friend
- (A) support
- (B) hurt
- (C) describe
- (D) deceive

27. a **desperate** feeling
- (A) sad
- (B) hopeful
- (C) confused
- (D) angry

28. an **eternal** flame
- (A) temporary
- (B) enormous
- (C) everlasting
- (D) warm

29. to **glimpse** a cougar
- (A) run from
- (B) capture
- (C) stare at
- (D) shoot

30. a **victorious** group of people
- (A) losing
- (B) large
- (C) committed
- (D) bold

MAKING NEW WORDS YOUR OWN

Lesson 15 | CONTEXT: People and Places

From Tipis to Igloos: How Native Americans Adapted to the Land

When you think of Native American homes, what image comes to mind? Some people may picture a cone-shaped tipi. The snow-block igloo is another Native American house. Housing styles depend somewhat on climate and the raw materials available. Tradition and patterns of use are other factors that go into the design of Native American houses. Houses are made to suit the lifestyles of the people who live in them. The Plains Indians, for example, moved often, so they built portable houses that they could take with them.

In the following exercises, you will have the opportunity to expand your vocabulary by reading about the traditional houses Native Americans make. Below are ten vocabulary words that will be used in these exercises.

| abundant | descriptive | establish | possess | survey |
| barrier | desirable | geology | prehistoric | terrain |

EXERCISE 1   *Mapping* ✍

Directions. In the item below, a vocabulary word is provided and used in a sentence. Take a guess at the word's meaning and write it in the box labeled **Your Guess**. Then look the word up in your dictionary and write the definition in the box labeled **Definition**. Finally, use your dictionary to find other forms of the word, such as adjective, noun, or verb forms. Write these words in the box labeled **Other Forms**.

Then, on a separate sheet of paper, draw your own map and follow the same instructions for each of the nine remaining vocabulary words.

1.

(abundant) ➜ Igloos are domed houses built from blocks of snow. Although snow is **abundant** in the Arctic, only certain kinds of snow can be used to make igloos.

Your Guess:

Other Forms:

Definition:

2.

barrier → The Plains peoples also took advantage of snow as a building material. In the winter, Plains peoples would bank snow around the bases of their tipis as **barriers** against wind and blowing snow.

3.

descriptive → To make a tipi, tightly stitched buffalo hides were stretched over long poles. In a **descriptive** passage, the Spanish explorer Juan de Oñate gives a detailed picture of a heavy rainstorm and says that no rain passed through the buffalo skin.

4.

desirable → Igloos can only be made in the winter when snow is plentiful. Tipis make **desirable** houses all year long because they can be lined for warmth in winter or opened up to the fresh air in summer.

5.

establish → The Pueblo peoples build their homes from stone, wood, and adobe. When a Pueblo woman married, her husband would **establish** a home for them by building a new room onto her family's house.

6.

geology → The **geology** of the Southwest can be seen in Pueblo houses. Because the homes are covered with adobe—earth mixed with water and straw—their walls are the color of the earth from which they are made.

7.

possess → Some Pueblo villages are built on high mesas. These towns **possess** breathtaking views of the surrounding mountains and valleys.

8.

prehistoric → Scientists believe that the Pueblo peoples are distant relatives of the **prehistoric** Anasazi. No written records exist to tell us about the Anasazi.

9.

survey → Scientists **survey** Anasazi ruins and compare them with modern Pueblo structures. Through this kind of careful examination, they are able to draw conclusions about how the Anasazi might have lived.

10.

terrain → Anasazi ruins blend smoothly into the **terrain** of the desert Southwest. These Native American houses often look like part of the land, like the canyon walls on which they are built.

EXERCISE 2   *Context Clues* ✍

Directions. Scan the definitions in Column A. Then think about how the boldface words are used in the sentences in Column B. To complete the exercise, match each definition in Column A with the correct vocabulary word from Column B. Write the letter of your choice on the line provided. Finally, write the vocabulary word on the line before the definition.

COLUMN A

_____ **11.** word: _____:
adj. concerned with describing; presented in detail

_____ **12.** word: _____:
n. the science of the physical nature and history of the earth; the physical characteristics of a certain feature of the earth, such as rock types, fossils, and so on

_____ **13.** word: _____:
n. the ground or a piece of ground; a piece of ground for some use

_____ **14.** word: _____:
adj. plentiful; more than enough

_____ **15.** word: _____:
v. to set up; to bring about; to prove

_____ **16.** word: _____:
n. a detailed study; *v.* to inspect or review in detail; to view or consider

_____ **17.** word: _____:
v. to have something; to have as an attribute or quality

_____ **18.** word: _____:
n. something that prevents passage; a blockade; anything that separates

_____ **19.** word: _____:
adj. before recorded history

_____ **20.** word: _____:
adj. worth wanting or having; worthwhile; pleasing, attractive

COLUMN B

(A) Meghan is a sixth-grader who needs information to **establish,** or set up, a theory on Native American homes.

(B) Meghan's theory is that the **abundant** water in one area or the lack of water in another area may affect Native American house styles.

(C) In a **geology** textbook, which is full of information about the physical features of the earth, Meghan reads that water is a scarce resource in much of the southwestern United States.

(D) Meghan learns that the Pueblos live in the Southwest. For centuries, they built attractive houses from earth, stone, water, and wood. Many of these homes are still **desirable** dwellings.

(E) In the library, Meghan finds a detailed, **descriptive** article about the Pueblos.

(F) Meghan reads that the building styles of the Pueblos are divided into two types. The eastern Pueblos live near the Rio Grande. The western Pueblos live on drier **terrain** in what is now New Mexico and Arizona.

(G) The lack of ground water is not much of a **barrier** to the western Pueblos. They are able to overcome the shortage by collecting rainwater.

(H) According to the article Meghan reads, the two groups **possess** different building methods. The western Pueblos, for example, use more stone and less water to build their homes.

(I) The article also discusses the Anasazi, the Pueblos' **prehistoric** ancestors. Meghan would like to study these ancient people.

(J) Meghan's well-researched **survey** supports her theory. She hopes her teacher will be happy with the results of her careful study.

EXERCISE 3   *Like Meanings and Opposite Meanings* ✍

Directions. For each item below, circle the letter of the choice that means the same, or about the same, as the boldface word.

21. a **geology** class
- (A) science of the earth's physical features
- (B) study of house design
- (C) study of ancient cultures of the earth
- (D) agricultural science

22. Meghan's **descriptive** essay
- (A) boring
- (B) detailed
- (C) exciting
- (D) dangerous

23. a **prehistoric** ax
- (A) before recorded history
- (B) before the American Revolution
- (C) after written language
- (D) after recorded history

24. a published **survey**
- (A) a law
- (B) a book about the ocean
- (C) a detailed study
- (D) a long poem

25. rugged **terrain**
- (A) a small cave
- (B) waterfalls
- (C) a state highway
- (D) an area of ground

Directions. For each item below, circle the letter of the choice that means the opposite, or about the opposite, of the boldface word.

26. **abundant** snow
- (A) very old
- (B) available
- (C) scarce
- (D) useful

27. **possess** sturdy houses
- (A) lack
- (B) build
- (C) decorate
- (D) own

28. a high **barrier**
- (A) collar
- (B) opening
- (C) wall
- (D) maintain

29. **establish** a cultural center
- (A) organize
- (B) make happen
- (C) govern
- (D) bring to an end

30. a **desirable** tipi
- (A) unwanted
- (B) interesting
- (C) practical
- (D) sturdy

MAKING NEW WORDS YOUR OWN

Lesson 16 | CONTEXT: People and Places
Kipling's Just So Stories: Myths of Nature

In *Just So Stories*, Rudyard Kipling (1865–1936) creates myths of the world's beginnings. These stories explain how the camel got his hump, why the elephant's trunk is so long, and how the leopard got its spots, among other things. Kipling lived and traveled in India in the late 1890s. There he wrote several books. Some of his other children's and young adult books are *The Jungle Book, Captains Courageous,* and *Kim.* The *Just So Stories* are some of his best-loved tales. His humorous descriptions, such as the "great-grey-green greasy Limpopo River," continue to delight readers today.

In the following exercises, you will have the opportunity to expand your vocabulary by reading about Kipling's *Just So Stories*. Below are ten vocabulary words that will be used in these exercises.

dramatic	feat	leisure	marvel	satisfy
extraordinary	irregular	lieutenant	numerous	vicinity

EXERCISE 1 *Mapping*

Directions. In the item below, a vocabulary word is provided and used in a sentence. Take a guess at the word's meaning and write it in the box labeled **Your Guess**. Then look the word up in your dictionary and write the definition in the box labeled **Definition**. Finally, use your dictionary to find other forms of the word, such as adjective, noun, or verb forms. Write these words in the box labeled **Other Forms**.

Then, on a separate sheet of paper, draw your own map and follow the same instructions for each of the nine remaining vocabulary words.

1.

(dramatic) ➡️ In "How the Whale Got His Throat," the mariner makes the whale very uncomfortable by jumping up and down. The mariner dances with **dramatic** gestures, as if he were on stage.

⬇️

Your Guess:

Other Forms:

⬇️

⬅️ **Definition:**

2.

extraordinary → Tegumai thinks his daughter Taffy is **extraordinary**. She is amazing because she comes up with the idea of writing a letter to her mother.

3.

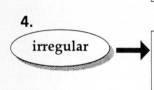
feat → In "The Beginning of the Armadillos," the hedgehog learns how to swim—an unusual **feat**. This remarkable act allows him to escape from the jaguar.

4.

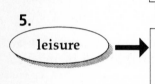
irregular → The Ethiopian gives the leopard his spots by pressing his fingers against the fur. The spots are not **irregular**, but are evenly spaced in groups of five.

5.

leisure → In "The Cat That Walked by Himself," the cat gains the right to live a life of **leisure**. Because the woman is grateful to him, he is fed without having to do any work.

6.

lieutenant → In "How the Camel Got His Hump," the Djinn acts like a **lieutenant** in the army. He orders the camel to go to work like the other animals.

7.

marvel → When the elephant's child returns from visiting the crocodile, his family is surprised by his appearance. They think his wonderful new trunk is a **marvel**.

8.

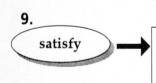
numerous → The Parsee places **numerous** cake crumbs inside the rhinoceros' skin. There are so many crumbs that the rhinoceros is very uncomfortable and itchy.

9.

satisfy → In "How the Whale Got His Throat," the whale cannot **satisfy** his hunger even though he eats all but one fish in the sea.

10.

vicinity → The hedgehog and tortoise live in the **vicinity** of the Amazon River. In this area, they find lots of food to eat.

EXERCISE 2 *Context Clues* ✍

Directions. Scan the definitions in Column A. Then think about how the boldface words are used in the sentences in Column B. To complete the exercise, match each definition in Column A with the correct vocabulary word from Column B. Write the letter of your choice on the line provided. Finally, write the vocabulary word on the line before the definition.

COLUMN A	COLUMN B
_____ **11.** word: _____: *adj.* pertaining to drama or theater; having the forced qualities of a drama; striking	(A) Taffy acts as a kind of **lieutenant,** or aide, to her father as they invent the alphabet together.
_____ **12.** word: _____: *n.* something that is wonderful or surprising; *v.* to be amazed at something	(B) In "The Butterfly That Stamped," a very **dramatic,** striking thing occurs when the butterfly stamps his foot. The palace disappears!
_____ **13.** word: _____: *adj.* not straight; uneven; not following established rule or method	(C) In "Old Man Kangaroo," the kangaroo is amazed. He **marvels** at the change in himself.
_____ **14.** word: _____: *v.* to fill the needs or requirements of; to free from doubt	(D) In "The Cat That Walked by Himself," the dog, horse, and cow all stay nearby, in the **vicinity** of the cave.
_____ **15.** word: _____: *n.* free and unoccupied time; spare time; freedom from work	(E) The mariner accomplishes a remarkable **feat** in "How the Whale Got His Throat." He uses his suspenders to tie a set of bars in the whale's throat.
_____ **16.** word: _____: *adj.* very many; consisting of many people or things	(F) The jaguar is confused when the hedgehog and tortoise act in an **irregular** way. They do not follow the rules that the jaguar's mother had told him.
_____ **17.** word: _____: *n.* a remarkable deed or accomplishment	(G) In "Old Man Kangaroo," the kangaroo has no **leisure** when he is being chased by the dingo. There is simply no time to rest.
_____ **18.** word: _____: *n.* the state of being close by; the area surrounding a particular place; the neighborhood of a place	(H) When the Ethiopian and the leopard enter the forest, they think the other animals look **extraordinary**. Each animal's appearance is different and unusual, with spots and stripes.
_____ **19.** word: _____: *adj.* markedly different from the usual; amazing; exceptional	(I) The elephant child is curious about so many things that they are too **numerous** to list.
_____ **20.** word: _____: *n.* an officer ranking below a captain; an aide or deputy	(J) The jaguar is confused by the tortoise and the hedgehog. He is never **satisfied,** or freed from doubt, about which is which.

EXERCISE 3 — *Like Meanings and Opposite Meanings* ✍

Directions. For each item below, circle the letter of the choice that means the same, or about the same, as the boldface word.

21. a **dramatic** appearance
   (A) ordinary
   (B) elegant
   (C) striking
   (D) meaningful

22. the **feat** of the camel
   (A) remarkable deed
   (B) hump
   (C) original owner
   (D) unusual appearance

23. **leisure** to learn the alphabet
   (A) desire
   (B) free time
   (C) request
   (D) requirement

24. the **lieutenant's** uniform
   (A) waiter's
   (B) student's
   (C) officer's
   (D) pilot's

25. the **vicinity** of the river
   (A) banks
   (B) village
   (C) fish
   (D) neighborhood

Directions. For each item below, circle the letter of the choice that means the opposite, or about the opposite, of the boldface word.

26. an **extraordinary** elephant child
   (A) usual
   (B) young
   (C) annoying
   (D) odd

27. **irregular** leopard's spots
   (A) uneven
   (B) brown
   (C) evenly spaced
   (D) widely spaced

28. to **marvel** about the rhinoceros' skin
   (A) be curious
   (B) be bored
   (C) be amazed
   (D) be scared

29. **numerous** fishes
   (A) few
   (B) a dozen
   (C) twenty
   (D) very many

30. to **satisfy** the elephant child's curiosity
   (A) free from doubt
   (B) not relieve
   (C) decrease
   (D) be shocked by

MAKING NEW WORDS YOUR OWN

Lesson 17 **CONTEXT: People and Places**

The Vikings: Adventuring to America

History books used to teach that Columbus discovered America. But Columbus wasn't the first person to come to America. Native Americans were already living in America when Columbus arrived. Today many people believe that Columbus and his men weren't even the first Europeans in America. A recent discovery indicates that the Vikings reached North America five hundred years before Columbus. Anne Stine, an archaeologist, discovered the remains of a Viking encampment in northern Newfoundland, an island off the eastern coast of Canada. Many scientists today believe that the Vikings did not stop in Newfoundland but traveled as far south as Massachusetts or New York.

In the following exercises, you will have the opportunity to expand your vocabulary by reading about the Vikings in America. Below are ten vocabulary words that will be used in these exercises.

ambitious	exclaim	honorable	portrait	wardrobe
envy	heir	oath	reign	yacht

EXERCISE 1 *Mapping*

Directions. In the item below, a vocabulary word is provided and used in a sentence. Take a guess at the word's meaning and write it in the box labeled **Your Guess**. Then look the word up in your dictionary and write the definition in the box labeled **Definition**. Finally, use your dictionary to find other forms of the word, such as adjective, noun, or verb forms. Write these words in the box labeled **Other Forms**.

Then, on a separate sheet of paper, draw your own map and follow the same instructions for each of the nine remaining vocabulary words.

1.

ambitious ➡ The people who lived in Scandinavia from the ninth to the twelfth centuries were known as Vikings. **Ambitious** young Viking men, that is, those who wanted to get ahead, traveled to find fortune.

Your Guess:

Other Forms:

Definition:

2.

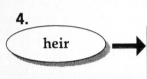

At that time, Scandinavia was not as rich as the rest of Europe, partly because the soil in Scandinavia was not as good for farming as that in France and England. For this reason, the Vikings may have **envied** their richer neighbors.

3.

The Vikings raided the countries to the south. Although the people of England and France loudly **exclaimed** their pain and misery, no one answered their cries for help, and the raids continued.

4.

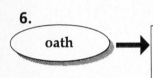

The Vikings also colonized new territory: The Viking Naddod laid claim to Iceland. His great-grandnephew, Erik the Red, was the **heir** to this family tradition of colonization. He colonized Greenland.

5.

Old Norse sagas, or legends, tell of the adventures of this **honorable** Viking family. These sagas indicate that Erik the Red and his son, Leif Eriksson, were especially respected.

6.

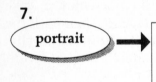

The Vikings were feared and hated throughout Europe for their warlike behavior and their cursing and swearing. To this day, they are remembered for their violent actions and loud **oaths**.

7.

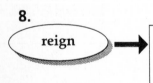

From the Norse legend *Erik's Saga,* we can piece together a **portrait** of Erik the Red. The picture that emerges is of a clever, brave, and confident man.

8.

Most Norse legends are written about the deeds of a king and the events that happened during the period of his **reign**.

9.

An important part of a Viking's **wardrobe** was his suit of armor, made of thick animal hides. His clothing also included a long, heavy shirt, leather shoes, and a leather helmet.

10.

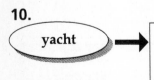

Viking ships were light and fast but were very different in design from today's **yachts,** which are used for pleasure cruises or racing. Viking ships carried horses, cows, pigs, and warriors on long, difficult journeys.

EXERCISE 2 *Context Clues*

Directions. Scan the definitions in Column A. Then think about how the boldface words are used in the sentences in Column B. To complete the exercise, match each definition in Column A with the correct vocabulary word from Column B. Write the letter of your choice on the line provided. Finally, write the vocabulary word on the line before the definition.

COLUMN A	COLUMN B

_____ **11.** word: _____:
n. a person who inherits another's property or traits

_____ **12.** word: _____:
n. dislike or uneasiness because of another person's possessions or advantages; *v.* to be jealous of

_____ **13.** word: _____:
n. a drawing, painting, sculpture, photograph, or description of someone

_____ **14.** word: _____:
n. one's collection of clothes; a closet, cupboard, or room for clothes

_____ **15.** word: _____:
adj. greatly desirous of something; eager; demanding great effort or skill

_____ **16.** word: _____:
v. to cry out; to speak suddenly in surprise or anger

_____ **17.** word: _____:
n. a formal declaration of honesty or loyalty; a swear word; a curse

_____ **18.** word: _____:
n. a small boat for pleasure or racing

_____ **19.** word: _____:
n. a power or rule over; a period of rule; *v.* to rule or have power over

_____ **20.** word: _____:
adj. worthy of being honored or respected; having a sense of right and wrong

(A) Long ago, the Vikings **reigned** over the huge northern island of Greenland. The Vikings also ruled Iceland.

(B) The settlement of Greenland—a harsh place with long, cold, dark winters—was an **ambitious** project. It took a great effort to carry out.

(C) Eventually the settlement was abandoned because no new people came to the colony, and the settlers left no **heirs** to inherit their property.

(D) Because life was hard in Greenland, the Greenlanders must have **envied** people who lived in warmer places.

(E) A piece of carved ivory that looks like a **portrait** of a Viking was discovered in an old Eskimo camp. This likeness is evidence that the Vikings had contact with the Eskimos.

(F) Until recently, there was no proof that the Vikings had traveled south along the Canadian coast—until one person promised to carry out her dream. She made an **oath** to discover the truth about the Vikings.

(G) Anne Stine is an archaeologist who is fascinated by the Vikings. One summer she sailed a **yacht** down Canada's coast.

(H) Stine **exclaimed** out loud with joy when she discovered the ruins of a Viking village in a meadow in Newfoundland.

(I) Stine made a careful study of the ruins. There were no signs of the clothing that made up the Viking's **wardrobes** because the cloth had all rotted.

(J) In their own way, Viking warriors were **honorable** men. They had their own concept of right and wrong: Right was bravery and travel, and wrong was giving up without a fight.

MAKING NEW WORDS YOUR OWN **69**

EXERCISE 3 Like Meanings and Opposite Meanings ✍

Directions. For each item below, circle the letter of the choice that means the same, or about the same, as the boldface word.

21. a solemn **oath**

(A) decision
(B) lecture
(C) comment
(D) declaration

22. an empty **wardrobe**

(A) closet for clothes
(B) large glass bottle
(C) small ship
(D) suitcase

23. **heir** to a fortune

(A) child
(B) inheritor
(C) judge
(D) lawyer

24. a life-size **portrait**

(A) clay mask
(B) mirror
(C) picture of someone
(D) suit of armor

25. a private **yacht**

(A) car
(B) beach
(C) meadow
(D) boat

Directions. For each item below, circle the letter of the choice that means the opposite, or about the opposite, of the boldface word.

26. the **ambitious** Viking

(A) halfhearted
(B) violent
(C) athletic
(D) eager

27. a feeling of **envy**

(A) jealousy
(B) sympathy
(C) pride
(D) desire

28. to **exclaim** with anger

(A) whisper
(B) scream
(C) threaten
(D) hope

29. **reign** justly

(A) organize
(B) dominate
(C) abuse
(D) serve

30. **honorable** leader

(A) worthy
(B) honest
(C) not respectable
(D) conquering

Name _____ Date _____ Class _____

MAKING NEW WORDS YOUR OWN

Lesson 18 | **CONTEXT: People and Places**

Desert Mysteries: Prehistoric Civilizations in the Southwestern United States

People have grown fruits and vegetables for thousands of years. But until about seven thousand years ago, our ancestors did not know how to grow food. The Cochise people of Mexico and the Southwestern United States were the first people to grow corn. We have learned about how the Cochise lived through the work of archaeologists and other scientists. Archaeologists study the things that ancient peoples have left behind. These artifacts include pottery, houses, and ancient garbage dumps. Studying these artifacts tells us something about how these early peoples lived.

In the following exercises, you will have the opportunity to expand your vocabulary by reading about the ancient civilizations of the Southwest. Below are ten vocabulary words that will be used in these exercises.

counterfeit	investment	luxurious	relate	solitary
galaxy	knapsack	ornamental	request	transparent

EXERCISE 1 *Mapping*

Directions. In the item below, a vocabulary word is provided and used in a sentence. Take a guess at the word's meaning and write it in the box labeled **Your Guess**. Then look the word up in your dictionary and write the definition in the box labeled **Definition**. Finally, use your dictionary to find other forms of the word, such as adjective, noun, or verb forms. Write these words in the box labeled **Other Forms**.

Then, on a separate sheet of paper, draw your own map and follow the same instructions for each of the nine remaining vocabulary words.

1.

counterfeit → People and museums are eager to own ancient carvings and pottery. For this reason, some dishonest people make **counterfeit** artifacts.

Your Guess:

Other Forms:

Definition:

HRW material copyrighted under notice appearing earlier in this work.

2.
galaxy

What were the beliefs of the ancient peoples of the Southwest? Did they think of the millions of stars in our **galaxy** as gods? We can never be certain what these people believed. We can, however, learn many things about how they lived.

3.
investment

The Hohokam were the descendants of the ancient Cochise. The Hohokam lived near rivers in southern Arizona. They made a huge **investment** of time and energy to create irrigation canals.

4.
knapsack

On a hike out to the ruins of the Hohokam city, you will need to carry water in a **knapsack**. Once, Hohokam canals flowed into the city. Now the only water around is what you carry on your back.

5.
luxurious

The Hohokam ruins are near present-day Phoenix, Arizona. Life in this ancient city was comfortable, even **luxurious**. Harvests were rich, so some people probably had time to relax.

6.
ornamental

Archaeologists have discovered decorative, **ornamental** jewelry and crafts made by the Hohokam.

7.
relate

Scientists **relate** these decorative objects to the lifestyle of the people who made them. One important connection is that fancy crafts take time to make. Based on this fact, scientists feel that the Hohokam must have had a lot of spare time.

8.
request

If you ask for information on the religious beliefs of the Hohokam, your **request** cannot be granted easily. Some archaeologists believe that the large, thick-walled Hohokam ruins were once temples. But others think they might have been forts.

9.
solitary

Imagine that you stand at the foot of one of these **solitary** buildings. You are struck by the loneliness of the place. Who built this massive structure with its five-foot-thick adobe walls? Where did these people go?

10.
transparent

The answer to this question is far from **transparent**. No one knows what happened to the great Hohokam civilization. By the time the Spanish arrived, the Hohokam cities had been abandoned.

EXERCISE 2 *Context Clues* ✍

Directions. Scan the definitions in Column A. Then think about how the boldface words are used in the sentences in Column B. To complete the exercise, match each definition in Column A with the correct vocabulary word from Column B. Write the letter of your choice on the line provided. Finally, write the vocabulary word on the line before the definition.

COLUMN A	COLUMN B

COLUMN A

_____ **11.** word: _____:
n. an imitation intended to deceive; *v.* to make an imitation in order to deceive; *adj.* made in imitation of something

_____ **12.** word: _____:
n. the act of asking for something; something asked for; *v.* to ask for

_____ **13.** word: _____:
n. a bag or case worn on the back

_____ **14.** word: _____:
adj. used as an ornament; decorative; without functional use

_____ **15.** word: _____:
adj. living or being alone; without others; single; only; lonely, empty

_____ **16.** word: _____:
n. property such as stocks purchased for future profit; time or effort spent with the expectation of some return

_____ **17.** word: _____:
adj. fond of or enjoying luxury; splendid; rich; comfortable; expensive

_____ **18.** word: _____:
adj. capable of being seen through; easily understood; very clear

_____ **19.** word: _____:
v. to tell the story of; to connect or associate; to have some connection to

_____ **20.** word: _____:
n. a group of stars; a brilliant collection

COLUMN B

(A) In social studies, Randy has learned about the ancient Anasazi people who once lived in the southwestern United States. He decides to take a bus trip to that area. He has packed a tent, clothes, and food into his **knapsack**.

(B) He visits the Anasazi cliff dwellings at Mesa Verde National Park. From the observation point, he looks through the **transparent** lenses of his binoculars at the famous Anasazi Cliff Palace.

(C) It will be hard to **relate** to his family the beauty of these ancient houses. A snapshot won't tell the whole story.

(D) After lunch, Randy decides to take a hike along the Petroglyph Trail. The trail is **solitary**; Randy doesn't meet anyone else on it.

(E) The trail leads to a large stone panel with markings cut into it. These markings are called petroglyphs. Randy wonders if the symbols have any meaning or if they are only **ornamental**.

(F) At the park museum, Randy asks a favor. He **requests** that a park ranger explain the petroglyphs to him.

(G) She tells Randy, "Archaeologists have made a great **investment** of time to answer that question. But so far, their efforts have not paid off."

(H) In the museum, Randy sees a whole **galaxy** of ancient Anasazi artifacts. He is especially amazed by the collection of Anasazi baskets.

(I) He wonders how the fragile baskets could have survived. The ranger assures him that they are not **counterfeit**. They are the real thing.

(J) Randy camps in the Mesa Verde campground. His tent is not a **luxurious** hotel room. But he feels that the splendor of nearby Cliff Palace is better than any four-star hotel.

EXERCISE 3 *Like Meanings and Opposite Meanings* ✍

Directions. For each item below, circle the letter of the choice that means the same, or about the same, as the boldface word.

21. the Milky Way **galaxy**
(A) the moons of Jupiter
(B) a large group of stars
(C) a constellation
(D) a star like the sun

22. a financial **investment**
(A) something bought for future profit
(B) a business expense
(C) a salary
(D) a person who buys stocks and bonds

23. carry my **knapsack**
(A) folding chair
(B) lantern
(C) backpack
(D) hammer

24. **request** a favorite song
(A) to offer
(B) to open
(C) to discard something
(D) to ask for something

25. **relate** a myth
(A) remember
(B) repeat
(C) tell
(D) shout happily

Directions. For each item below, circle the letter of the choice that means the opposite, or about the opposite, of the boldface word.

26. a **counterfeit** artifact
(A) broken
(B) genuine
(C) ancient
(D) worthless

27. designed to be **ornamental**
(A) useful
(B) cheap
(C) expensive
(D) pleasing

28. a **solitary** example
(A) bland
(B) excellent
(C) multiple
(D) important

29. the **transparent** lake
(A) easily reached
(B) deep
(C) very clouded
(D) inviting

30. the **luxurious** temple
(A) large
(B) restored
(C) foreign
(D) plain

MAKING NEW WORDS YOUR OWN

Lesson 19 | **CONTEXT: People and Places**

Haystacks and Waterlilies: Impressions of Monet

French painter Claude Monet (1840–1926) led a movement called Impressionism. He painted his personal response to—his impression of—natural and human-made objects. At first, Monet and other Impressionist painters were not accepted by the public. But eventually people came to appreciate Impressionist art, and Monet became successful. He made enough money from his work to buy land in the country. In 1883, Monet moved from Paris to an estate at Giverny. Here, he painted his famous pictures of gardens and waterlilies.

In the following exercises, you will have the opportunity to expand your vocabulary by reading about Claude Monet. Below are ten vocabulary words that will be used in these exercises.

| appropriate | contribute | gorgeous | inviting | ordinarily |
| assume | cultivate | hearty | occasion | quantity |

EXERCISE 1   *Mapping*

Directions. In the item below, a vocabulary word is provided and used in a sentence. Take a guess at the word's meaning and write it in the box labeled **Your Guess**. Then look the word up in your dictionary and write the definition in the box labeled **Definition**. Finally, use your dictionary to find other forms of the word, such as adjective, noun, or verb forms. Write these words in the box labeled **Other Forms**.

Then, on a separate sheet of paper, draw your own map and follow the same instructions for each of the nine remaining vocabulary words.

1.

appropriate → Monet exhibited a painting called *Impression: Sunrise* in 1874. A critic **appropriated** the title. Taking it for his own use, he coined the term Impressionism.

Your Guess:

Other Forms:

Definition:

2.

assume

Monet is very popular today. However, you should not **assume**, or accept as true, that he was popular during his lifetime before you study the facts.

3.
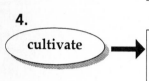
contribute

Monet **contributed** greatly to the world of art. He gave other artists a new way of looking at light and nature.

4.

cultivate

When he moved to Giverny, Monet was able to **cultivate** a beautiful garden. He loved to grow plants.

5.
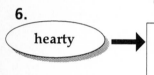
gorgeous

The Art Institute of Chicago has several of Monet's most **gorgeous** paintings of waterlilies. I have never seen anything more magnificent!

6.

hearty

Monet had a **hearty** relationship with his children. Except for an occasional bad temper, he was warm and friendly with all of them.

7.

inviting

Some of Monet's paintings are especially **inviting**. Looking at the waterlilies, for instance, you almost feel tempted to walk into the water.

8.
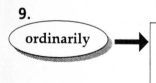
occasion

For Monet, as for most artists, every sale of a painting was an **occasion**, a special cause for celebration.

9.
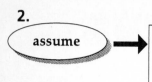
ordinarily

When he moved to the country, Monet's life fell into a pattern. He **ordinarily** woke up around four or five in the morning to see what the weather was like. If it looked like a sunny day, he would get out of bed and begin painting.

10.
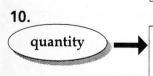
quantity

Monet was his own harshest critic and destroyed hundreds of pictures. Fortunately, a large **quantity** of paintings still remain for our pleasure today.

EXERCISE 2   Context Clues ✍

Directions. Scan the definitions in Column A. Then think about how the boldface words are used in the sentences in Column B. To complete the exercise, match each definition in Column A with the correct vocabulary word from Column B. Write the letter of your choice on the line provided. Finally, write the vocabulary word on the line before the definition.

COLUMN A	COLUMN B

COLUMN A

_____ **11.** word: _____:
adj. right for the purpose; suitable; proper; *v*. to take for one's own or exclusive use

_____ **12.** word: _____:
adj. very warm and friendly; enthusiastic; satisfying and plentiful; strong and healthy

_____ **13.** word: _____:
n. a favorable time; an opportunity; a special time or event for celebration

_____ **14.** word: _____:
v. to take upon oneself; to undertake; to put on; to suppose something to be a fact; to take for granted

_____ **15.** word: _____:
adj. magnificent; splendid; beautiful

_____ **16.** word: _____:
adv. usually; in a normal manner

_____ **17.** word: _____:
n. an amount; a portion

_____ **18.** word: _____:
v. to prepare and use land for growing crops; to grow plants, crops; to improve or develop

_____ **19.** word: _____:
adj. tempting; attractive; enticing

_____ **20.** word: _____:
v. to give to a common fund or cause; to assist in bringing something about

COLUMN B

(A) Another school of painting in fashion about the same time as Impressionism was Realism. Realist artists **ordinarily** tried to make their paintings look exactly like their subjects. They usually painted things almost as the things would appear in a photograph.

(B) Sometimes it takes time to develop a liking for a certain style of painting. Have you **cultivated** an appreciation of Monet's art? Or do you prefer Realist painting?

(C) Monet's early critics did not feel his paintings were **appropriate**. These critics felt the Impressionists made improper use of their subjects.

(D) Public approval of Impressionism **contributed** to Monet's success. This approval helped bring about acceptance by art critics.

(E) Monet became a successful artist by the late 1880s. He was able to buy his country estate with a portion, or **quantity,** of his income.

(F) At Giverny, Monet built a **gorgeous** bridge in the waterlily garden. He painted this beautiful bridge many times.

(G) Generally, Monet was not attracted by images of the city. He found nature a more **inviting** subject.

(H) Living in the country gave Monet a big appetite. He ate a **hearty,** satisfying breakfast every morning before setting about his work.

(I) Monet loved to take trips. Any event away from his home became an **occasion** for travel.

(J) Monet **assumed** the responsibility for his large family. He took it upon himself to provide for them, and his success made it possible for him to do so.

EXERCISE 3 Like Meanings and Opposite Meanings ✍

Directions. For each item below, circle the letter of the choice that means the same, or about the same, as the boldface word.

21. to **assume** a big project
    (A) work on
    (B) undertake
    (C) ask about
    (D) finish

22. an **occasion** for a celebration
    (A) costume
    (B) poor reason
    (C) opportunity
    (D) ordinary time

23. to **cultivate** relationships with other artists
    (A) develop
    (B) end
    (C) watch
    (D) ruin

24. a **hearty** approach to life
    (A) cautious
    (B) unhappy
    (C) uninteresting
    (D) enthusiastic

25. a **quantity** of paint
    (A) splash
    (B) amount
    (C) gallon
    (D) cup

Directions. For each item below, circle the letter of the choice that means the opposite, or about the opposite, of the boldface word.

26. an **appropriate** question
    (A) suitable
    (B) confusing
    (C) improper
    (D) interesting

27. **gorgeous** waterlilies
    (A) beautiful
    (B) wilted
    (C) ugly
    (D) yellow

28. an **inviting** story
    (A) unappealing
    (B) long
    (C) brief
    (D) familiar

29. to **contribute** a small amount
    (A) find
    (B) give
    (C) take away
    (D) ask for

30. **ordinarily** pleasant
    (A) with enthusiasm
    (B) unusually
    (C) daily
    (D) rarely

MAKING NEW WORDS YOUR OWN

Lesson 20 **CONTEXT: People and Places**

Island Hopping in the Caribbean

When you think of the Caribbean, you probably think of clear, turquoise water, palm trees, and beaches of pure, white sand. The Caribbean islands—Jamaica, Cuba, and Puerto Rico are the largest—are famous for colorful fish and coral and for rare tropical birds. Because the islands are separated from each other by water, each island has its own culture, history, and languages. People speak Spanish in Puerto Rico and Cuba, but French is spoken in Haiti. And people on the island of Aruba speak a language called Papiamento.

In the following exercises, you will have the opportunity to expand your vocabulary by reading about the Caribbean islands. Below are ten vocabulary words that will be used in these exercises.

boast	disadvantage	export	import	precipitation
contrast	eliminate	forefathers	inaccurate	tradition

EXERCISE 1 *Mapping* 👈

Directions. In the item below, a vocabulary word is provided and used in a sentence. Take a guess at the word's meaning and write it in the box labeled **Your Guess**. Then look the word up in your dictionary and write the definition in the box labeled **Definition**. Finally, use your dictionary to find other forms of the word, such as adjective, noun, or verb forms. Write these words in the box labeled **Other Forms**.

Then, on a separate sheet of paper, draw your own map and follow the same instructions for each of the nine remaining vocabulary words.

1.

boast → Carnival celebrations are popular throughout the Caribbean. Carnival takes place on the island of Trinidad from late February to early March. Trinidadians **boast** about their Carnival, proudly claiming that it is the best celebration in all the world.

Your Guess:

Other Forms:

Definition:

2.

contrast ➤ The lush vegetation of Trinidad forms a **contrast** to the dry, rocky landscape of Aruba. These islands are very different as they are seven hundred miles apart.

3.

disadvantage ➤ Sunny weather is nice, but rain is important too. One **disadvantage** of Aruba's dry climate is that there is very little fresh water on the island.

4.

eliminate ➤ The St. Vincent parrot is a rare parrot that lives only on the island of St. Vincent. This species is in danger of extinction because the destruction of island forests threatens to **eliminate** the parrot's natural habitat.

5.

export ➤ Bananas, which are grown on many of the islands and sold all over the world, are a major Caribbean **export**.

6.

forefathers ➤ The Caribs lived in the Caribbean islands long before Columbus arrived in the Americas. The Caribs are the **forefathers**, or ancestors, of many Caribbean islanders.

7.

import ➤ There are not many farms on the island of St. Eustatius. So, people who live on St. Eustatius must **import** most of their food from other islands.

8.

inaccurate ➤ Shipwrecks, caused by storms and the **inaccurate** calculations of navigators, are common in the Caribbean. Navigators can easily misjudge the distance to the shore during a storm.

9.

precipitation ➤ On the beaches of Jamaica, the weather is almost always warm and clear. But high in the Blue Mountains there is much **precipitation** in the form of both rain and snow.

10.

tradition ➤ Brightly painted houses are a Caribbean **tradition**. People have believed for a long time that bright, cheerful colors keep away evil spirits.

EXERCISE 2 *Context Clues* ✎

Directions. Scan the definitions in Column A. Then think about how the boldface words are used in the sentences in Column B. To complete the exercise, match each definition in Column A with the correct vocabulary word from Column B. Write the letter of your choice on the line provided. Finally, write the vocabulary word on the line before the definition.

COLUMN A	COLUMN B

COLUMN A

_____ **11.** word: _____:
v. to talk proudly about oneself; to brag

_____ **12.** word: _____:
v. to show differences between; *n.* a striking difference; the effect of a striking difference, as in photography

_____ **13.** word: _____:
n. something brought in from another country or place; importance; *v.* to bring in goods from another country

_____ **14.** word: _____:
n. the handing down of stories, beliefs, or customs from generation to generation; a custom

_____ **15.** word: _____:
n. a drawback; a handicap

_____ **16.** word: _____:
n. a bringing on suddenly; a sudden fall or rush; snow, rain, or sleet

_____ **17.** word: _____:
n. something sent to another place or country; *v.* to carry or send goods to another country for sale

_____ **18.** word: _____:
n. male ancestors

_____ **19.** word: _____:
v. to take out, remove, get rid of; to take out of consideration

_____ **20.** word: _____:
adj. not correct; not exact

COLUMN B

(A) The relaxed life style of my cousins in the Virgin Islands is such a **contrast** to the hustle and bustle of my life here in New York City.

(B) My brother ran into the water at St. Thomas Beach with **precipitation**. He was in such a hurry that he didn't watch where he was going, and he stepped on a jellyfish.

(C) Our cousins told us an old story about Sir Francis Drake, who lived on St. Thomas in the 1600s. According to **tradition**, the explorer used Magen Bay Beach as a lookout.

(D) "Mountain chicken" is an **inaccurate** name for the dish my aunt Gladys made for us— mountain chicken is really frog legs.

(E) My uncle Marcus told me that tourism is of great **import** in the Virgin Islands. The economies of the islands depend on tourism.

(F) Some islanders do not like the changes that the tourist industry brings. Yet tourism will probably never be **eliminated** because it is so important to the island economy.

(G) On St. Barts, many of the ways of the **forefathers** are disappearing. A few of the older islanders are the last to carry on the practices of their ancestors.

(H) The island of Grand Cayman **boasts** the world's only sea turtle farm. To check the truth of this claim, we went to see the farm.

(I) Sea turtle meat is not usually **exported** to other countries. Instead, it is sold to restaurants on the island.

(J) A girl I met speaks English, Dutch, and Papiamento. She was surprised that I only speak one language, but I told her that in New York it's not a **disadvantage** to know only English.

EXERCISE 3 _Like Meanings and Opposite Meanings_ ☞

Directions. For each item below, circle the letter of the choice that means the same, or about the same, as the boldface word.

21. boast about a skill
- (A) worry
- (B) talk
- (C) brag
- (D) know

22. a Jamaican **tradition**
- (A) celebration
- (B) custom
- (C) culture
- (D) history

23. Carib **forefathers**
- (A) grandchildren
- (B) ancestors
- (C) fishermen
- (D) relations

24. heavy **precipitation**
- (A) a surprise
- (B) rainfall
- (C) evaporation
- (D) pressure

25. export bananas
- (A) send to another country
- (B) return to the farmers
- (C) eat a great deal of
- (D) use as a medicine

Directions. For each item below, circle the letter of the choice that means the opposite, or about the opposite, of the boldface word.

26. a strong **contrast**
- (A) difference
- (B) dislike
- (C) similarity
- (D) opinion

27. an unfortunate **disadvantage**
- (A) handicap
- (B) aid
- (C) disaster
- (D) inability

28. import oil
- (A) send to another country
- (B) offer for sale
- (C) increase the price of
- (D) set on fire

29. an **inaccurate** statement
- (A) important
- (B) false
- (C) funny
- (D) correct

30. eliminate a choice
- (A) keep
- (B) create
- (C) think about
- (D) get rid of

MAKING NEW WORDS YOUR OWN

Lesson 21 | **CONTEXT:** Ecology and Environment
Down to the Sea with Jacques Cousteau

The sea has always held mysteries for people. Jacques Cousteau (b. 1910), a French under-water explorer, has revealed some of these mysteries to us. Cousteau's interest in the sea started with his service in the French Navy. His friendship with two other sailors led to their working together for many years. They studied the shark and the whale, dove for sunken treasure, and explored a coral sea. What made all of these adventures possible was a ship named *Calypso* and the scuba tank which Cousteau and Emile Gagnan invented.

In the following exercises, you will have the opportunity to expand your vocabulary by reading about Cousteau's ship, *Calypso*. Below are ten vocabulary words that will be used in these exercises.

| appreciate | entertain | inform | mammoth | theme |
| braille | genuine | inspiration | text | visual |

EXERCISE 1 *Mapping*

Directions. In the item below, a vocabulary word is provided and used in a sentence. Take a guess at the word's meaning and write it in the box labeled **Your Guess**. Then look the word up in your dictionary and write the definition in the box labeled **Definition**. Finally, use your dictionary to find other forms of the word, such as adjective, noun, or verb forms. Write these words in the box labeled **Other Forms**.

Then, on a separate sheet of paper, draw your own map and follow the same instruction for each of the nine remaining vocabulary words.

1.

appreciate →

> The *Calypso* was an old United States minesweeper being used as a ferry after World War II. On his expeditions, Cousteau learned to **appreciate** such a vessel. He understood the worth of a ship that could hold a crew of thirty people, a helicopter, and a hot-air balloon.

Your Guess:

Other Forms:

Definition:

2.

braille ➤ Cousteau's inventions and his ship made it easier for people to learn about the sea. The *Calypso* helped to open the sea to people much as the system of **braille** opened the world of books to the blind.

3.

entertain ➤ In 1893, the first underwater photograph was taken. Sixty-two years later, Cousteau **entertained** audiences with his award-winning movies about the sea. The films *The Silent World* and *World Without Sun* held the interest of thousands of viewers.

4.

genuine ➤ In 1959, *Calypso* acquired a two-person exploration submarine. It had no propeller and it could take divers to depths of 1150 feet—a chance for some real, **genuine** adventure.

5.

inform ➤ The films made by the crew of *Calypso* have served to **inform** viewers about underwater life. Audiences learned about life forms they never knew existed.

6.

 **inspiration** ➤ Cousteau's work aboard *Calypso* is an **inspiration** to amateurs and scientists alike. He has had a strong influence on others who wish to explore the sea.

7.

 **mammoth** ➤ A 139-foot-long ship may seem **mammoth** to some. *Calypso,* however, is rather small compared to many other ships, although it has two engines, a repair workshop, and walk-in refrigerators.

8.

text ➤ In 1967, *Calypso* set out on a three-year expedition. During this trip, the first twelve films of the TV series, *The Undersea World of Jacques Cousteau,* were filmed. A **text,** or written work, about the sea may be interesting, but a film is really gripping.

9.

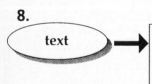 **theme** ➤ Cousteau has also written books about his adventures. The **theme,** or subject, of his work is the fascinating world beneath the sea. *Diving Companions,* for example, talks about two sea lions living aboard *Calypso.*

10.

visual ➤ The many photographs in Cousteau's books are a **visual** treat for the reader. It is exciting to actually see photographs of creatures mentioned by Cousteau in his writing.

EXERCISE 2 Context Clues ✍

Directions. Scan the definitions in Column A. Then think about how the boldface words are used in the sentences in Column B. To complete the exercise, match each definition in Column A with the correct vocabulary word from Column B. Write the letter of your choice on the line provided. Finally, write the vocabulary word on the line before the definition.

COLUMN A

_____ **11.** word: _____:
adj. connected with sight; having qualities that can be seen

_____ **12.** word: _____:
n. a topic, subject, or main idea of a written work, sermon, speech, and so on

_____ **13.** word: _____:
v. to give knowledge of something to; to tell someone something

_____ **14.** word: _____:
n. an inhaling; a strong influence; a stimulus to creativity

_____ **15.** word: _____:
n. a type of extinct elephant; *adj.* huge

_____ **16.** word: _____:
adj. real; true; authentic; honest

_____ **17.** word: _____:
v. to hold the interest of and give pleasure to; to amuse; to think about or consider; to give hospitality to guests

_____ **18.** word: _____:
n. a written work; the main part of a piece of writing

_____ **19.** word: _____:
v. to think well of; to understand; to recognize the worth of and to be grateful for; to raise the price or value of

_____ **20.** word: _____:
n. a system of writing for the blind in which the fingers are used to read

COLUMN B

(A) I dive off *Calypso*. I swim underwater with a scuba tank on my back. "Is this a **genuine** experience? Am I really here?" I ask myself.

(B) "That sea elephant over there reminds me of the long-extinct **mammoth**, a woolly elephant. Am I dreaming?"

(C) I **appreciate** all the tips and advice that the crew gave me. I am grateful because it is my first solo dive. I begin to adjust to the light. Many strange sights float past me.

(D) The crew **informed** me just last night that I had to find the lost treasure. But why didn't they tell me sooner?

(E) Suddenly, a shark crosses my path. I **entertain** the idea of going back to the surface and to the safety of the ship. Then I think about the importance of my mission.

(F) My dive has been an **inspiration** to me. I suddenly feel creative! I'm going to write a book about my adventures.

(G) What will my book be about? The **theme** will be the wonders of the sea, but its exact title will have to wait until I write it.

(H) My vision-impaired sister wants my first book to be put into **braille**, a system of writing that she can read with her fingers. She says she can't wait to read it.

(I) The **text**, or the words, of the book will be easy to put into braille with a special typewriter.

(J) The **visual** part of the book, the photographs and drawings I make, will appear in full color. I wake up. . . . Cousteau's book, *The Shark: Splendid Savage of the Sea,* lies next to my bed. I guess it was only a dream.

EXERCISE 3 *Like Meanings and Opposite Meanings* ✍

Directions. For each item below, circle the letter of the choice that means the same, or about the same, as the boldface word.

21. an **inspiration** to us
  (A) burden
  (B) comfort
  (C) bitter disappointment
  (D) strong influence

22. the **visual** image
  (A) painted
  (B) something that can be seen
  (C) connected with touch
  (D) invisible to the human eye

23. the **theme** of the story
  (A) last paragraph
  (B) hidden threat
  (C) main idea
  (D) level of interest

24. to read **braille**
  (A) a system of writing for the blind
  (B) a very ancient form of writing
  (C) a military code
  (D) sign language

25. read the **text**
  (A) written work
  (B) title
  (C) introduction
  (D) sign language

Directions. For each item below, circle the letter of the choice that means the opposite, or about the opposite, of the boldface word.

26. a **mammoth** whale
  (A) gentle
  (B) tiny
  (C) intelligent
  (D) endangered

27. to **appreciate** someone's help
  (A) scorn
  (B) understand
  (C) protect
  (D) imagine

28. to be **entertained** by dolphins
  (A) interested
  (B) studied
  (C) photographed
  (D) bored

29. **genuine** interest
  (A) valuable
  (B) strong
  (C) fake
  (D) real

30. **inform** the captain
  (A) withhold facts from
  (B) speak to quietly
  (C) answer directly
  (D) discuss openly with

MAKING NEW WORDS YOUR OWN

Lesson 22 **CONTEXT: Ecology and Environment**

What's the Forecast for Brazil's Rain Forest?

A tropical rain forest receives rain all year long and is very warm. It has hundreds of species of tall trees—some as high as two hundred feet! The largest tropical rain forest in the world is located in Brazil's Amazon region. Many valuable woods and plants are found in this rain forest, as well as hundreds of species of animals. Today, Brazil's rain forest is threatened. Scientists worry that the mass cutting of trees may affect the world's climate. They are also worried that many species of plants and animals may become extinct. People all around the world are trying to work with Brazil to slow the destruction of the rain forest.

In the following exercises, you will have the opportunity to expand your vocabulary by reading about Brazil's rain forest. Below are ten vocabulary words that will be used in these exercises.

| campaign | conscience | furious | plot | urge |
| characteristic | doubtless | juvenile | reduction | widespread |

EXERCISE 1 *Mapping*

Directions. In the item below, a vocabulary word is provided and used in a sentence. Take a guess at the word's meaning and write it in the box labeled **Your Guess**. Then look the word up in your dictionary and write the definition in the box labeled **Definition**. Finally, use your dictionary to find other forms of the word, such as adjective, noun, or verb forms. Write these words in the box labeled **Other Forms**.

Then, on a separate sheet of paper, draw your own map and follow the same instructions for each of the nine remaining vocabulary words.

1.

campaign → A **campaign** to save the rain forests is growing throughout the world. People hope to achieve their goal of saving the tropical forests through a series of planned actions.

Your Guess:

Other Forms:

Definition:

2.
characteristic →

A major **characteristic** of Brazil's rain forest is the canopy. This unique feature is formed by the overlapping tops of trees.

3.
conscience →

You must decide for yourself whether the destruction of the rain forest should be stopped. Let your **conscience** help you decide what is right and what is wrong.

4.
doubtless →

Doubtless, many miners, farmers, and others will resist efforts to save the rain forest. These people are concerned about their livelihoods and are afraid of what will happen if their activities are limited by the government.

5.
furious →

Many of Brazil's farmers become extremely angry when they are told not to burn down trees in the rain forest. They feel that they have a right to earn a living and are **furious** when people tell them they can't farm there.

6.
juvenile →

In the forest, **juvenile** trees are dwarfed by taller ones. These young trees have to struggle to find sunlight.

7.
plot →

Farmers have burned trees on certain **plots** in the rain forest. They then plant crops on these small areas of ground.

8.
reduction →

Less burning of the rain forest would lead to a **reduction** in the amount of carbon dioxide in the air. Too much carbon dioxide might lead to global warming.

9.
urge →

I **urge** you to find out as much as you can about the tropical rain forests. Once you have, you may want to persuade others to do the same.

10.
widespread →

Scientists worry that the destruction of the rain forests will have **widespread** effects. In fact, they expect the effects to be felt all around the world.

EXERCISE 2 *Context Clues*

Directions. Scan the definitions in Column A. Then think about how the boldface words are used in the sentences in Column B. To complete the exercise, match each definition in Column A with the correct vocabulary word from Column B. Write the letter of your choice on the line provided. Finally, write the vocabulary word on the line before the definition.

COLUMN A

_____ **11.** word: _____:
adj. young, immature, childish; suitable or characteristic of young persons or children; *n.* a young person, child, or youth

_____ **12.** word: _____:
adv. certainly; probably; *adj.* sure

_____ **13.** word: _____:
n. a lessening; anything made by lessening something; the amount by which something is made smaller

_____ **14.** word: _____:
n. a small area of ground marked off for special use; a plan to do something dishonest; a story line; *v.* to plan secretly

_____ **15.** word: _____:
adj. occurring over a wide area; widely distributed or spread

_____ **16.** word: _____:
adj. full of rage; violently angry; intense

_____ **17.** word: _____:
n. a series of planned actions to achieve a goal; *v.* to promote a person actively for political office; to promote a cause

_____ **18.** word: _____:
adj. typical; *n.* a distinguishing feature

_____ **19.** word: _____:
v. to beg or plead; to persuade; to call forth; *n.* an impulse to do a certain thing

_____ **20.** word: _____:
n. a knowledge or sense of right and wrong, with a leaning toward doing right

COLUMN B

(A) Some people **plot** to smuggle endangered birds and other animals into the United States. They make their plans secretly because smuggling is a crime.

(B) If you were running for political office in Brazil, would you **campaign** to save the rain forest? Or would you promote some other cause?

(C) **Doubtless**, much of Brazil's rain forest will be cut down, probably within the next few years.

(D) A **characteristic** or typical day in the rain forest is very warm and humid. There's always a good chance that it will rain.

(E) **Juveniles** in the United States might not understand how the destruction of the rain forest touches them. It is hard for young people to see how something happening thousands of miles away can change their lives.

(F) One environmentalist recently had an **urge** to threaten Brazilian officials. Fortunately, he controlled that impulse.

(G) A **reduction** in the number of trees in the rain forest means that fewer birds can nest there. Fewer trees will cause problems for monkeys and other animals, too.

(H) The rain forest frequently experiences **furious,** or violent, thunderstorms.

(I) Cattle ranching and farming are becoming **widespread** in Brazil. Throughout the rain forest, huge ranches are appearing.

(J) The **consciences** of Brazil's elected officials will probably seal the fate of the rain forest. They have to balance what is right today with what is right for the future.

EXERCISE 3 *Like Meanings and Opposite Meanings* ✍

Directions. For each item below, circle the letter of the choice that means the same, or about the same, as the boldface word.

21. a **campaign** to save the rain forest
(A) goal
(B) series of planned actions
(C) desire
(D) end result

22. the **conscience** of the voters
(A) knowledge
(B) concerns
(C) sense of right and wrong
(D) lack of power

23. a **furious** biologist
(A) active
(B) well-educated
(C) secretive
(D) extremely angry

24. the **plot** of a novel about Brazil
(A) author
(B) publisher
(C) story line
(D) last chapter

25. an **urge** to speak
(A) impulse
(B) request
(C) permission
(D) reason

Directions. For each item below, circle the letter of the choice that means the opposite, or about the opposite, of the boldface word.

26. a **characteristic** gesture
(A) kind
(B) unusual
(C) inexperienced
(D) American

27. **doubtless**, action must be taken
(A) eagerly
(B) maybe
(C) sadly
(D) impatiently

28. a **juvenile** farmer
(A) elderly
(B) poor
(C) native
(D) hard-working

29. a **reduction** of species
(A) increase
(B) count
(C) small number
(D) decrease

30. **widespread** logging
(A) environmentally safe
(B) very limited
(C) restricted
(D) widely practiced

MAKING NEW WORDS YOUR OWN

Lesson 23 CONTEXT: Ecology and Environment
Jean of the Environment: Jean Craighead George

"Save the whales!" "Recycle your plastic!" Today, the environment is a major topic of conversation, study, and even advertising. People used to look for ways to use nature's forces and products. Now we search for ways to save the environment. Some people insist that we can do both, but others are not so sure. Jean Craighead George (b. 1919) helps children learn about the environment while entertaining them with her novels and nonfiction books. George explores the Yu'pik and Inupiat cultures in Alaska and the Seminole culture in Florida. Her 1959 book, *My Side of the Mountain,* is the story of a boy who survives in the wilderness by living in a hollow tree trunk for a year.

In the following exercises, you will have the opportunity to expand your vocabulary by reading about Jean Craighead George and the environment. Below are ten vocabulary words that will be used in these exercises.

applaud	inexpensive	persuade	remedy	temporary
guidance	issue	protest	revolution	villain

EXERCISE 1 *Mapping* ✍

Directions. In the item below, a vocabulary word is provided and used in a sentence. Take a guess at the word's meaning and write it in the box labeled **Your Guess**. Then look the word up in your dictionary and write the definition in the box labeled **Definition**. Finally, use your dictionary to find other forms of the word, such as adjective, noun, or verb forms. Write these words in the box labeled **Other Forms**.

Then, on a separate sheet of paper, draw your own map and follow the same instructions for each of the nine remaining vocabulary words.

1.

(applaud) ➔ Book reviewers **applaud** Jean Craighead George's writing. In fact, *Julie of the Wolves,* a novel about a Native Alaskan girl, received further praise: It was awarded the Newbery Medal in 1972.

Your Guess:

Other Forms:

Definition:

2.
guidance  → Under George's **guidance,** her children carried out projects to learn more about nature. With their mother's advice, one son started his own chemical-free garden.

3.
inexpensive → Fortunately, there are many **inexpensive** ways to become a naturalist. You can make a bird feeder, study trees on the way home from school, plant some flowers, or start a bug collection. All of these are very low-cost ways of starting an environmental project.

4.
issue → In her 1971 book, *Who Really Killed Cock Robin? An Ecological Mystery,* George talks about the **issue** of chemical pollution and its far-reaching effects. The question of pollution and other current environmental topics are often themes in George's books.

5.
persuade → George does not try to **persuade,** or convince, people to care about nature. She merely takes us to spend the winter with a pack of wolves or to search for food with baby alligators.

6.
protest → Some people **protest,** or demonstrate, against environmental dangers. Others study or write about them. Jean Craighead George has chosen to both study and write about nature.

7.
remedy → Knowledge is a **remedy** for many environmental problems, but knowledge cannot cure the ills without action.

8.
revolution → Some people think it will take a **revolution** to bring about the drastic changes needed to save our planet, but people like George work to bring about change in a peaceful way.

9.
temporary → In *One Day in the Alpine Tundra,* George gives us a glimpse of a meadow in the mountains of Wyoming. Damage to the fragile world of plants and animals there may be only **temporary.** But how can we be sure the damage won't be permanent?

10.
villain → George avoids blaming **villains** in her stories. Instead of pointing to specific "bad guys," she coaxes her readers to understand the impact of their actions on nature.

EXERCISE 2 *Context Clues*

Directions. Scan the definitions in Column A. Then think about how the boldface words are used in the sentences in Column B. To complete the exercise, match each definition in Column A with the correct vocabulary word from Column B. Write the letter of your choice on the line provided. Finally, write the vocabulary word on the line before the definition.

COLUMN A

_____ **11.** word: _____:
adj. costing little; low-priced; cheap

_____ **12.** word: _____:
v. to put forth or distribute; to publish; *n.* a question to be decided; something put out in many copies; offspring

_____ **13.** word: _____:
v. to cause to do something; to convince

_____ **14.** word: _____:
v. to speak strongly against; to object; *n.* an objection; a demonstration against

_____ **15.** word: _____:
v. to show enjoyment or approval by clapping hands; to praise

_____ **16.** word: _____:
n. leadership; advice and assistance

_____ **17.** word: _____:
n. a person who commits great crimes; a wicked or evil person; a criminal

_____ **18.** word: _____:
n. the movement of an object around another object; a turning motion; the forceful overthrow of a government; complete or radical change

_____ **19.** word: _____:
n. a cure or correction; *v.* to cure or correct

_____ **20.** word: _____:
adj. lasting for only a certain time; not permanent

COLUMN B

(A) Dear Ms. George:
Our sixth-grade class plans to **issue** a video magazine on the environment. We will put the first one out next month and would like to have your opinion on our ideas.

(B) The magazine will be **inexpensive,** because our costs are low. The only profit we seek is a healthier world.

(C) We plan to report on environmental **protests** because we think that people are interested in knowing who speaks out against polluters.

(D) We will ask how the protesters plan to **remedy** the problems that concern them. Then we will compare their solutions with those offered by experts in the environmental field.

(E) Do you think protesters can **persuade** people to change their old habits, or do you think that demonstrating is not the way to convince people to change?

(F) What if everyone started to recycle plastic? We think it would be a real **revolution,** and we hope our video magazine will help bring about this great change.

(G) In the video, we will also offer our audience some **guidance** on recycling. We believe people need some direction and advice in this area.

(H) After all, our planet is not a **temporary** home. If we plan on the human race being here for good, we need to care for the earth.

(I) We will also name some of the **villains** in the environmental game, such as people who pollute our air, soil, or water.

(J) We hope that students will **applaud** when they see our video. We hope that adults will be clapping for us, too.

EXERCISE 3 *Like Meanings and Opposite Meanings* ✍

Directions. For each item below, circle the letter of the choice that means the same, or about the same, as the boldface word.

21. issue a new book
   (A) publish
   (B) write
   (C) buy
   (D) read

22. a violent **revolution**
   (A) disaster
   (B) overthrow of the government
   (C) complete stop
   (D) election of the president

23. helpful **guidance**
   (A) question
   (B) work
   (C) advice
   (D) knowledge

24. persuade them to change
   (A) begin
   (B) attempt
   (C) wish
   (D) convince

25. applaud her effort
   (A) understand
   (B) watch
   (C) approve of
   (D) help

Directions. For each item below, circle the letter of the choice that means the opposite, or about the opposite, of the boldface word.

26. remedy the situation
   (A) correct
   (B) worsen
   (C) explain
   (D) notice

27. an **inexpensive** product
   (A) necessary
   (B) cheap
   (C) costly
   (D) dangerous

28. protest the decision
   (A) approve of
   (B) object to
   (C) make
   (D) change

29. the evil **villain**
   (A) citizen
   (B) writer
   (C) criminal
   (D) hero

30. a **temporary** solution
   (A) permanent
   (B) brief
   (C) sudden
   (D) poor

MAKING NEW WORDS YOUR OWN

Lesson 24 CONTEXT: Ecology and Environment
Balancing Society and the Environment: Global Warming

Global warming is caused by a blanket of carbon dioxide and other gases that surrounds the earth. This blanket is part of the earth's atmosphere and has warmed the earth for many thousands of years. Originally, the gases were produced by natural processes on earth. For example, a volcanic eruption releases a lot of carbon dioxide into the air. Some of this gas is used up by green plants or absorbed by the ocean. The rest of the gas rises up into the atmosphere and becomes part of the blanket. Many scientists believe this natural process is being upset by the activities of modern society. They tell us that the earth is getting warmer.

In the following exercises, you will have the opportunity to expand your vocabulary by reading about global warming. Below are ten vocabulary words that will be used in these exercises.

adjust	candidate	disgust	employer	hazard
ballot	corporation	dissolve	foul	merchandise

EXERCISE 1 *Mapping* ✍

Directions. In the item below, a vocabulary word is provided and used in a sentence. Take a guess at the word's meaning and write it in the box labeled **Your Guess**. Then look the word up in your dictionary and write the definition in the box labeled **Definition**. Finally, use your dictionary to find other forms of the word, such as adjective, noun, or verb forms. Write these words in the box labeled **Other Forms**.

Then, on a separate sheet of paper, draw your own map and follow the same instructions for each of the nine remaining vocabulary words.

1.

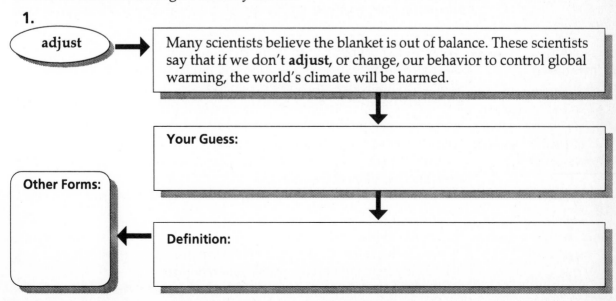

adjust → Many scientists believe the blanket is out of balance. These scientists say that if we don't **adjust,** or change, our behavior to control global warming, the world's climate will be harmed.

Your Guess:

Other Forms:

Definition:

2.

ballot →
One way that we can change our behavior is by conserving, or saving, energy. Because our government can make laws that deal with conservation, people can express their views on the environment through the **ballot**, or vote.

3.

candidate →
Many **candidates** who run for government offices want to protect the environment. They feel that a healthy, balanced environment is in everyone's best interest.

4.

corporation →
Scientists say that some industries contribute to the greenhouse effect more than others. Some **corporations** burn a lot of coal, oil, or gas. Studies show that firms that cut down trees and plants may also contribute to the greenhouse effect.

5.

disgust →
Many people feel **disgust** at the sight of litter on the highway. But other threats to the environment do not seem sickening at all but are useful. Refrigerators and automobiles are two examples.

6.

dissolve →
Cars make global warming worse by using fossil fuel that releases gases into the air. Scientists say that to reduce global warming, we must change our everyday habits. Our environmental problems will not just **dissolve**, or fade away, into thin air.

7.

employer →
But changing our behavior is difficult, especially when a company that is a major **employer** is forced to make changes that lead to a loss of jobs.

8.

foul →
We must not continue to **foul** our environment. Environmentalists say that we can help stop pollution and global warming if we develop cleaner technologies and conserve energy.

9.

hazard →
The blanket of gases is becoming thicker, environmentalists say. As a result, the earth is getting warmer. Global warming is a **hazard**, endangering plants and animals.

10.

merchandise →
Environmentalists tell us that one way to protect the environment is to use products that help stop global warming. These products are known as environmentally friendly **merchandise**.

EXERCISE 2 *Context Clues* ✍

Directions. Scan the definitions in Column A. Then think about how the boldface words are used in the sentences in Column B. To complete the exercise, match each definition in Column A with the correct vocabulary word from Column B. Write the letter of your choice on the line provided. Finally, write the vocabulary word on the line before the definition.

COLUMN A	COLUMN B
_____ **11.** word: _____: *n.* a danger; an obstacle; *v.* to attempt	(A) When gasoline is burned, carbon dioxide is released. Carbon dioxide breaks up, or **dissolves,** into the air. This process adds to the greenhouse effect.
_____ **12.** word: _____: *v.* to break up; to disappear	(B) In everyday life, it is almost impossible to notice carbon dioxide. Unlike many gases, it has no **foul** smell. Carbon dioxide is odorless.
_____ **13.** word: _____: *n.* a ticket by which a vote is cast; a list of people running for office	(C) **Employers** can help to cut down on pollution by encouraging the people who work for them to carpool or ride buses to their jobs.
_____ **14.** word: _____: *v.* to change so as to fit; to become used to	(D) Many **corporations** encourage workers to ride bicycles to work. These firms provide special parking spaces for the bikes.
_____ **15.** word: _____: *adj.* offensive to the senses; dirty; evil; unfavorable; (in baseball) not fair; *v.* to cause or to become dirty or rotten	(E) Not all products that are **merchandised** as environmentally safe are truly safe. We must not be fooled by this tricky method of selling goods.
_____ **16.** word: _____: *n.* a person who seeks or is proposed for an office, award, and so on; a person or thing destined for a certain end	(F) If you want to buy environmentally friendly goods, do not just **hazard** a guess as to which products are really safe. Educate yourself.
_____ **17.** word: _____: *n.* goods that are bought and sold; *v.* to trade on or advertise a particular product	(G) It may be hard to **adjust** to a new way of shopping. Many people are not used to looking for environmentally friendly products.
_____ **18.** word: _____: *n.* a business firm or organization that is run by a group of people and that has many of the legal rights of an individual	(H) Environmentalists say that we must work to reduce global warming. If we do not, the earth will become a **candidate** for worldwide environmental problems—a sad destiny for all of us.
_____ **19.** word: _____: *n.* a person, business firm, and so on, that hires people to work for wages or salary	(I) In an election, environmental laws are often an item on the **ballot.** Some people vote based on how the laws will impact on jobs. Others consider the laws' effects on the environment.
_____ **20.** word: _____: *n.* a feeling of extreme distaste or dislike; *v.* to sicken	(J) Pollution **disgusts** most people. If we do not change our behavior, say environmentalists, pollution will become even more sickening.

EXERCISE 3 Like Meanings and Opposite Meanings

Directions. For each item below, circle the letter of the choice that means the same, or about the same, as the boldface word.

21. the store's **merchandise**
    - (A) location
    - (B) goods
    - (C) popularity
    - (D) recycling bin

22. **adjust** the temperature
    - (A) study scientifically
    - (B) increase
    - (C) correct or change
    - (D) lower gradually

23. mark the **ballot**
    - (A) legal contract
    - (B) sworn statement by a politician
    - (C) ticket by which a vote is cast
    - (D) driver's license

24. the new **corporation**
    - (A) tax system
    - (B) government agency that studies the law
    - (C) court of law
    - (D) business firm

25. the **candidate** for president
    - (A) person who seeks office
    - (B) president's trusted advisor
    - (C) someone who studies the weather
    - (D) famous person

Directions. For each item below, circle the letter of the choice that means the opposite, or about the opposite, of the boldface word.

26. to **dissolve** salt in water
    - (A) stay solid
    - (B) eat with water
    - (C) use as fuel
    - (D) study carefully

27. an understanding **employer**
    - (A) high school teacher
    - (B) neighbor
    - (C) worker
    - (D) partner

28. health **hazard**
    - (A) risk
    - (B) mistake
    - (C) mystery
    - (D) safety

29. filled with **disgust**
    - (A) pleasure
    - (B) sense of doubt
    - (C) feeling of hatred
    - (D) shock

30. a **foul** smell
    - (A) pleasing
    - (B) dim
    - (C) incredible
    - (D) hopeful

MAKING NEW WORDS YOUR OWN

Lesson 25 | **CONTEXT:** Ecology and Environment
The Arabian Oryx and Other Endangered Species

Have you ever heard of the Arabian oryx? It's a kind of antelope with long, straight horns and is one of the few animals that lives in the Arabian desert. For years, it has been hunted for sport. As a result, the oryx has nearly been wiped out. Today, only a handful of oryx live in a wildlife park in Phoenix, Arizona, and in a private reserve in Arabia. Many species have become extinct, or wiped out, while the populations of others have declined. What can be done to save these animals? What can *you* do?

In the following exercises, you will have the opportunity to expand your vocabulary by reading about endangered wildlife. Below are ten vocabulary words that will be used in these exercises.

absorb	cooperate	mourning	omit	security
complaint	debt	offense	regret	tension

EXERCISE 1 *Mapping* ✍

Directions. In the item below, a vocabulary word is provided and used in a sentence. Take a guess at the word's meaning and write it in the box labeled **Your Guess**. Then look the word up in your dictionary and write the definition in the box labeled **Definition**. Finally, use your dictionary to find other forms of the word, such as adjective, noun, or verb forms. Write these words in the box labeled **Other Forms**.

Then, on a separate sheet of paper, draw your own map and follow the same instructions for each of the nine remaining vocabulary words.

1.

absorb → Because so many of the earth's species are threatened with extinction today, it's hard to **absorb** all the facts about them. It takes some time for the information to sink in.

Your Guess:

Other Forms:

Definition:

2.

Many **complaints** are filed against people who export endangered animals like the woolly monkey. These protests rarely lead to action, however.

3.

Several nations began to **cooperate** in wildlife conservation after the United Nations was formed in 1945. They realized they needed to work together to protect endangered species.

4.

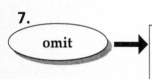

The Nature Conservancy and other groups have been buying wilderness land from countries that are in **debt**. These countries then use the money to pay what they owe, and land that endangered species live on is protected.

5.

When endangered species in zoos do not bear live young, there is great **mourning,** or grief for the loss.

6.

Some biologists have taken the **offense** in the fight to save endangered animals. They think more animals might become extinct unless the problems are attacked head on.

7.

It would be a mistake to **omit** the Japanese crested ibis and the noisy scrub bird from the endangered list. They are both in danger of extinction.

8.

regret

Those who have nearly wiped out the oryx should **regret** their actions. I wonder how many of them feel sorry about what they have done?

9.

security

Some endangered animals only find **security** in zoos, where they are protected from hunters and other dangers.

10.

tension

People await the return of the whooping cranes to the Texas coast every year with great **tension**. They feel a strain not knowing how many birds will survive the long journey from Canada.

EXERCISE 2 Context Clues ✍

Directions. Scan the definitions in Column A. Then think about how the boldface words are used in the sentences in Column B. To complete the exercise, match each definition in Column A with the correct vocabulary word from Column B. Write the letter of your choice on the line provided. Finally, write the vocabulary word on the line before the definition.

COLUMN A

_____ **11.** word: _____:
n. a protest; a written or spoken expression of pain, annoyance, or discontent

_____ **12.** word: _____:
n. the expression of grief at someone's death; the period during which one grieves for the dead; *adj.* of grief

_____ **13.** word: _____:
v. to soak up; to take up the attention of

_____ **14.** word: _____:
n. a strain; a state of strained relations

_____ **15.** word: _____:
v. to feel sorry about or mourn; to feel remorseful; *n.* a troubled feeling

_____ **16.** word: _____:
n. something owed by one person to another; the state of owing

_____ **17.** word: _____:
v. to leave out

_____ **18.** word: _____:
n. the feeling of being safe or certain; safety; an organization that guards an area; an assurance of repayment of a loan or debt

_____ **19.** word: _____:
v. to work with others for a shared cause or purpose

_____ **20.** word: _____:
n. a crime; the feeling of hurt; something that greatly upsets; the side that attacks

COLUMN B

(A) There was a period of **mourning** when the last Carolina parakeet died in 1910. Many people grieved the loss of this beautiful bird.

(B) The hunting of the Javan rhinoceros is a serious **offense**, or crime.

(C) One way to help endangered animals is to send a written **complaint** to your local newspaper. Your letter should express your feelings about the trouble these animals are in.

(D) Many endangered animals live with a false sense of **security**. They may not be aware that their numbers are dangerously low.

(E) **Tension** exists between poachers and those who want to protect endangered animals. These strained relations have sometimes resulted in violent conflicts.

(F) Scientists and government officials have **cooperated** to help the wild nenes of Hawaii. By working together, they have helped increase the population of this bird from just a few to about two thousand.

(G) Feeling troubled about extinct animals will not bring them back. But **regret** can cause people to act to protect today's endangered species.

(H) Because humans have caused many species' disappearance, some environmentalists feel that we owe a **debt** to those species that remain.

(I) When talking about endangered animals, do not **omit** the Bali tiger of Indonesia. Such a grand creature should not be overlooked.

(J) Scientists are **absorbed** with the study of the pink pigeon of Mauritius. They pay close attention to how many chicks are hatched each year.

EXERCISE 3 *Like Meanings and Opposite Meanings* ✍

Directions. For each item below, circle the letter of the choice that means the same, or about the same, as the boldface word.

21. the biologists' **complaint**
    (A) supporting statement
    (B) explanation
    (C) protest
    (D) interview

22. a large **debt**
    (A) antelope
    (B) popular movement
    (C) beetle
    (D) amount owed

23. to **cooperate** to help the oryx
    (A) work together
    (B) protest
    (C) think of ways
    (D) decide

24. **mourning** extinct animals
    (A) painting
    (B) looking for
    (C) studying
    (D) grieving for

25. to **absorb** the information
    (A) present
    (B) soak up
    (C) dismiss
    (D) ask about

Directions. For each item below, circle the letter of the choice that means the opposite, or about the opposite, of the boldface word.

26. to **regret** the outcome
    (A) feel worried about
    (B) feel sorry about
    (C) feel afraid of
    (D) feel good about

27. to **omit** the giant panda
    (A) hunt
    (B) include
    (C) study
    (D) sketch

28. **security** for all animals
    (A) protection
    (B) hope
    (C) danger
    (D) zoos

29. the battle's **offense**
    (A) fighters
    (B) winners
    (C) losers
    (D) defense

30. **tension** between biologists and poachers
    (A) state of ease
    (B) discussions
    (C) state of strain
    (D) payment of debt

MAKING NEW WORDS YOUR OWN

Lesson 26 | **CONTEXT:** Ecology and Environment
Peter Rabbit Would Have Been Proud of Beatrix Potter

Do the names Peter Rabbit, Flopsy, Mopsy, and Cottontail ring a bell? Few characters have delighted children more. They were all created by Beatrix Potter (1866–1943), a quiet woman who dearly loved both animals and children. Potter also loved the Lake District of England and wanted to preserve it. In her later years she became involved with the National Trust, which bought and cared for land so that the countryside would not be damaged by development. Potter bought as much land as she could and willed it to the Trust when she died and so helped protect the beautiful English countryside.

In the following exercises, you will have the opportunity to expand your vocabulary by reading about Beatrix Potter. Below are ten vocabulary words that will be used in these exercises.

amateur	intrusion	privacy	resident	simplify
duplicate	keen	rebel	self-respect	sympathy

EXERCISE 1 *Mapping*

Directions. In the item below, a vocabulary word is provided and used in a sentence. Take a guess at the word's meaning and write it in the box labeled **Your Guess**. Then look the word up in your dictionary and write the definition in the box labeled **Definition**. Finally, use your dictionary to find other forms of the word, such as adjective, noun, or verb forms. Write these words in the box labeled **Other Forms**.

Then, on a separate sheet of paper, draw your own map and follow the same instructions for each of the nine remaining vocabulary words.

1.

(amateur) →

In addition to writing and illustrating children's books, Beatrix Potter was an **amateur** scientific illustrator. Her hobby involved painting watercolors of plants and fungi.

Your Guess:

Other Forms:

Definition:

2.

duplicate → In her artwork, Potter tried to **duplicate** nature. She wanted the drawings to look exactly like what she saw.

3.

intrusion → Potter was a very private person who did not want **intrusion**, or interference, in her personal life.

4.

keen → Potter was always **keen** about animals and nature. Everyone around her was aware of her strong feelings on these subjects.

5.

privacy → Potter wrote her journals in code to protect her **privacy**. She wanted to be sure that the details of her personal life could not be made public.

6.

rebel → As a child, Potter always obeyed her parents and other adults; she was never a **rebel**.

7.

resident → As a **resident** of the Lake Country, Potter had a special interest in it. She wanted to preserve the area that was her home.

8.

self-respect → Potter had healthy, positive feelings about herself and her accomplishments. She probably developed this strong sense of **self-respect** early in life.

9.

simplify → Potter told stories about her pet rabbit, Peter. To make sure the stories would be easy for children to understand, she **simplified** her language.

10.

sympathy → Potter was in **sympathy** with the aims of the National Trust. She shared their belief that the Lake Country should be preserved.

EXERCISE 2 *Context Clues*

Directions. Scan the definitions in Column A. Then think about how the boldface words are used in the sentences in Column B. To complete the exercise, match each definition in Column A with the correct vocabulary word from Column B. Write the letter of your choice on the line provided. Finally, write the vocabulary word on the line before the definition.

COLUMN A	COLUMN B

COLUMN A

_____ **11.** word: _____:
n. a person who resists authority; *v.* to resist authority or control

_____ **12.** word: _____:
adj. exactly alike; *n.* an exact copy; *v.* to make an exact copy

_____ **13.** word: _____:
v. to make easier or less complex

_____ **14.** word: _____:
adj. living in a place for a period of time; *n.* a person who lives in a place

_____ **15.** word: _____:
n. a beginner, not a professional; *adj.* of or done by someone acting for pleasure rather than for pay

_____ **16.** word: _____:
n. the act of forcing oneself on others; an unasked-for interruption

_____ **17.** word: _____:
n. a withdrawal from public company; one's private life; secrecy

_____ **18.** word: _____:
n. a sameness in feeling; a feeling of agreement with an idea

_____ **19.** word: _____:
n. a high regard for oneself and one's worth as a person

_____ **20.** word: _____:
adj. sharp; shrewd; strongly felt; enthusiastic

COLUMN B

(A) Potter wanted children to have **self-respect,** to have a sense of their own worth.

(B) Potter first told the story of Peter Rabbit in a letter. **Duplicates** of the story, along with exact copies of her original pictures, were later printed in a book.

(C) Potter was concerned about the **intrusion** of developers into the rural Lake Country. By buying land and preserving it, she blocked their attempt to force themselves into the area.

(D) Potter had a **keen,** or sharp, sense of pleasure in the way of life in the countryside.

(E) Potter was an **amateur** naturalist. She studied nature for her own pleasure.

(F) Although she enjoyed her **privacy,** Potter also enjoyed the company of others.

(G) Potter had **sympathy** with those who felt it was important to preserve the countryside. She shared their belief in its worth.

(H) As an adult, Potter became a **rebel.** She resisted the control of developers in the countryside.

(I) Potter wanted to give the parcels of land she bought to the National Trust. To **simplify** the process, she left all the land to the Trust when she died, rather than hand it over bit by bit while she was still alive.

(J) A **resident** conservationist, Potter picked up litter and planted trees in her own neighborhood during the last ten years of her life.

EXERCISE 3   *Like Meanings and Opposite Meanings* ☞

Directions. For each item below, circle the letter of the choice that means the same, or about the same, as the boldface word.

21. to **duplicate** Potter's journal

(A) copy
(B) decode
(C) create
(D) read

22. an unwelcome **intrusion**

(A) group
(B) interruption
(C) following
(D) question

23. keen about Peter Rabbit

(A) enthusiastic
(B) worried
(C) friendly
(D) afraid

24. not lacking **self-respect**

(A) selfishness
(B) bravery
(C) high regard for oneself
(D) care for others

25. a **sympathy** with children

(A) shared understanding
(B) desired result
(C) playfulness
(D) loneliness

Directions. For each item below, circle the letter of the choice that means the opposite, or about the opposite, of the boldface word.

26. an **amateur** writer

(A) professional
(B) intelligent
(C) unknown
(D) poor

27. a desire for **privacy**

(A) friendship
(B) children
(C) secrecy
(D) company

28. to **rebel** against nature

(A) obey
(B) resist
(C) speak
(D) study

29. a **resident** children's author

(A) popular
(B) quiet
(C) young
(D) visiting

30. to **simplify** the language for children

(A) newly invent
(B) listen to
(C) make harder
(D) speak clearly

MAKING NEW WORDS YOUR OWN

Lesson 27 | CONTEXT: Ecology and Environment

Pandas: Cute Isn't Everything

Have you ever seen a giant panda at a wildlife park? They are adorable, with black ears, noses, and eye patches. If you have seen one you are lucky, for they are very rare. Pandas live in the mountain forests of China, where they eat mostly bamboo shoots. There used to be thousands of them. Today, only about a thousand wild pandas live in a small area. In 1972, China gave two pandas—Ling-Ling and Hsing-Hsing—to the United States. The Chinese government has also loaned pandas to a few U.S. wildlife parks. No panda cubs born in U.S. zoos have survived.

In the following exercises, you will have the opportunity to expand your vocabulary by reading about pandas. Below are ten vocabulary words that will be used in these exercises.

| captivity | eavesdrop | migrate | prohibit | threat |
| decrease | massacre | prey | survival | tragedy |

EXERCISE 1 *Mapping* ✍

Directions. In the item below, a vocabulary word is provided and used in a sentence. Take a guess at the word's meaning and write it in the box labeled **Your Guess**. Then look the word up in your dictionary and write the definition in the box labeled **Definition**. Finally, use your dictionary to find other forms of the word, such as adjective, noun, or verb forms. Write these words in the box labeled **Other Forms**.

Then, on a separate sheet of paper, draw your own map and follow the same instructions for each of the nine remaining vocabulary words.

1.

(captivity) → Only a few giant pandas live in **captivity** today. Although they are not free, they are safe and protected.

Your Guess:

Other Forms:

Definition:

2.

(decrease) ➔ The number of giant pandas in the wild has **decreased**. It has fallen to about one thousand and may continue to fall.

3.

(eavesdrop) ➔ Scientists have attached radio collars to some pandas in the wild. As the pandas wander around, scientists can listen to these radios and **eavesdrop** on the activities of the pandas.

4.

(massacre) ➔ The **massacre** of pandas by hunters has been a terrible thing. Hundreds of them have been killed at a time.

5.

(migrate) ➔ Pandas have had to **migrate** as forests have been cut down. If they don't move from place to place, they won't be able to find food.

6.

(prey) ➔ Giant pandas have been the **prey** of hunters, who have shot them for their fur.

7.

(prohibit) ➔ The Chinese government now **prohibits** hunting the giant panda. It wants to prevent the panda from dying out completely.

8.

(survival) ➔ The **survival** of giant pandas in the wild depends on the supply of bamboo. When the bamboo dies off, many pandas die of starvation.

9.

(threat) ➔ People are a **threat** to the giant pandas. Even if people do not hunt the animals, they can cause great harm to the pandas by cutting down forests.

10.

(tragedy) ➔ It is always a **tragedy** when a panda dies in the wild. But because there are so few pandas, the death of a young panda is an even worse disaster.

EXERCISE 2 *Context Clues*

Directions. Scan the definitions in Column A. Then think about how the boldface words are used in the sentences in Column B. To complete the exercise, match each definition in Column A with the correct vocabulary word from Column B. Write the letter of your choice on the line provided. Finally, write the vocabulary word on the line before the definition.

COLUMN A

_____ **11.** word: _____:
n. to listen secretly to a private conversation

_____ **12.** word: _____:
n. imprisonment; the condition of being held against one's will

_____ **13.** word: _____:
n. the act or fact of living or existing

_____ **14.** word: _____:
n. an animal hunted and killed for food by another animal; a person or thing that is hunted; *v.* to hunt or kill for food; to rob; to weigh heavily (upon)

_____ **15.** word: _____:
v. to become smaller; to lessen; *n.* a lessening

_____ **16.** word: _____:
n. a statement or action of intended harm; an indication of danger

_____ **17.** word: _____:
v. to refuse to permit; to prevent

_____ **18.** word: _____:
n. an event bringing great suffering; a disaster; a serious play about events of great harm, suffering, or disaster

_____ **19.** word: _____:
n. a large-scale killing; an overwhelming defeat; *v.* to kill many; to defeat overwhelmingly

_____ **20.** word: _____:
v. to move from one place to another

COLUMN B

(A) The dangers facing the giant pandas **prey,** or weigh heavily, on the minds of environmentalists.

(B) When the pandas run out of food, they sometimes **migrate** from the mountain forests to farmland to find more to eat.

(C) The **survival** of the giant pandas cannot be taken for granted. Without our help, they may not live.

(D) The Chinese government has made **threats** to those who think about hunting pandas. The government warns that hunters will be severely punished.

(E) A **decrease,** or lessening, of human settlements in the mountains would probably help the giant pandas.

(F) About forty giant pandas live in **captivity** around the world. If they could choose, I'm sure they'd rather live in freedom in the mountain forests of China!

(G) The story of the little panda cub crushed by its mother is very sad. It is a subject for a **tragedy,** a play about a disaster.

(H) Hungry wild pandas are sometimes captured and fed to **prohibit** them from starving.

(I) At wildlife parks with pandas, you can always **eavesdrop** on other people and listen to them talk about how cute the little bears are.

(J) How could hunters **massacre** so many pandas? I don't understand how anyone could kill these adorable animals.

EXERCISE 3 *Like Meanings and Opposite Meanings* 👆

Directions. For each item below, circle the letter of the choice that means the same, or about the same, as the boldface word.

21. the **captivity** of endangered species
  (A) freedom
  (B) health
  (C) imprisonment
  (D) value

22. to **eavesdrop** secretly
  (A) listen
  (B) leave
  (C) whisper
  (D) hunt

23. to **massacre** defenseless animals
  (A) rescue
  (B) protect
  (C) kill many
  (D) tame a few

24. the lion **preys**
  (A) escapes
  (B) is killed
  (C) sleeps
  (D) hunts

25. a **threat** of harm
  (A) example
  (B) repeat
  (C) fear
  (D) statement

Directions. For each item below, circle the letter of the choice that means the opposite, or about the opposite, of the boldface word.

26. a **decrease** in the number of pandas
  (A) reversal
  (B) lessening
  (C) increase
  (D) change

27. to **migrate** in search of food
  (A) move around
  (B) make noises
  (C) stay put
  (D) roll over

28. to **prohibit** hunting
  (A) expect
  (B) allow
  (C) dislike
  (D) license

29. **survival** in zoos
  (A) dying off
  (B) existing
  (C) breeding
  (D) playing

30. the **tragedy** of the rare panda
  (A) disaster
  (B) story
  (C) death
  (D) comedy

MAKING NEW WORDS YOUR OWN

Lesson 28 | CONTEXT: Ecology and Environment

Catching the Sun for Energy

Where does unlimited, free energy come from? Well, it comes from the sun, which we often take for granted. As the earth gets more crowded and there are fewer energy resources, people are starting to look toward the sun.

Imagine living in a solar house! Its enormous windows face the south. Your water is heated by flat plates that collect heat from the sun. In the summertime your home could be air-conditioned with solar power. Solar energy can also be used to generate electricity. Engineers have even created cars that run on solar power!

In the following exercises, you will have the opportunity to expand your vocabulary by reading about solar energy. Below are ten vocabulary words that will be used in these exercises.

benefit	reckless	responsibility	suburbs	unite
obvious	resemble	severe	unfortunate	vocal

EXERCISE 1 *Mapping* ✍

Directions. In the item below, a vocabulary word is provided and used in a sentence. Take a guess at the word's meaning and write it in the box labeled **Your Guess**. Then look the word up in your dictionary and write the definition in the box labeled **Definition**. Finally, use your dictionary to find other forms of the word, such as adjective, noun, or verb forms. Write these words in the box labeled **Other Forms**.

Then, on a separate sheet of paper, draw your own map and follow the same instructions for each of the nine remaining vocabulary words.

1.

benefit ➔ A clear **benefit** of solar energy is that it does not cause pollution. This is an improvement over the burning of oil and coal.

Your Guess:

Other Forms:

Definition:

2.

obvious →

It is **obvious** that we will have to develop new kinds of energy. Clearly, the earth is running out of fuels like oil, which cannot be renewed.

3.

reckless →

We can no longer be **reckless** with the earth's resources. We must be responsible and think about the future.

4.

resemble →

Solar homes **resemble** homes that are powered by electricity. From the outside, they look very much the same, but flat panels on the roof usually tell you that a home uses solar power.

5.

responsibility →

The **responsibility** for developing clean energy sources lies with us. We have a duty to protect the environment now so that future generations can enjoy it later.

6.

severe →

There were **severe** shortages of oil and natural gas during the 1970s and 1980s. These serious shortages sped up the development of solar technology.

7.

suburbs →

New solar homes are being built in many American **suburbs**. It is often less expensive to build them outside the city limits.

8.

unfortunate →

It is **unfortunate** that so few people make use of solar energy. It is unlucky for our environment that we remain tied to oil and gas.

9.

unite →

Solar furnaces are made up of several mirrors that **unite** to focus the sun's rays on one spot. Bringing together energy collected by these mirrors can generate electricity.

10.

vocal →

Many builders are **vocal** about the advantages of solar energy. They speak out about its low cost and the lack of pollution.

EXERCISE 2 *Context Clues*

Directions. Scan the definitions in Column A. Then think about how the boldface words are used in the sentences in Column B. To complete the exercise, match each definition in Column A with the correct vocabulary word from Column B. Write the letter of your choice on the line provided. Finally, write the vocabulary word on the line before the definition.

COLUMN A	COLUMN B

_____ **11.** word: _____:
n. the areas just outside a city; the towns surrounding a city

_____ **12.** word: _____:
adj. easy to see or understand; evident

_____ **13.** word: _____:
adj. capable of making sounds; connected to the voice; inclined to express oneself with speech

_____ **14.** word: _____:
adj. having or bringing bad luck; not favorable; unlucky

_____ **15.** word: _____:
n. something that adds to the improvement of a condition; an event held to raise money for a cause; *v.* to do good to

_____ **16.** word: _____:
adj. careless; not caring about future results

_____ **17.** word: _____:
n. the state of being dependable; an obligation; a duty

_____ **18.** word: _____:
v. to bring or join together for a common cause; to make into one

_____ **19.** word: _____:
v. to be similar to; to look like

_____ **20.** word: _____:
adj. serious; strict or very critical

(A) The first solar home was built in a Chicago **suburb** in 1940, just outside the city.

(B) A **benefit** was recently held to raise money for solar energy research. The governor was the guest of honor.

(C) The tone of the governor's speech was **severe**. Looking very serious, she told us that we should support solar energy research.

(D) Before the event, **vocal** supporters of solar energy formed a rally. You could hear their voices from several blocks away.

(E) People who use use solar energy for cooking should be very careful. If they are **reckless**, they could easily burn the food.

(F) Scientists and engineers have **united** to study solar energy. Together they have made progress.

(G) Sadly, we use only a small fraction of the solar energy that reaches the earth. It is **unfortunate** that we have not found more ways to harness it.

(H) Everyone should accept the **responsibility** of saving energy. This is an important duty.

(I) Solar cells power many small electronic devices, such as calculators. One **obvious** advantage to these types of calculators is that you never need to replace the batteries. But a clear drawback is that they need a certain amount of light to work.

(J) Solar energy is caused by nuclear reactions that take place in the sun. These **resemble**, or seem to be like, the reactions that take place in nuclear bombs.

EXERCISE 3   *Like Meanings and Opposite Meanings* ✍

Directions. For each item below, circle the letter of the choice that means the same, or about the same, as the boldface word.

21. to **benefit** the environment
(A) do good for
(B) speak out for
(C) clean up
(D) write about

22. to **resemble** nuclear energy
(A) create
(B) control
(C) contrast with
(D) be similar to

23. a **responsibility** to future generations
(A) letter
(B) duty
(C) friend
(D) release

24. a **severe** shortage of funding
(A) improved
(B) unknown
(C) serious
(D) mild

25. to **unite** different groups
(A) form
(B) split apart
(C) speak to
(D) bring together

Directions. For each item below, circle the letter of the choice that means the opposite, or about the opposite, of the boldface word.

26. an **obvious** advantage
(A) cheap
(B) related
(C) unclear
(D) free

27. **reckless** use of resources
(A) careful
(B) gradual
(C) careless
(D) generous

28. homes in the **suburbs**
(A) national parks
(B) inner city
(C) mountains
(D) seashore

29. an **unfortunate** event
(A) expected
(B) lucky
(C) exciting
(D) popular

30. a **vocal** supporter
(A) elderly
(B) shouting
(C) tired
(D) silent

MAKING NEW WORDS YOUR OWN

Lesson 29 | CONTEXT: Ecology and Environment
For the People and for the Future: U.S. National Parks

If not for Yellowstone's famous geysers, we might not have a National Park System. In 1870, fabulous tales of these geysers prompted General Henry D. Washburn to visit the **area**. There, he wondered what the future would bring to Yellowstone. Judge Cornelius **Hedges** suggested that the land should be protected from mining and lumbering. Two **years later,** Yellowstone became the first national park. Today, many types of natural and historic sites are preserved. The birthplace of Booker T. Washington, prehistoric Native American **cliff** dwellings, and sea-bird breeding grounds all have a place in the National Park System.

In the following exercises, you will have the opportunity to expand your vocabulary by reading about America's national parks. Below are ten vocabulary words that will be used in these exercises.

anthem	courteous	justify	promotion	rehearsal
compliment	engage	nominate	qualify	specify

EXERCISE 1 *Mapping* ✍

Directions. In the item below, a vocabulary word is provided and used in a sentence. Take a guess at the word's meaning and write it in the box labeled **Your Guess**. Then look the word up in your dictionary and write the definition in the box labeled **Definition**. Finally, use your dictionary to find other forms of the word, such as adjective, noun, or verb forms. Write these words in the box labeled **Other Forms**.

Then, on a separate sheet of paper, draw your own map and follow the same instructions for each of the nine remaining vocabulary words.

1.

(anthem) → Have you ever heard the song "America the Beautiful"? It is probably the best-known **anthem** to the magnificence of the United States. Do you recall the memorable words praising the sky and mountains?

Your Guess:

Other Forms:

Definition:

2.

Those words of praise are not simply a formal **compliment**. Instead, they express the heartfelt feelings of millions of people. We Americans treasure our land and its resources.

3.

In fact, America was the first nation to have a national park. Now, over 350 parks are protected. **Courteous** park rangers politely give visitors information about the natural features of the parks.

4.

In the parks, anyone can find sights to **engage** the senses. What tourist has not been drawn in and captured by the majesty of the Grand Canyon?

5.

Today, nature has become even more precious. Many animals have become endangered. Fragile beaches are at risk. What reason can **justify** their destruction?

6.

To protect our natural wealth, we must **nominate** and elect people who will conserve our heritage. The future depends on how we manage our resources today.

7.

The parks offer a rich variety of recreational activities. The National Park Service need not attract visitors through advertising or other types of **promotion**. In fact, the parks regularly fill up and have to turn campers away.

8.

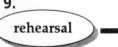

Most parks require an entrance fee. However, people sixty-two years of age or older can enter free with a Golden Age Passport. Likewise, people with physical impairments may **qualify** for a Golden Access Passport and free entry.

9.

(rehearsal)

If you want to visit a national park, be sure to plan ahead. New campers are often surprised at the hardship. If you want to set up a wilderness camp, you might plan a **rehearsal** near your home as practice for the real thing.

10.

(specify)

In some areas, cabins, motels, and hotels are available. But make your reservations months early! And remember to **specify** dates and your exact needs.

EXERCISE 2 *Context Clues*

Directions. Scan the definitions in Column A. Then think about how the boldface words are used in the sentences in Column B. To complete the exercise, match each definition in Column A with the correct vocabulary word from Column B. Write the letter of your choice on the line provided. Finally, write the vocabulary word on the line before the definition.

COLUMN A

_____ **11.** word: _____:
n. a song of praise or devotion

_____ **12.** word: _____:
n. something said in admiration, praise, or flattery; *v.* to congratulate; to praise

_____ **13.** word: _____:
n. a repeating for practice before a future performance or event; a practice

_____ **14.** word: _____:
v. to name or appoint to an office or position; to name as a candidate for an office

_____ **15.** word: _____:
v. to draw into or involve; to enter in conflict with; to take part in; to hire

_____ **16.** word: _____:
n. an advancement in rank or pay; the furthering of a cause; the advertisement of a product or event

_____ **17.** word: _____:
adj. polite and considerate towards others; well-mannered

_____ **18.** word: _____:
v. to show to be just and right; to show to be reasonable and lawful

_____ **19.** word: _____:
v. to define, mention, or describe in detail; state definitely

_____ **20.** word: _____:
v. to explain by narrowing down or describing the specific characteristics of; to be fit for a position

COLUMN B

(A) Before I give an oral report, I like to have a **rehearsal**. So I asked my mother to listen to my draft.

(B) "Imagine the last notes of the national **anthem** fading away," I told her, to set the tone. Then I began my speech.

(C) "Ladies and gentlemen, I would like to tell you about one of our great national parks, Big Bend. Its beauty alone **justifies** its membership in our National Parks System.

(D) "Let me **specify** the benefits it offers the American people. Over 800,000 acres of unspoiled land await visitors. The park contains desert, springs, and of course, the Rio Grande.

(E) "During my visit, we **engaged** a guide to lead us through some of the rougher country. This hired guide led us through Boquillas Canyon.

(F) "Our friendly and **courteous** guide told us that fossils can also be found in the park.

(G) The preservation of our parks' wildlife is important to our future. Countless ecological studies have provided specific data that **qualify** that claim.

(H) For this reason, all the wildlife at Big Bend—beaver, deer, and the rare panther—are well protected. I **compliment** the staff of Big Bend for their good work.

(I) "They guard some of our most priceless treasures. In my opinion, they should all receive **promotions**, as well as a raise in pay.

(J) "I hope that we continue to **nominate**, or appoint, such responsible people to safeguard the future of this great bend in the Rio Grande."

EXERCISE 3 *Like Meanings and Opposite Meanings* 👈

Directions. For each item below, circle the letter of the choice that means the same, or about the same, as the boldface word.

21. justify your actions
(A) plan ahead
(B) describe in detail
(C) show reasons for
(D) recall to mind

22. proudly **nominate**
(A) approach boldly
(B) accept a prize
(C) name as a candidate
(D) give a speech

23. a hurried **rehearsal**
(A) funeral
(B) practice
(C) turnaround
(D) a type of automobile

24. the national **anthem**
(A) constitution
(B) military
(C) song
(D) flag

25. to **qualify** a statement
(A) announce
(B) research
(C) argue
(D) explain

Directions. For each item below, circle the letter of the choice that means the opposite, or about the opposite, of the boldface word.

26. to **specify** details
(A) generalize
(B) measure
(C) memorize
(D) omit

27. her **promotion** of the project
(A) hurrying
(B) creation
(C) opinion
(D) blocking

28. a nice **compliment**
(A) insult
(B) tragedy
(C) beginning
(D) essay

29. engage in conflict
(A) draw swords
(B) withdraw
(C) bully
(D) maintain

30. courteous attitude
(A) polite
(B) foolish
(C) rude
(D) serious

MAKING NEW WORDS YOUR OWN

Lesson 30 | CONTEXT: Ecology and Environment
Making the Great Lakes Great Again

Superior, Michigan, Huron, Erie, and Ontario are the five Great Lakes. These lakes border eight states: Minnesota, Wisconsin, Michigan, Illinois, Indiana, Ohio, Pennsylvania, and New York. The Great Lakes are among the fifteen largest lakes in the world. If you stand on the shore of any one of the five Great Lakes, it will seem as if you are standing at the edge of an ocean—in fact, the lakes are so large that they are sometimes called inland seas. Today, these lakes are the scene of a conflict—a conflict between humans and the environment.

In the following exercises, you will have the opportunity to expand your vocabulary by reading about the Great Lakes. Below are ten vocabulary words that will be used in these exercises.

apologize	associate	frantic	hesitate	reservoir
application	ballad	gallant	impatience	superior

EXERCISE 1 | *Mapping* ✍

Directions. In the item below, a vocabulary word is provided and used in a sentence. Take a guess at the word's meaning and write it in the box labeled **Your Guess**. Then look the word up in your dictionary and write the definition in the box labeled **Definition**. Finally, use your dictionary to find other forms of the word, such as adjective, noun, or verb forms. Write these words in the box labeled **Other Forms**.

Then, on a separate sheet of paper, draw your own map and follow the same instructions for each of the nine remaining vocabulary words.

1.

apologize → Industry and development are the major polluters of the Great Lakes. Some companies **apologize** for past pollution. But regrets do not solve the problem.

↓

Your Guess:

↓

Other Forms:

Definition:

2.

application → Scientists hope that the **application** of new technology will help to reduce the effects of pollution. Putting these new technologies into practice may help cut pollution at its source.

3.

associate → Are your friends and classmates concerned about pollution? Talk to the people you **associate** with about the pollution problem in the Great Lakes.

4.

ballad → Some folk singers have written **ballads** about the pollution of the Great Lakes. These songs tell of the history of the Great Lakes and of the lakes' current troubles.

5.

frantic → Many people who live near the Great Lakes are very concerned with the safety of their homes. As water levels in the lakes rise steadily, lake-shore residents are **frantic** with worry that they will lose their homes to the lake.

6.

gallant → Some of these people are making **gallant** efforts to reduce water levels. Unfortunately, these bold attempts to control water levels could further harm the delicate ecosystem of the Great Lakes.

7.

hesitate → Lakeshore homeowners feel that there is no time to lose. They call for quick action, urging the government not to **hesitate** in reducing water levels.

8.

impatience → It's not hard to understand the **impatience** of these homeowners. They hate any delay because in a few years' time their houses may be swallowed by the lakes.

9.

reservoir → But some people feel that protecting the environment should come first. They point out that pollution in the Great Lakes is threatening water supplies—high levels of toxic chemicals have been found in the water **reservoirs**.

10.

superior → Today, knowledge of the Great Lakes' environmental problems is **superior** to that of any time in the past. Thanks to modern science, we have the best and most thorough knowledge of the lakes ever.

EXERCISE 2 Context Clues

Directions. Scan the definitions in Column A. Then think about how the boldface words are used in the sentences in Column B. To complete the exercise, match each definition in Column A with the correct vocabulary word from Column B. Write the letter of your choice on the line provided. Finally, write the vocabulary word on the line before the definition.

COLUMN A	COLUMN B
_____ **11.** word: _____: *v.* to join with others; to connect different things together; *n.* a person with whom one works; *adj.* having less than full status	(A) It is a sunny fall day on Lake Erie. Sixteen sixth-grade students are filled with **impatience** as they line up to climb aboard a small tugboat. They can't wait to start their trip!
_____ **12.** word: _____: *adj.* showy and lively in appearance; brave, noble, and daring	(B) Finally, the captains of the boat arrive. They regret their lateness and they **apologize**.
_____ **13.** word: _____: *v.* to express regret for a fault or wrong	(C) The captains are Pat and Chuck Potter. The **gallant** Chuck makes a great show of helping the teacher aboard; the trip is ready to begin.
_____ **14.** word: _____: *adj.* wild with anger, pain, or worry	(D) The Potters are **reservoirs** of valuable information about the Great Lakes area. They have a great supply of facts and figures memorized.
_____ **15.** word: _____: *n.* a place where water is collected and stored ; a large supply of something	(E) Pat points out some foamy water at the base of a low dam. She asks the students what they **associate** with foam. In this case, she says, they should connect it with pollution.
_____ **16.** word: _____: *n.* a romantic song or poem that tells a story in short stanzas with repetition	(F) The students don't **hesitate** at guessing the source of the pollution. They instantly remember the nearby factories.
_____ **17.** word: _____: *v.* to pause or stop momentarily; to delay because of feeling unsure	(G) Pat points out a fertilizer plant. "That plant has just filled out an **application** for a new waste dump."
_____ **18.** word: _____: *adj.* high or higher in order, status, or rank; greater in quality or value	(H) "The old dump has already killed the surrounding plants. We're working at a **frantic** pace to see that no new dumps are allowed. We are trying to beat the clock."
_____ **19.** word: _____: *n.* the method of putting something to use; continued effort; a form to be filled out with information	(I) Pat reminds us that U.S. regulations on pollution are **superior** to those in Canada, so some U.S. companies go there to dump their wastes. The less strict Canadian rules give the companies less trouble.
_____ **20.** word: _____: *n.* annoyance because of delay; restless eagerness to do something	(J) On the return trip, we make up a sad song. We call it "The Song of the Inland Seas," a **ballad** that tells the history of trade and shipping on the Great Lakes.

EXERCISE 3 — Like Meanings and Opposite Meanings ✍

Directions. For each item below, circle the letter of the choice that means the same, or about the same, as the boldface word.

21. the polluted **reservoir**
(A) river that runs into one of the Great Lakes
(B) treatment plant for polluted water
(C) a factory that creates smog
(D) place where something is collected and stored

22. the **application** of new technology
(A) use
(B) discovery
(C) understanding
(D) scientific method

23. the sad **ballad**
(A) ancient legend
(B) romantic song
(C) history
(D) historic revolution

24. her business **associate**
(A) admirer
(B) office
(C) enemy
(D) partner

25. do not **hesitate**
(A) wait briefly
(B) fall suddenly
(C) enter quickly
(D) cry loudly

Directions. For each item below, circle the letter of the choice that means the opposite, or about the opposite, of the boldface word.

26. to **apologize** for one's actions
(A) have regret
(B) be proud
(C) resist
(D) repeat

27. the **gallant** offer
(A) sincere
(B) shocking
(C) brave
(D) cowardly

28. our growing **impatience**
(A) anger
(B) patience
(C) impossibility
(D) unhappiness

29. a **frantic** attempt
(A) violent
(B) foolish
(C) frenzied
(D) calm

30. a **superior** method
(A) faster
(B) uncertain
(C) worse
(D) better

UNDERSTANDING NEW WORDS AND THEIR USES

Building Your Vocabulary

One way to build your vocabulary is to learn the different meanings of a single word. Another way is to learn how to make new words by learning prefixes and suffixes. A third way is to learn about the origins of words: Learning about the origins of words will help you remember the words' meanings. The following exercises will help you build on, and remember, vocabulary.

EXERCISE 1 *Multimeaning*

Words often have more than one meaning. In a Multimeaning exercise, you will read a boldface vocabulary word in a sentence. You will then read four more sentences that use the same vocabulary word. Your job is to choose the sentence that uses the vocabulary word in the same way as it is used in the first sentence. Here's an example of a Multimeaning exercise:

The fog of nineteenth-century London was, in fact, **foul** air caused by pollution.

(A) Soot from the city's many chimneys would also **foul** the air.

(B) In this setting, Detective Sherlock Holmes tracks down **foul** murderers and other evil-doers.

(C) Nothing keeps Holmes from the chase. He goes out into the streets of London even in a thunderstorm or other **foul** weather.

(D) Waste dumped into London's river Thames had made the waterway **foul**.

In the first sentence, the air was **foul** because of pollution. Pollution makes things dirty or impure. **Foul** is used as an adjective to mean dirty or impure. How does this compare to the uses of the word in choices A, B, C, and D?

- In choice A, **foul** is a verb meaning to pollute or make dirty.
- In choice B, **foul** means evil, not dirty.
- In choice C, **foul** is used to describe weather, and it means unfavorable or stormy.
- In the correct choice, D, **foul** again describes something made dirty or impure.

EXERCISE 2 *Word Analysis*

Prefixes and Suffixes

The following items will give you practice in identifying the kinds of prefixes and suffixes that you will run into again and again as you read. In each of these items, you will read two words. Both words will contain the same prefix or suffix. You will be asked to identify the choice that describes the meaning of the prefix or suffix as it is used in both words. Here's an example of a prefix exercise:

reclaim   **re**write

(A) after
(B) with
(C) before
(D) again

Hint #1 The second word will usually be a word that you already know well. For example, you probably already know that *rewrite* means "to write again."

Hint #2 The first word or its root (in this case, *claim*) is a word you learned in *Making New Words Your Own*. When you remember that *rewrite* means "to write again," you can guess that *reclaim* means "to claim again." That leads you to the correct choice, D.

Note: The table below lists some common prefixes and suffixes. These lists will help you to complete the exercises on *Prefixes* and *Suffixes* in the lessons that follow.

Prefix	Definition	Suffix	Definition
anti-	against; opposite; reverse	-able, -ible	able to be; capable of being
co-	together; equally; joint(ly)	-al, -ial	of, like, pertaining to; suitable for; the act or process of
de-	away from, down; entirely; undo	-ant	a person or thing that has or does
dis-	away; apart; opposite of; not; lack of	-er	one who; that which
extra-	outside; beyond; besides	-ery	place for; act, practice, or occupation of
hyper-	more than normal, too much	-ess	female
im-	in; into; on; toward; not	-ic	of; characterized, caused, or produced by
in-	in; into; on; toward; not	-ion	act, condition, or result of
ir-	in; into; on; toward; not	-ish	of or belonging to; characterized by; somewhat
mis-	wrong; bad; not	-ism	act, practice, or result of; example of
non-	not; opposite of	-ity	condition; state of being
pre-	before; in front of	-ive	of; relating to; belonging to; tending to
re-	back; again	-ize	make; cause to be
self-	of the self	-ment	result, act, process, or state of
semi-	half; partly	-ous	having; like; full of
sub-	under; beneath	-y	characterized by
un-	not; lack of; opposite of		

Word Origins

Many words in the English language come from Greek, Latin, French, and other languages. Word Origins exercises will give you practice in learning the roots of vocabulary words. In these exercises, you will be asked to identify the choice that best completes the sentence.

Here's an example of a Word Origins exercise:

debt decrease definite descriptive

The Latin word *crescere*, "to grow," combined with the prefix *de-*, "away," gives us the word ____.

Hint #1 Compare the Latin root to the list of words provided above the item. If you remove *de-* from all of the choices, the part of the word left that most resembles the Latin root would be *-crease*, from the word *decrease*.

Hint #2 The choices in Word Origins will be vocabulary words you studied in *Making New Words Your Own*. In the introduction to *Making New Words Your Own*, you learned that to decrease means to grow smaller. *Decrease* is the correct response.

UNDERSTANDING NEW WORDS AND THEIR USES

Lesson 1 | CONTEXT: Amazing Nature

Has Anyone Seen the Abominable Snowman?

EXERCISE 1 *Multimeaning* ✍️

Directions. Read each numbered sentence below. Then circle the letter of the choice that uses the boldface word in the same way as it is used in the numbered sentence.

1. Would you like to **interview** the author of the new best-selling book about the Abominable Snowman?
   (A) During his **interview** for the job of forest ranger, my brother was asked his opinion about Bigfoot.
   (B) Following the most recent sighting of the Loch Ness monster, the police granted an **interview** to the national news media.
   (C) If I could go to Africa, I would **interview** some people who claim to have seen a dinosaur in Lake Telle.
   (D) The **interview** on the morning talk show revealed some fascinating information about huge flying reptiles seen in Asia.

2. The morning **session** of the conference included a talk by a scientist who studies unusual sea creatures.
   (A) During its fall **session,** the college offered a course on mysterious creatures of the world.
   (B) The conference's most interesting **session,** which was held from ten to eleven o'clock, was about the book *On the Track of Unknown Animals* by Bernard Heuvelmans.
   (C) It was just after a **session** of wood-chopping that Mr. Brehm claims to have seen Bigfoot.
   (D) A bill to protect the Bigfoots was proposed when the state's legislature was in **session** from August to September.

EXERCISE 2 *Word Analysis* ✍️

Prefixes

Directions. Read each numbered pair of words below. Then circle the letter of the choice that best describes the meaning of the boldface prefix as it is used in each pair.

3. **in**definite   **in**complete
   (A) not
   (B) less
   (C) very
   (D) beyond

4. **un**expectedly   **un**interested
   (A) very
   (B) with
   (C) not
   (D) greater than

Suffixes

Directions. Read each numbered pair of words below. Then circle the letter of the choice that best describes the meaning of the boldface suffix as it is used in each pair.

5. summar**ize**   magnet**ize**
   (A) undo
   (B) without
   (C) person who does
   (D) make

6. reli**able**   undeni**able**
   (A) full of
   (B) practice of
   (C) able to be
   (D) about

Word Origins

Directions. Read each of the following sentences. Then, from the vocabulary list below, choose the word that best completes the sentence. Write the word in the blank.

astonish	doubtful	majority	summarize
conference	innumerable	navigator	symbol
definite	interview	quote	twilight
deny	journalism	reliable	unexpectedly
descendant	legend	session	vivid

7. The Middle English word *astonien*, meaning "to stun," carries over into Modern English as the word _____.

8. The Latin word *denagare* means "to say no," as does the English word

   _____.

9. By combining the Latin word *numerus*, meaning "number," the prefix *in-*, meaning "not," and the suffix *-able*, meaning "able to be," we get the English word

   _____.

10. The Middle English word *liht*, meaning "to shine," is combined with the Old English word *twi* to form the Modern English word _____.

UNDERSTANDING NEW WORDS AND THEIR USES

Lesson 2 | CONTEXT: Amazing Nature

Traveling Down Tornado Alley

EXERCISE 1 *Multimeaning*

Directions. Read each numbered sentence below. Then circle the letter of the choice that uses the boldface word in the same way as it is used in the numbered sentence.

1. To see a good **demonstration** of how a tornado forms, go to the Mid-America Museum in Hot Springs, Arkansas.
   (A) Following the deadly tornadoes, the people staged a **demonstration** in front of city hall to protest the city's safety procedures.
   (B) After our home was destroyed by a tornado, we appreciated the community's sincere **demonstration** of concern.
   (C) The salesperson's **demonstration** failed to convince us that the fence could withstand a tornado.
   (D) The **demonstration** against the new law was postponed because a tornado was sighted south of town.

2. The tornado's 200-mile-per-hour winds ripped the little store right off its **foundation**.
   (A) The tornado picked up a car and set it down on the **foundation** of a nearby house that had been blown away.
   (B) The family established the charitable **foundation** to help victims of natural disasters such as tornadoes.
   (C) There is a **foundation** in actual events for describing one section of the country as Tornado Alley.
   (D) The **foundation** of our Emergency Readiness Team is the preparedness of its members.

EXERCISE 2 *Word Analysis*

Prefixes

Directions. Read each numbered pair of words below. Then circle the letter of the choice that best describes the meaning of the boldface prefix as it is used in each pair.

3. **un**declared   **un**happy
   (A) against
   (B) extremely
   (C) not
   (D) into

4. **co**incidental   **co**operate
   (A) together
   (B) able
   (C) without
   (D) act

Suffixes

Directions. Read each numbered pair of words below. Then circle the letter of the choice that best describes the meaning of the boldface suffix as it is used in each pair.

5. detec**tion**   depress**ion**
(A) like
(B) state of
(C) person who does
(D) study of

6. predict**able**   forgett**able**
(A) not capable of being
(B) against
(C) capable of being
(D) act of

Word Origins

Directions. Read each of the following sentences. Then, from the vocabulary list below, choose the word that best completes the sentence. Write the word in the blank.

aviation	demonstration	exception	locally
bombard	departure	fatal	miraculous
collapse	detect	foundation	mischievous
collide	disastrous	ignore	nuisance
declare	disturb	incident	predict

7. The Middle English word *nusance*, meaning "annoyance," became the Modern English word _____.

8. We get a hint of the meaning of the word _____ when we learn that the Latin word *avis* means "bird."

9. The Latin word *ignorare*, meaning "not to know," or "to disregard," is related to our word _____.

10. You may recognize the French word *bombe*, meaning "bomb," in the Modern English word _____.

UNDERSTANDING NEW WORDS AND THEIR USES

Lesson 3 | CONTEXT: Amazing Nature

Tangled in a Spider's Web

EXERCISE 1 *Multimeaning*

Directions. Read each numbered sentence below. Then circle the letter of the choice that uses the boldface word in the same way as it is used in the numbered sentence.

1. I would like you to **escort** me through the passage—it is full of spiders.
   (A) My sister's **escort** for the prom looks like Jeff Daniels, the actor who starred in the movie *Arachnophobia,* which is about the fear of spiders.
   (B) I had to **escort** my little brother and his Cub Scout troop through the museum's spider house.
   (C) As their **escort**, I told the group the common name for each spider, such as the wolf spider and the crab spider.
   (D) When the museum's rare spider collection was transferred to another museum, it was given a police **escort**.

2. Since the 1950s, each **generation** of young readers has enjoyed the book *Charlotte's Web* by E. B. White.
   (A) The speaker said that the **generation,** or production, of new pesticides is harmful to spiders.
   (B) Some scientists have spent their careers studying the **generation,** or procreation, of spiders.
   (C) I think our **generation** is less frightened of spiders than people my grandparents' age, but I could be wrong.
   (D) The university's **generation** of money for research into spider habits was slow.

EXERCISE 2 *Word Analysis*

Prefixes

Directions. Read each numbered pair of words below. Then circle the letter of the choice that best describes the meaning of the boldface prefix as it is used in each pair.

3. **re**involve   **re**read
   (A) lacking
   (B) with
   (C) not
   (D) again

4. **im**mobile   **im**patient
   (A) very
   (B) toward
   (C) not
   (D) with

Suffixes

Directions. Read each numbered pair of words below. Then circle the letter of the choice that best describes the meaning of the boldface suffix as it is used in each pair.

5. hero**ic**   fantas**tic**

    (A) unrelated to
    (B) state of being
    (C) of or related to
    (D) somewhat

6. separa**tion**   comple**tion**

    (A) act of
    (B) unable to
    (C) able to
    (D) full of

Word Origins

Directions. Read each of the following sentences. Then, from the vocabulary list below, choose the word that best completes the sentence. Write the word in the blank.

abdomen	dread	generation	maximum
caution	error	gratitude	mobile
commotion	escort	heroic	paralysis
competition	flexible	hoist	previous
congratulate	foe	involve	separation

7. Not much was changed in the Middle English word *fo*, meaning "enemy," to make our Modern English word _____.

8. From the Greek word *paralyein*, meaning "to weaken," we get our English word _____.

9. The Latin word *errare*, which means "to go astray," gives us the English word _____.

10. We can still see the Latin word *congratulari*, meaning "to rejoice with someone," in the English word _____.

UNDERSTANDING NEW WORDS AND THEIR USES

Lesson 4 | **CONTEXT:** Amazing Nature
Wild About Animals

EXERCISE 1 *Multimeaning*

Directions. Read each numbered sentence below. Then circle the letter of the choice that uses the boldface word in the same way as it is used in the numbered sentence.

1. I became curious about beavers when my teacher made **reference** to the amazing dams they build using wood and mud.
   (A) *Wild Animals of North America,* published by the National Geographic Society, is an excellent **reference** book.
   (B) My cousin Tanya, a dolphin trainer, received a glowing **reference** from her former boss for her new job with the sea-life park.
   (C) I'm going to **reference** Dr. Nabors, a retired biologist, for my report about weaver ants.
   (D) Your **reference** to armadillos jumping when they are startled reminded me of a funny cartoon.

2. During our trip to Australia, we saw three kangaroos **vault** over a fence.
   (A) Drawings of cats, which were sacred to the ancient Egyptians, were found on the inner walls of the **vault**.
   (B) The **vault** of the snow leopard is a wonder to behold.
   (C) Wouldn't you like to see a snow leopard **vault** across a snowy canyon?
   (D) The photographer kept the negatives of the award-winning pictures of the duckbill platypus in a **vault** at the bank.

EXERCISE 2 *Word Analysis*

Prefixes

Directions. Read each numbered pair of words below. Then circle the letter of the choice that best describes the meaning of the boldface prefix as it is used in each pair.

3. **dis**comfort   **dis**approve
   (A) for
   (B) after
   (C) not
   (D) into

4. **de**regulate   **de**frost
   (A) undo
   (B) do the same as
   (C) do more than
   (D) state of

Suffixes

Directions. Read each numbered pair of words below. Then circle the letter of the choice that best describes the meaning of the boldface suffix as it is used in each pair.

5. imita**tive**   competi**tive**
   (A) tending to
   (B) resulting in
   (C) not like
   (D) one who does

6. conceal**ment**   excite**ment**
   (A) state of
   (B) without being
   (C) suitable for
   (D) resulting in

Word Origins

Directions. Read each of the following sentences. Then, from the vocabulary list below, choose the word that best completes the sentence. Write the word in the blank.

assault	disguise	impostor	regulate
conceal	earnest	inhale	requirement
dainty	gasp	linger	terminal
discomfort	hibernate	portion	vacuum
discourage	imitate	reference	vault

7. The Latin word *imponere,* meaning "place up on," has given us the English word

_____.

8. Our English word _____ comes from the Old Norse word *geispa,* which means "a short catching of the breath."

9. The Latin word *partio,* meaning "part," evolved into the English word _____

_____ .

10. The Middle English word *deinte,* which means "excellent," gives us the Modern English word _____ .

UNDERSTANDING NEW WORDS AND THEIR USES

Lesson 5 | **CONTEXT:** Amazing Nature

Einstein Started Somewhere, Too

EXERCISE 1 *Multimeaning*

Directions. Read each numbered sentence below. Then circle the letter of the choice that uses the boldface word in the same way as it is used in the numbered sentence.

1. This year, a **toll** of one dollar was charged to process each entry in the regional science fair.
   - (A) I wanted to call my friend in Seattle to tell him about the science fair, but the **toll** was too much.
   - (B) Working night and day on her science fair entry really has taken a **toll** on Janice's health.
   - (C) For her project, Sabina decided to **toll** church bells and measure the time of sound vibrations.
   - (D) The rainstorm took a heavy **toll** on the number of people willing to come out to the science fair.

2. Because I don't have my driver's **license**, one of my parents drove me to the beach to get sea water for my experiment.
   - (A) "Who gave you **license** to use my bowls and measuring cups for your experiment?" my mother asked.
   - (B) One of my experiments involved cooking fresh-caught fish, so I had to get a fishing **license**.
   - (C) In order for the Fish and Game Department to **license** me, I had to have parental permission.
   - (D) My sister joked that the letters on our car **license** plate, YAE, must stand for "Young Albert Einstein."

EXERCISE 2 *Word Analysis*

Prefixes

Directions. Read each numbered pair of words below. Then circle the letter of the choice that best describes the meaning of the boldface prefix as it is used in each pair.

3. **anti**static   **anti**freeze
   - (A) between
   - (B) for
   - (C) against
   - (D) together

4. **un**manned   **un**told
   - (A) beneath
   - (B) very
   - (C) not
   - (D) across

Suffixes

Directions. Read each numbered pair of words below. Then circle the letter of the choice that best describes the meaning of the boldface suffix as it is used in the pair.

5. suspic**ious**   courag**eous**
   (A) one who does
   (B) state of
   (C) away from
   (D) full of

6. surg**ery**   robb**ery**
   (A) act, practices, or occupation of
   (B) extremely
   (C) one who does
   (D) of or pertaining to

Word Origins

Directions. Read each of the following sentences. Then, from the vocabulary list below, choose the word that best completes the sentence. Write the word in the blank.

automation	lunar	pry	stray
bureau	nephew	ransom	surgery
flammable	particle	receipt	suspicion
gossip	pharmacy	resign	toll
license	pierce	static	unmanned

7. The Old English word *godsibbe*, meaning "godparent," later came to be *godsip*, meaning "good friend." In Modern English, this word has become _____, something good friends often do.

8. *Raunson*, meaning "to buy back," is a Middle English word that became the Modern English word _____.

9. From the Latin word *recipere*, meaning "to receive," we get the word _____— a paper we receive to show we have paid for something.

10. The Latin word *nepos*, meaning "grandson or nephew," became the English word _____.

UNDERSTANDING NEW WORDS AND THEIR USES

Lesson 6 | **CONTEXT:** People and Places

A Career in Anthropology

EXERCISE 1 *Multimeaning* ✍️

Directions. Read each numbered sentence below. Then circle the letter of the choice that uses the boldface word in the same way as it is used in the numbered sentence.

1. If you choose a **career** in anthropology, you could study people's physical or cultural characteristics.
   (A) You might study how in some cultures most people **career** through life, while in other cultures people prefer a slower pace.
   (B) The science of anthropology has moved through this century in full **career**, making rapid progress.
   (C) L.S.B. Leakey (1903–1972), who did much research in Africa, was a **career** anthropologist and archaeologist.
   (D) Mary Catherine Bateson (b. 1939), the daughter of famed anthropologist Margaret Mead (1901–1978), entered the same **career** as her mother.

2. An anthropologist's life can be extremely interesting, but there is always some **routine** involved with every job.
   (A) In her field work, Margaret Mead's **routine** varied somewhat with the locations.
   (B) The **routine** lives of members of a society are the raw materials anthropologists use in their work.
   (C) The actors presented a **routine** based on Margaret Mead's first encounters with young Samoan girls.
   (D) Traveling to faraway islands was **routine** business for Margaret Mead.

EXERCISE 2 *Word Analysis* ✍️

Prefixes

Directions. Read each numbered pair of words below. Then circle the letter of the choice that best describes the meaning of the boldface prefix as it is used in each pair.

3. **pre**determined   **pre**arranged
   (A) against
   (B) into
   (C) before
   (D) after

4. **self**-confidence   **self**-guiding
   (A) regarding others
   (B) doubly
   (C) not of the self
   (D) of the self

Name _____ Date _____ Class _____

Suffixes

Directions. Read each numbered pair of words below. Then circle the letter of the choice that best describes the meaning of the boldface suffix as it is used in each pair.

5. react**ion**   confu**sion**
   (A) result of
   (B) capable of
   (C) without
   (D) before

6. respect**able**   think**able**
   (A) incapable of being
   (B) nearly
   (C) capable of being
   (D) full of

Word Origins

Directions. Read each of the following sentences. Then, from the vocabulary list below, choose the word that best completes the sentence. Write the word in the blank.

analyze	determination	notion	respectable
biography	document	offspring	routine
career	essential	profession	scholar
debate	generous	publicity	self-confidence
destination	identical	reaction	thorough

7. The Latin word *notio,* meaning "coming to know," has added one letter and changed meaning to become the English word _____.

8. We can easily see the French word *publicite,* meaning "public information," in the English word _____.

9. The French word *analyser,* which means "to separate into basic principles," gives us the English word _____.

10. There is not much difference in the Old English word *ofspring,* meaning "to spring from," and the Modern English word _____.

HRW material copyrighted under notice appearing earlier in this work.

UNDERSTANDING NEW WORDS AND THEIR USES

Lesson 7 **CONTEXT: People and Places**

Mexico City: Then and Now

EXERCISE 1 *Multimeaning*

Directions. Read each numbered sentence below. Then circle the letter of the choice that uses the boldface word in the same way as it is used in the numbered sentence.

1. Have you read about the **conduct** of the Aztecs during the terrible two-year drought that began in 1450?
   - (A) It was the great King Montezuma I (1390?–1469?) who had to **conduct** the Aztecs' efforts to survive the drought years.
   - (B) It was also up to the king to **conduct** the many military battles that extended the empire from the Pacific Ocean to the Gulf of Mexico.
   - (C) Aztec parents taught their children important rules about **conduct**.
   - (D) The musician will **conduct** his own composition, "Warriors of the Sun."

2. While hurrying through Mexico City's Chapultepec Park, did you **glimpse** the giant cypress known as the Tree of Montezuma?
   - (A) Our tour allowed time for only a **glimpse** of the Alameda, the city's central park.
   - (B) Fortunately, we had time for much more than a **glimpse** of the unearthed Great Temple of the Aztecs.
   - (C) The air was hazy, so it was difficult to **glimpse** the mountains surrounding Mexico City.
   - (D) Even a **glimpse** of the snow-covered peaks is impressive.

EXERCISE 2 *Word Analysis*

Prefixes

Directions. Read each numbered pair of words below. Then circle the letter of the choice that best describes the meaning of the boldface prefix as it is used in each pair.

3. **re**ignite   **re**capture
   - (A) before
   - (B) never
   - (C) first
   - (D) again

4. **un**interrupted   **un**wanted
   - (A) after
   - (B) half
   - (C) not
   - (D) again

Suffixes

Directions. Read each numbered pair of words below. Then circle the letter of the choice that best describes the meaning of the boldface suffix as it is used in each pair.

5. manage**ment**   arrange**ment**
  (A) unable to
  (B) act or state of
  (C) one who
  (D) into

6. sacrific**ial**   resident**ial**
  (A) not related to
  (B) state of
  (C) pertaining to
  (D) resulting in

Word Origins

Directions. Read each of the following sentences. Then, from the vocabulary list below, choose the word that best completes the sentence. Write the word in the blank.

architect	desperate	ignite	realm
betray	district	interrupt	sacrifice
ceremony	eternal	management	scheme
conduct	fragrant	plead	victim
consent	glimpse	quarantine	victorious

7. From the Greek word *architekton,* meaning "chief carpenter," comes the English word _____.

8. The Modern English word _____ comes from the Middle English word *realme. Realme,* in turn, comes from the Latin word *regere,* meaning "to rule."

9. The Medieval Latin word *districtus,* meaning "an area of jurisdiction or rule," became the Modern English word _____.

10. Originally, the English word _____ meant "to isolate for forty days," because it came from the Italian word *quarantina,* meaning "forty days."

UNDERSTANDING NEW WORDS AND THEIR USES

Lesson 8 | CONTEXT: People and Places
Rocky Roads and Snake River Canyon

EXERCISE 1 *Multimeaning*

Directions. Read each numbered sentence below. Then circle the letter of the choice that uses the boldface word in the same way as it is used in the numbered sentence.

1. The magazine editors made a **survey** about people's knowledge of the Rocky Mountains.
   (A) It would be a big job to **survey** all 3,000 miles of the Rocky Mountains.
   (B) The **survey** proves that a wide variety of animals make the Rockies their home.
   (C) Government officials said they will **survey** the damage caused by forest fires in the Southern Rockies.
   (D) The Geological Service has to **survey** the mountains with instruments before section markers are put in place.

2. Many **dramatic** views of the mountains can be seen while traveling the Going-to-the-Sun Road in Glacier National Park.
   (A) At a local theater, we saw a **dramatic** production about mountaineers in the Rockies.
   (B) The lead actor, who made many sly comments that only the audience was supposed to understand, was a master of **dramatic** irony.
   (C) As we sat around the bonfire in our Rocky Mountain camp, each of us took turns giving **dramatic** tellings of our earlier camping experiences.
   (D) Float trips near Jackson, Wyoming, provide views of some **dramatic** scenes in the Snake River Canyon.

EXERCISE 2 *Word Analysis*

Prefixes

Directions. Read each numbered pair of words below. Then circle the letter of the choice that best describes the meaning of the boldface prefix as it is used in each pair.

3. **extra**ordinary   **extra**terrestrial
   (A) less than
   (B) beyond
   (C) part of
   (D) different from

4. **ir**regular   **ir**responsible
   (A) between
   (B) within
   (C) extremely
   (D) not

Suffixes

Directions. Read each numbered pair of words below. Then circle the letter of the choice that best describes the meaning of the boldface suffix as it is used in each pair.

5. establish**ment**   govern**ment**
   (A) process of
   (B) possession of
   (C) lack of
   (D) of or relating to

6. marvel**ous**   nerv**ous**
   (A) state of
   (B) within
   (C) full of
   (D) without

Word Origins

Directions. Read each of the following sentences. Then, from the vocabulary list below, choose the word that best completes the sentence. Write the word in the blank.

abundant	establish	leisure	prehistoric
barrier	extraordinary	lieutenant	satisfy
descriptive	feat	marvel	survey
desirable	geology	numerous	terrain
dramatic	irregular	possess	vicinity

7. The Old French word *fait,* meaning "an act or deed," has become the English word

   _____.

8. The Old French word *barriere,* meaning "bar," has become the English word

   _____.

9. The Middle English word *liue,* meaning "place," was combined with a form of the Latin word *tenir* meaning "to hold," to form the word *lutenand,* which then evolved into the Modern English word _____.

10. The Latin words *vicus,* meaning "village," and *vicnus,* meaning "hear," helped form the English word _____.

UNDERSTANDING NEW WORDS AND THEIR USES

Lesson 9 | CONTEXT: People and Places
Dazzled by Diamonds

EXERCISE 1 | *Multimeaning*

Directions. Read each numbered sentence below. Then circle the letter of the choice that uses the boldface word in the same way as it is used in the numbered sentence.

1. Did the empress **request** her garnet or her opal earrings?
   (A) The sign in the museum states that detailed information about the queen's jewels is available on **request**.
   (B) The tour guide told a legend about one king's **request** that grains of solid gold be sprinkled in the duck pond.
   (C) Please **request** that the tour guide find out whether the emeralds are from Colombia.
   (D) Teresa's **request** is to see the pear-shaped Spoonmaker Diamond.

2. The dishonest man's plan was to **counterfeit** bills and use them to buy jewels.
   (A) Did he really **counterfeit** the jewels by using plastic and paint?
   (B) The saleswoman could tell that the customers' interest in the gems was **counterfeit**.
   (C) Experts verified that the three diamonds from South Africa were not **counterfeit**.
   (D) The **counterfeit** was detected quickly by the experienced jeweler.

EXERCISE 2 | *Word Analysis*

Prefixes

Directions. Read each numbered pair of words below. Then circle the letter of the choice that best describes the meaning of the boldface prefix as it is used in each pair.

3. **un**ambitious   **un**friendly
   (A) less
   (B) not
   (C) always
   (D) again

4. **co**rrelate   **co**operate
   (A) nearly
   (B) together
   (C) of or relating to
   (D) having the quality of being

Suffixes

Directions. Read each numbered pair of words below. Then circle the letter of the choice that best describes the meaning of the boldface suffix as it is used in the pair.

5. invest**ment**   pave**ment**
  (A) one who does
  (B) result of
  (C) into
  (D) bringing about

6. heir**ess**   princ**ess**
  (A) female
  (B) male
  (C) one who does
  (D) without

Word Origins

Directions. Read each of the following sentences. Then, from the vocabulary list below, choose the word that best completes the sentence. Write the word in the blank.

ambitious	heir	oath	request
counterfeit	honorable	ornamental	solitary
envy	investment	portrait	transparent
exclaim	knapsack	reign	wardrobe
galaxy	luxurious	relate	yacht

7. If you know that the *j* in the Dutch word *jaghte-schip* ("chasing ship") is pronounced as a *y*, then you will know the origin of the English word _____.

8. The Modern English word _____ comes from the Middle English word *galaxie*. *Galaxie*, in turn, comes from the Greek word *galaxias*, meaning "Milky Way."

9. The Middle English word *oth*, meaning "a solemn vow," became the Modern English word _____.

10. The Middle English word *knappen*, "to eat," and the Dutch word *zac*, or "sack," were combined to make the Dutch word *knapzak*. This word eventually came into Modern English as the word _____.

UNDERSTANDING NEW WORDS AND THEIR USES

Lesson 10 CONTEXT: People and Places

Japan and The Japanese

EXERCISE 1 *Multimeaning*

Directions. Read each numbered sentence below. Then circle the letter of the choice that uses the boldface word in the same way as it is used in the numbered sentence.

1. I **assume** you know that the Japanese islands are located along the "Ring of Fire."
   (A) Did his uncle **assume** the debts of the soybean farm in southern Japan?
   (B) He will **assume** the management of the farm, too.
   (C) The teacher should not **assume** that everyone in the class knows the names of Japan's four main islands.
   (D) The women will **assume** traditional Japanese robes called kimonos.

2. It would be interesting to **contrast** farming methods in Japan with those in China.
   (A) The book shows the basic **contrast** between the public gardens and parks in Japan and those in the United States.
   (B) The **contrast** in this picture of Tokyo is not very good, so I can't identify the details.
   (C) In **contrast**, the fishing industry in Japan is modern.
   (D) Will she **contrast** Mount Fuji with other volcanoes in Japan?

EXERCISE 2 *Word Analysis*

Prefixes

Directions. Read each numbered pair of words below. Then circle the letter of the choice that best describes the meaning of the boldface prefix as it is used in each pair.

3. **dis**advantage   **dis**loyalty
   (A) like
   (B) opposite of
   (C) distant
   (D) different

4. **in**accurate   **in**correct
   (A) not
   (B) into
   (C) extremely
   (D) often

Suffixes

Directions. Read each numbered pair of words below. Then circle the letter of the choice that best describes the meaning of the boldface suffix as it is used in each pair.

5. hearty   sticky
   (A) belief or practice
   (B) without
   (C) capable of
   (D) characterized by

6. tradition**al**   music**al**
   (A) belief or practice of
   (B) unlike
   (C) of, like, suitable for
   (D) without

Word Origins

Directions. Read each of the following sentences. Then, from the vocabulary list below, choose the word that best completes the sentence. Write the word in the blank.

appropriate	cultivate	gorgeous	occasion
assume	disadvantage	hearty	ordinarily
boast	eliminate	import	precipitation
contrast	export	inaccurate	quantity
contribute	forefathers	inviting	tradition

7. We get the English word _____ from the Latin word *quantus*, meaning "how great."

8. The English word _____ comes from the Latin word *importare*, meaning "to bring in."

9. We can see the Old French word *gorgias*, meaning "beautiful, glorious," in the English word _____.

10. The English word _____ comes from the Latin noun *occasios*, which means "accidental opportunity" or "fit time."

UNDERSTANDING NEW WORDS AND THEIR USES

| Lesson 11 | **CONTEXT: Ecology and Environment** |

Writers with a Message

EXERCISE 1 | *Multimeaning*

Directions. Read each numbered sentence below. Then circle the letter of the choice that uses the boldface word in the same way as it is used in the numbered sentence.

1. In Bill Peet's book *Farewell to Shady Glade*, the animals want to preserve their small **plot**.
   (A) A brave rabbit wants to **plot** an attack against the humans' machines.
   (B) The old raccoon says such a **plot** won't work because the machines are too powerful.
   (C) The **plot** of the book revolves around the animals' move to a new Shady Glade.
   (D) You'll be glad to hear that the animals find a safe, new **plot** to call their own.

2. Would it be a **mammoth** task for you to write your own picture book about the environment?
   (A) The main character in your book could be a woolly **mammoth** that arrives in the modern world.
   (B) This animal from the past could view pollution as a **mammoth** problem facing the modern world.
   (C) Perhaps the **mammoth** would want to tackle some polluting companies.
   (D) If you want, you could try drawing your **mammoth** in the style of Dr. Seuss.

EXERCISE 2 | *Word Analysis*

Prefixes

Directions. Read each numbered pair of words below. Then circle the letter of the choice that best describes the meaning of the boldface prefix as it is used in each pair.

3. **sub**text   **sub**marine
   (A) under, beneath
   (B) away from or out of
   (C) above or atop
   (D) less

4. **un**characteristic   **un**able
   (A) over
   (B) very
   (C) not
   (D) into

Suffixes

Directions. Read each numbered pair of words below. Then circle the letter of the choice that best describes the meaning of the boldface suffix as it is used in each pair.

5. inform**ant**   assist**ant**
   (A) one who does
   (B) capable of being
   (C) between
   (D) one who does not

6. visual**ize**   computer**ize**
   (A) make, cause to be
   (B) not seeing
   (C) do away with
   (D) state of

Word Origins

Directions. Read each of the following sentences. Then, from the vocabulary list below, choose the word that best completes the sentence. Write the word in the blank.

appreciate	doubtless	inspiration	test
braille	entertain	juvenile	theme
campaign	furious	mammoth	urge
characteristic	genuine	plot	visual
conscience	inform	reduction	widespread

7. The Latin word *juvenis*, meaning "young," will help you understand the English word
   _____.

8. Two Middle English words, *widen*, meaning "wide," and *spreden*, meaning "spread," were combined to form the word _____.

9. The Greek word *thema*, meaning "what is laid down," has come into the English language as the word _____.

10. The Latin word *conscientia* means "consciousness, moral sense." From it we get the English word _____.

UNDERSTANDING NEW WORDS AND THEIR USES

Lesson 12 | CONTEXT: Ecology and Environment
Trash Talk

EXERCISE 1 | Multimeaning

Directions. Read each numbered sentence below. Then circle the letter of the choice that uses the boldface word in the same way as it is used in the numbered sentence.

1. Do you get upset when people **foul** the landscape with trash?
   (A) There are many ways to **foul** the environment, and littering is one of them.
   (B) Littering is a **foul** crime.
   (C) My dad picks up litter along our road each Saturday, even in **foul** weather.
   (D) Even a **foul** baseball, when no one claims it, can become garbage.

2. The committee will **issue** the results of its public survey about trash and recycling next week.
   (A) Thank goodness people have started making an **issue** out of garbage!
   (B) In what **issue** of *Newsweek* did you find the newest figures on the amount of trash produced yearly in the world?
   (C) Does the city plan to **issue** new recycling guidelines?
   (D) The mayor called the latest garbage solution "the **issue** of an unimaginative committee."

EXERCISE 2 | Word Analysis

Prefixes

Directions. Read each numbered pair of words below. Then circle the letter of the choice that best describes the meaning of the boldface prefix as it is used in each pair.

3. **mis**guidance   **mis**fortune
   (A) very
   (B) bad
   (C) previous
   (D) total

4. **in**expensive   **in**capable
   (A) not
   (B) extremely
   (C) under
   (D) state of being

Suffixes

Directions. Read each numbered pair of words below. Then circle the letter of the choice that best describes the meaning of the boldface suffix as it is used in each pair.

5. corpor**ation**   desper**ation**
  (A) not existing
  (B) state of being
  (C) quality of
  (D) capable of

6. employ**er**   destroy**er**
  (A) full of
  (B) having the quality of
  (C) state of being
  (D) one who or that which

Word Origins

Directions. Read each of the following sentences. Then, from the vocabulary list below, choose the word that best completes the sentence. Write the word in the blank.

adjust	disgust	hazard	protest
applaud	dissolve	inexpensive	remedy
ballot	employer	issue	revolution
candidate	foul	merchandise	temporary
corporation	guidance	persuade	villain

7. The Latin word *villanus*, meaning "farm servant," has changed in spelling and meaning to become the English word _____.

8. It is easy to see the Latin word *applaudere*, meaning "to clap hands," in the English word _____.

9. The Middle French word *desgoust*, meaning "distaste," is similar in spelling to the English word _____.

10. The Latin word *persuadere*, which means "to urge," has come into English as the word _____.

UNDERSTANDING NEW WORDS AND THEIR USES

Lesson 13 | **CONTEXT:** Ecology and Environment
A Visit to the Adirondacks

EXERCISE 1 *Multimeaning*

Directions. Read each numbered sentence below. Then circle the letter of the choice that uses the boldface word in the same way as it is used in the numbered sentence.

1. Having her dogs in her home in the woods gave ecologist Anne LaBastille, the author of *Woodswoman,* a feeling of **security**.
   (A) My mother used her cottage in the Adirondacks as **security** for the loan.
   (B) If you lived in an isolated cabin in the woods, you couldn't call **security** for protection.
   (C) Knowing that neighbors are close in the woods would give me a sense of **security**.
   (D) Of course, **security** was tight during the 1980 Winter Olympics in the Adirondacks.

2. The **offense** in the battle against polluters in the Adirondacks includes the National Wildlife Federation.
   (A) The author might take **offense** if I said I didn't want to be a woodswoman like her.
   (B) During a football game at our family reunion in the Adirondacks, my brothers and I played **offense** against our cousins' defense.
   (C) Destroying forests in the Adirondacks is, of course, a serious **offense**.
   (D) Campers without concern for the environment are an **offense** to environmentalists everywhere.

EXERCISE 2 *Word Analysis*

Prefixes

Directions. Read each numbered pair of words below. Then circle the letter of the choice that best describes the meaning of the boldface prefix as it is used in each pair.

3. **co**operate   **co**pilot
   (A) without
   (B) away from
   (C) with, together
   (D) extra

4. **non**resident   **non**believer
   (A) always
   (B) somewhat
   (C) without
   (D) not

Suffixes

Directions. Read each numbered pair of words below. Then circle the letter of the choice that best describes the meaning of the boldface suffix as it is used in each pair.

5. absorb**able**   market**able**
   - (A) act or state of
   - (B) capable of being
   - (C) not capable of being
   - (D) one who

6. amateur**ish**   self**ish**
   - (A) not including
   - (B) that which belongs to
   - (C) unlike
   - (D) characterized by

Word Origins

Directions. Read each of the following sentences. Then, from the vocabulary list below, choose the word that best completes the sentence. Write the word in the blank.

absorb	duplicate	omit	security
amateur	intrusion	privacy	self-respect
complaint	keen	rebel	simplify
cooperate	mourning	regret	sympathy
debt	offense	resident	tension

7. From the Latin word *tensio*, meaning "tense," we get the English word

   _____.

8. We can easily see the Latin word *privatus*, meaning "belonging to oneself, not the state," in the English word _____.

9. The English word _____, comes from the Latin word *complangere*, meaning "to beat the breast," an action that shows dismay or suffering.

10. The Old English word *cene*, meaning "wise, learned," became the Middle English word *kene* and the Modern English word _____.

UNDERSTANDING NEW WORDS AND THEIR USES

Lesson 14 | CONTEXT: Ecology and Environment

Appreciating the Elephant

EXERCISE 1 *Multimeaning* ✍️

Directions. Read each numbered sentence below. Then circle the letter of the choice that uses the boldface word in the same way as it is used in the numbered sentence.

1. A total worldwide ban on the ivory trade would be a **benefit** to elephants.
   (A) Of course, people who trade in ivory for a living would not **benefit** from such a ban.
   (B) Tourists who come to see elephants at Kenya's Amboseli National Park are a **benefit** to the country's economy.
   (C) Many causes can **benefit** from holding a fund-raising event.
   (D) More than a million dollars was raised at the **benefit** for endangered elephants.

2. Elephants are especially threatened today by a **decrease** in available land for their herds.
   (A) Elephant herds may **decrease** because they don't have enough land and food.
   (B) I hope world wildlife agencies do not **decrease** their funds and efforts to save the elephants.
   (C) The **decrease** in the habitats of both the Indian and African elephants is shocking.
   (D) My interest in elephant preservation will never **decrease**.

EXERCISE 2 *Word Analysis* ✍️

Prefixes

Directions. Read each numbered pair of words below. Then circle the letter of the choice that best describes the meaning of the boldface prefix as it is used in each pair.

3. **re**unite   **re**do
   (A) again
   (B) not
   (C) after
   (D) against

4. **un**fortunate   **un**lucky
   (A) under
   (B) very
   (C) not
   (D) into

Suffixes

Directions. Read each numbered pair of words below. Then circle the letter of the choice that best describes the meaning of the boldface suffix as it is used in each pair.

5. captivity   neces**sity**
   (A) in
   (B) without
   (C) state of being
   (D) full of

6. sur**val**   re**val**
   (A) make
   (B) one who does
   (C) act or process of
   (D) position of

Word Origins

Directions. Read each of the following sentences. Then, from the vocabulary list below, choose the word that best completes the sentence. Write the word in the blank.

benefit	migrate	resemble	threat
captivity	obvious	responsibility	tragedy
decrease	prey	severe	unfortunate
eavesdrop	prohibit	suburb	unite
massacre	reckless	survival	vocal

7. In Latin, *sub* means "near," and *urbs* means "city." Our word for a residential area near a city is _____.

8. The Greek word *tragoidia*, meaning "goat song," has come into the English language as the word _____. It may help to know that it is related to a form of singing in Greek plays.

9. The English word _____ comes from the Old French word *macacre*, meaning "slaughterhouse."

10. The Latin word *severus*, meaning "stern or exacting," has come into English as the word _____.

UNDERSTANDING NEW WORDS AND THEIR USES

Lesson 15 | **CONTEXT: Ecology and Environment**
Chief Seattle: Words for the Wise

EXERCISE 1 *Multimeaning*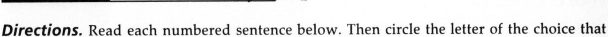

Directions. Read each numbered sentence below. Then circle the letter of the choice that uses the boldface word in the same way as it is used in the numbered sentence.

1. An **associate** of my father's has a book containing many of Chief Seattle's thoughts about "this beautiful land."
   (A) The new **associate** professor of history knows a lot about this great chief, who led the Susquamish peoples of the Pacific Northwest in the 1800s.
   (B) Wouldn't it have been interesting to have been an **associate** of Chief Seattle?
   (C) Do you **associate** Chief Seattle's name with the city of Seattle?
   (D) I prefer to **associate** with people who share Chief Seattle's views about the environment.

2. The professor received a **promotion** after finishing his study of Chief Seattle.
   (A) **Promotion** for the new book about Chief Seattle was especially heavy in Washington.
   (B) In my opinion, Chief Seattle's views need more **promotion**. If more people were aware of them, our environment might get better protection.
   (C) In 1962, many people were involved in the **promotion** of a world's fair in Seattle.
   (D) A friend of ours got a **promotion** for helping design city parks during the fair.

EXERCISE 2 *Word Analysis*

Prefixes

Directions. Read each numbered pair of words below. Then circle the letter of the choice that best describes the meaning of the boldface prefix as it is used in each pair.

3. **im**patience   **im**politeness
   (A) very
   (B) over
   (C) not
   (D) often

4. **re**nominate   **re**run
   (A) against
   (B) really
   (C) never
   (D) again

Suffixes

Directions. Read each numbered pair of words below. Then circle the letter of the choice that best describes the meaning of the boldface suffix as it is used in each pair.

5. apolo**gize**   American**ize**
   (A) without
   (B) to make
   (C) full of
   (D) to take away

6. specific**ity**   possibi**lity**
   (A) condition or state of being
   (B) practice, act, or occupation of
   (C) study of
   (D) with, together

Word Origins

Directions. Read each of the following sentences. Then, from the vocabulary list below, choose the word that best completes the sentence. Write the word in the blank.

anthem	compliment	hesitate	qualify
apologize	courteous	impatience	rehearsal
application	engage	justify	reservoir
associate	frantic	nominate	specify
ballad	gallant	promotion	superior

7. We get our English word _____ from the Old French word *engagier*, meaning "to pledge."

8. Our word _____, meaning "a song of praise or loyalty," comes from the Greek word *antiphonos*, meaning "sounding back."

9. We can still see the Latin word *qualificare*, meaning "to attribute a quality to," in the English word _____.

10. The English word _____ comes from the French word *réserver*, meaning "to reserve."

CONNECTING NEW WORDS AND PATTERNS

Why We Practice Analogies

Practice with analogies builds logic skills. To answer analogy questions correctly, you think about two words and discover the relationship between them; then you match that relationship with one shared by another pair of words. In addition, when you study analogies, you think about the precise meanings of words and fix these definitions in your memory.

Understanding Word Analogies

A word analogy is a comparison between two pairs of words. Here's how word analogies are written:

EXAMPLE 1   FIND : LOCATE :: lose : misplace

The colon (:) stands for the phrase "is related to." Here's how to read the relationships in Example 1:

> FIND [is related to] LOCATE
> lose [is related to] misplace

The double colon [::] between the two pairs of words stands for the phrase "in the same way that." Here's how to read the complete analogy:

> FIND [is related to] LOCATE
> [in the same way that]
> lose [is related to] misplace

Here's another way:

> FIND is to LOCATE as lose is to misplace.

A properly constructed analogy, then, tells us that the relationship between the first pair of words is the same as the relationship between the second pair of words. In Example 1, *find* and *locate* are synonyms, just as *lose* and *misplace* are synonyms.

Let's look at another example:

EXAMPLE 2   GIFT : JOY :: grief : tears

What's the relationship here? A *gift* causes *joy*, just as *grief* causes *tears*. These two pairs of words have the same relationship, a cause-and-effect relationship. The chart on page 156 will help you to identify analogy relationships. No chart could list all possible relationships between words, but the twelve relationships on the chart are the ones most often used. Also, they are the only relationships used in the analogy lessons.

TYPES OF ANALOGIES		
RELATIONSHIP	**EXAMPLE**	**EXPLANATION**
Synonym	DRY : ARID :: find : locate	*Dry* is similar in meaning to *arid,* just as *find* is similar in meaning to *locate.*
Antonym	KIND : CRUEL :: find : lose	A *kind* action is the opposite of a *cruel* action, just as *finding* something is the opposite of *losing* it.
Cause and Effect	GIFT : JOY :: rain : flood	A *gift* can cause *joy,* just as *rain* can cause a *flood.*
Part and Whole	CHAPTER : BOOK :: fender : automobile	A *chapter* is a part of a *book,* just as a *fender* is a part of an *automobile.*
Classification	POLKA : DANCE :: frog : amphibian	A *polka* may be classified as *dance,* just as a *frog* may be classified as an *amphibian.*
Characteristic Quality	PUPPIES : FURRY :: fish : slippery	*Puppies* are *furry,* just as *fish* are *slippery.*
Degree	CHUCKLE : LAUGH :: whimper : cry	A *chuckle* is a little *laugh,* just as a *whimper* is a little *cry.*
Function	KNIFE : CUT :: pen : write	The function of a *knife* is to *cut,* just as the function of a *pen* is to *write.*
Performer and Action	AUTHOR : WRITE :: chef : cook	You expect an *author* to *write,* just as you expect a *chef* to *cook.*
Performer and Object	CASHIER : CASH :: plumber : pipe	A *cashier* works with *cash,* just as a *plumber* works with *pipe.*
Action and Object	BOIL : EGG :: throw : ball	You *boil* an *egg,* just as you *throw* a *ball.*
Location	FISH : SEA :: moose : forest	A *fish* can be found in the *sea,* just as a *moose* can be found in a *forest.*

A Process for Solving Analogies

Your job in solving multiple-choice analogy questions is to identify the relationship between the first two words and then to find the pair of words that has the most similar relationship. Keep in mind that a word pair has the same relationship no matter in which order the two words appear. For example, both CHAPTER : BOOK and BOOK : CHAPTER have a part-and-whole relationship. Here is a hint for identifying relationships: Try using word pairs in the explanation sentences on the chart. When a word pair makes sense in the explanation sentence for a particular relationship, you have found the relationship that the two words have to each other.

Here's a process that will help you with analogy questions:

Answering Analogy Questions: A 4-Step Method

1. Identify the relationship between the capitalized pair of words.
2. Identify the relationship between the pair of words in each possible answer.
3. Eliminate answer choices that have relationships that do not match the relationship between the capitalized words.
4. Choose the remaining possible answer. This answer will have the same relationship as the capitalized pair.

Let's apply this pattern to a sample question.

EXAMPLE 3

WRITE : PEN :: _F_   [*Function*]

(A) toe : foot _PW_   [*Part and Whole*—does not match]
(B) toss : salad _AO_   [*Action and Object*—does not match]
(C) gymnast : mat _PO_   [*Performer and Object*—does not match]
(D) sky : blue _CQ_   [*Characteristic Quality*—does not match]
(E) shine : sun __F_   [*Function*—does match]

None of relationships (A)–(D) match that of the capitalized pair. They can be eliminated. Choice (E) must be the correct answer. Notice that the words make sense in the explanation sentence: The function of a *pen* is to *write* just as the function of the *sun* is to *shine*.

A Final Word

Analogies are easier and more fun if you tackle them with a sense of adventure. Allow yourself to discover the relationship between the first pair of words and to explore the relationships between the words in the answer choices. Keep in mind that some words can represent more than one part of speech and that many words have several meanings. Remember, these little verbal puzzles call for flexibility as well as logic.

CONNECTING NEW WORDS AND PATTERNS

Lesson 1 ANALOGIES

Directions. On each line, write the letter or letters that describe the type of relationship the words have to each other. Choose from the following types:

S synonym	A antonym	PW part and whole	PA performer and action
F function	L location	CE cause and effect	PO performer and object
D degree	C classification	CQ characteristic quality	AO action and object

Circle the letter of the pair of words that has the same relationship as the capitalized words. Each relationship is used no more than once in each numbered item.

1. CONFERENCE : MEETING :: _____
   (A) core : apple _____
   (B) people : persons _____
   (C) old : young _____
   (D) firefighter : fire engine _____
   (E) vegetable : garden _____

2. DESCENDANT : ANCESTOR :: _____
   (A) history : past _____
   (B) anger : rage _____
   (C) violinist : violin _____
   (D) cup : handle _____
   (E) inside : outside _____

3. DOUBTFUL : UNSURE :: _____
   (A) detective : investigate _____
   (B) nonfiction : fiction _____
   (C) hurt : harmed _____
   (D) famous : celebrity _____
   (E) whale : ocean _____

4. INNUMERABLE : FEW :: _____
   (A) calm : peaceful _____
   (B) safe : dangerous _____
   (C) long : longer _____
   (D) fork : utensil _____
   (E) juice : sweet _____

5. JOURNALISM : INFORM :: _____
   (A) comedy : amuse _____
   (B) shirt : blouse _____
   (C) singer : microphone _____
   (D) crave : eat _____
   (E) musician : pianist _____

6. LEGEND : MYTH :: _____
   (A) page : book _____
   (B) errors : anger _____
   (C) rhythm : beat _____
   (D) upset : calm _____
   (E) author : write _____

7. MAJORITY : MINORITY :: _____
   (A) throw : ball _____
   (B) brim : hat _____
   (C) odd : even _____
   (D) photographer : camera _____
   (E) puddle : wet _____

8. NAVIGATOR : STEER :: _____
   (A) chauffeur : drive _____
   (B) cut : knife _____
   (C) buckle : belt _____
   (D) private : personal _____
   (E) elephant : large _____

9. SYMBOL : FLAG :: _____
   (A) headboard : bed _____
   (B) typhoon : damage _____
   (C) mechanic : wrench _____
   (D) politician : senator _____
   (E) asleep : awake _____

10. VIVID : LIVELY :: _____
    (A) special : ordinary _____
    (B) necessary : needed _____
    (C) shrub : yard _____
    (D) armor : protect _____
    (E) drizzle : downpour _____

CONNECTING NEW WORDS AND PATTERNS

Lesson 2 | ANALOGIES

Directions. On each line, write the letter or letters that describe the type of relationship the words have to each other. Choose from the following types:

S synonym	A antonym	PW part and whole	PA performer and action
F function	L location	CE cause and effect	PO performer and object
D degree	C classification	CQ characteristic quality	AO action and object

Circle the letter of the pair of words that has the same relationship as the capitalized words. Each relationship is used no more than once in each numbered item.

1. AVIATION : SCIENCE :: _____
- (A) plant : sow _____
- (B) minerals : earth _____
- (C) typing : skill _____
- (D) handlebar : bike _____
- (E) circle : round _____

2. COLLIDE : CRASH :: _____
- (A) toss : throw _____
- (B) face : clock _____
- (C) diet : weight loss _____
- (D) painter : paintbrush _____
- (E) break : repair _____

3. DEPARTURE : ARRIVAL :: _____
- (A) teacher : textbook _____
- (B) sip : juice _____
- (C) left : right _____
- (D) joke : laughter _____
- (E) book : shelf _____

4. DISTURB : BOTHER :: _____
- (A) show : display _____
- (B) write : erase _____
- (C) shoes : protect _____
- (D) deer : forest _____
- (E) flannel : fabric _____

5. FATAL : HARMFUL :: _____
- (A) dictionary : book _____
- (B) clouds : sky _____
- (C) brilliant : bright _____
- (D) secretary : intercom _____
- (E) heel : boot _____

6. FOUNDATION : STRUCTURE :: _____
- (A) addition : subtraction _____
- (B) yardstick : measure _____
- (C) opera : opera house _____
- (D) introduction : essay _____
- (E) whale : large _____

7. IGNORE : DISREGARD :: _____
- (A) steel : hard _____
- (B) grow : shrink _____
- (C) glance : peek _____
- (D) English : language _____
- (E) overspending : debt _____

8. INCIDENT : EVENT :: _____
- (A) employer : hire _____
- (B) car : automobile _____
- (C) piano : instrument _____
- (D) range : mountain _____
- (E) farmer : tractor _____

9. MISCHIEVOUS : WELL-BEHAVED :: _____
- (A) goodness : praise _____
- (B) troublesome : difficult _____
- (C) messy : neat _____
- (D) wash : dishes _____
- (E) red : color _____

10. NUISANCE : ANNOYING :: _____
- (A) gull : beach _____
- (B) medical bag : doctor _____
- (C) collar : jacket _____
- (D) riddle : puzzling _____
- (E) bull : animal _____

CONNECTING NEW WORDS AND PATTERNS

Lesson 3 ANALOGIES

Directions. On each line, write the letter or letters that describe the type of relationship the words have to each other. Choose from the following types:

S synonym	A antonym	PW part and whole	PA performer and action
F function	L location	CE cause and effect	PO performer and object
D degree	C classification	CQ characteristic quality	AO action and object

Circle the letter of the pair of words that has the same relationship as the capitalized words. Each relationship is used no more than once in each numbered item.

1. ABDOMEN : BODY :: _____
   (A) trunk : elephant _____
   (B) furry : gorilla _____
   (C) empty : vacant _____
   (D) stressed : relaxed _____
   (E) hunter : kill _____

2. CAUTION : CARELESSNESS :: _____
   (A) movement : motion _____
   (B) sprinkle : pour _____
   (C) sound : silence _____
   (D) fire : hot _____
   (E) noun : grammar _____

3. COMMOTION : DISTURBANCE :: _____
   (A) person : crowd _____
   (B) rapid : slow _____
   (C) value : worth _____
   (D) work : pay _____
   (E) scissors : cut _____

4. FLEXIBLE : RUBBER :: _____
   (A) uprising : revolt _____
   (B) invisible : ghost _____
   (C) nervous : calm _____
   (D) boredom : yawn _____
   (E) nurse : thermometer _____

5. FOE : FRIEND :: _____
   (A) genie : grant _____
   (B) player : team _____
   (C) beginning : conclusion _____
   (D) broccoli : vegetable _____
   (E) wash : scour _____

6. GRATITUDE : FAVOR :: _____
   (A) crane : lift _____
   (B) salt : saltshaker _____
   (C) anger : insult _____
   (D) legs : table _____
   (E) salesperson : sell _____

7. HEROIC : RESCUER :: _____
   (A) honest : truthful _____
   (B) musician : oboe _____
   (C) photographer : shoot _____
   (D) teeth : bite _____
   (E) royal : prince _____

8. HOIST : CRANE :: _____
   (A) east : direction _____
   (B) transport : truck _____
   (C) compass needle : magnetic _____
   (D) inquire : ask _____
   (E) pass : fail _____

9. MAXIMUM : GREATEST :: _____
   (A) least : smallest _____
   (B) cool : freezing _____
   (C) close : door _____
   (D) star : bright _____
   (E) funniest : saddest _____

10. PREVIOUS : NEXT :: _____
    (A) student : notebook _____
    (B) suggest : insist _____
    (C) rushing : clumsiness _____
    (D) certain : sure _____
    (E) boring : entertaining _____

CONNECTING NEW WORDS AND PATTERNS

Lesson 4 ANALOGIES

Directions. On each line, write the letter or letters that describe the type of relationship the words have to each other. Choose from the following types:

S synonym	A antonym	PW part and whole	PA performer and action
F function	L location	CE cause and effect	PO performer and object
D degree	C classification	CQ characteristic quality	AO action and object

Circle the letter of the pair of words that has the same relationship as the capitalized words. Each relationship is used no more than once in each numbered item.

1. ASSAULT : INJURY :: _____
   (A) instrument : clarinet _____
   (B) repair : improvement _____
   (C) knob : television _____
   (D) celebrate : grieve _____
   (E) wish : desire _____

2. DAINTY : LACE :: _____
   (A) open : close _____
   (B) swift : fast _____
   (C) tablecloth : cover _____
   (D) waiter : restaurant _____
   (E) sparkling : diamond _____

3. DISGUISE : EXPOSE :: _____
   (A) bore : entertain _____
   (B) location : place _____
   (C) driver : truck _____
   (D) search : find _____
   (E) chef : bake _____

4. EARNEST : JOKING :: _____
   (A) sadness : emotion _____
   (B) exercise : sweat _____
   (C) steady : regular _____
   (D) pretty : beautiful _____
   (E) noisy : quiet _____

5. GASP : SURPRISE :: _____
   (A) short : tall _____
   (B) trot : gallop _____
   (C) happiness : emotion _____
   (D) tears : sorrow _____
   (E) tour : journey _____

6. HIBERNATE : BEAR :: _____
   (A) scissors : cut _____
   (B) method : system _____
   (C) injury : pain _____
   (D) hurt : heal _____
   (E) travel : tourist _____

7. INHALE : AIR :: _____
   (A) farmer : silo _____
   (B) maple : tree _____
   (C) surprised : shocked _____
   (D) rake : leaves _____
   (E) rubber band : stretchy _____

8. LINGER : WAIT :: _____
   (A) sneeze : dust _____
   (B) talk : chat _____
   (C) play : work _____
   (D) gymnast : tumble _____
   (E) tiger : meat eating _____

9. REQUIREMENT : NECESSITY :: _____
   (A) help : assistance _____
   (B) boat : ocean _____
   (C) arrive : depart _____
   (D) waiter : menu _____
   (E) game : fun _____

10. VACUUM : EMPTY :: _____
    (A) jumble : mess _____
    (B) North America : continent _____
    (C) lightning : bright _____
    (D) finger : hand _____
    (E) mirror : reflect _____

CONNECTING NEW WORDS AND PATTERNS

Lesson 5 | ANALOGIES

Directions. On each line, write the letter or letters that describe the type of relationship the words have to each other. Choose from the following types:

S synonym   A antonym   PW part and whole   PA performer and action
F function   L location   CE cause and effect   PO performer and object
D degree   C classification   CQ characteristic quality   AO action and object

Circle the letter of the pair of words that has the same relationship as the capitalized words. Each relationship is used no more than once in each numbered item.

1. AUTOMATION : SYSTEM :: ____
   (A) spill : stain ____
   (B) strange : familiar ____
   (C) cuff : pants ____
   (D) pitcher : ball ____
   (E) democracy : government ____

2. BUREAU : AGENCY :: ____
   (A) divide : multiply ____
   (B) piece : section ____
   (C) sofa : living room ____
   (D) arm : chair ____
   (E) bed : furniture ____

3. FLAMMABLE : GASOLINE :: ____
   (A) asleep : awake ____
   (B) ginger : spice ____
   (C) notebook : binder ____
   (D) startle : terrify ____
   (E) absorbent : cotton ____

4. LUNAR : MOONLIKE :: ____
   (A) candidate : speech ____
   (B) truth : lie ____
   (C) sunny : bright ____
   (D) warm : boiling ____
   (E) oven : bake ____

5. PHARMACY : MEDICINES :: ____
   (A) pretzel : salty ____
   (B) tailor : needle ____
   (C) kitchen : spices ____
   (D) notes : music ____
   (E) wild : tame ____

6. PIERCE : HOLE :: ____
   (A) wet : dry ____
   (B) shoot : target ____
   (C) dew : dampness ____
   (D) build : carpenter ____
   (E) fan : cool ____

7. PRY : CROWBAR :: ____
   (A) shave : razor ____
   (B) quilt : stitched ____
   (C) split : divide ____
   (D) pound : nail ____
   (E) guitar : instrument ____

8. RESIGN : APPLY :: ____
   (A) flood : damage ____
   (B) ask : beg ____
   (C) divide : combine ____
   (D) snow : cold ____
   (E) apple : orchard ____

9. STATIC : STATUE :: ____
   (A) face : watch ____
   (B) easygoing : strict ____
   (C) salty : ocean ____
   (D) poem : literature ____
   (E) nose : smell ____

10. SUSPICION : TRUST :: ____
    (A) boredom : interest ____
    (B) musician : orchestra ____
    (C) autumn : fall ____
    (D) glue : sticky ____
    (E) book : library ____

CONNECTING NEW WORDS AND PATTERNS

Lesson 6 ANALOGIES

Directions. On each line, write the letter or letters that describe the type of relationship the words have to each other. Choose from the following types:

S synonym	A antonym	PW part and whole	PA performer and action
F function	L location	CE cause and effect	PO performer and object
D degree	C classification	CQ characteristic quality	AO action and object

Circle the letter of the pair of words that has the same relationship as the capitalized words. Each relationship is used no more than once in each numbered item.

1. BIOGRAPHY : STORY :: _____
   (A) smooth : bumpy _____
   (B) able : talented _____
   (C) cement : strong _____
   (D) biology : science _____
   (E) free : independent _____

2. DEBATE : ARGUE :: _____
   (A) select : choose _____
   (B) language : Spanish _____
   (C) encourage : prevent _____
   (D) pit : peach _____
   (E) director : movie _____

3. DOCUMENT :
   BIRTH CERTIFICATE :: _____
   (A) coin : toss _____
   (B) pig : fat _____
   (C) soaked : damp _____
   (D) dependable : reliable _____
   (E) book : dictionary _____

4. ESSENTIAL : UNNECESSARY :: _____
   (A) constant : uninterrupted _____
   (B) cushions : sofa _____
   (C) grinning : frowning _____
   (D) study : learn _____
   (E) ruler : measure _____

5. GENEROUS : STINGY :: _____
   (A) tent : campground _____
   (B) fuzzy : blurry _____
   (C) anger : emotion _____
   (D) rude : polite _____
   (E) observer : binoculars _____

6. IDENTICAL : SIMILAR :: _____
   (A) writer : pencil _____
   (B) mayor : city hall _____
   (C) smart : intelligent _____
   (D) peak : valley _____
   (E) boiling : warm _____

7. PROFESSION : TEACHING :: _____
   (A) sheriff : arrest _____
   (B) speak : talk _____
   (C) want : crave _____
   (D) coaching : improvement _____
   (E) fabric : silk _____

8. ROUTINE : UNUSUAL :: _____
   (A) edge : rim _____
   (B) animal : dog _____
   (C) planned : unexpected _____
   (D) rules : order _____
   (E) pen pal : letter _____

9. SCHOLAR : READ :: _____
   (A) book : index _____
   (B) police officer : badge _____
   (C) mat : gymnasium _____
   (D) tell : say _____
   (E) pilot : fly _____

10. THOROUGH : COMPLETE :: _____
    (A) preparation : readiness _____
    (B) snow : cold _____
    (C) salad : toss _____
    (D) broad : wide _____
    (E) deep : shallow _____

CONNECTING NEW WORDS AND PATTERNS

Lesson 7 ANALOGIES

Directions. On each line, write the letter or letters that describe the type of relationship the words have to each other. Choose from the following types:

S synonym	A antonym	PW part and whole
F function	L location	CE cause and effect
D degree	C classification	CQ characteristic quality

PA performer and action
PO performer and object
AO action and object

Circle the letter of the pair of words that has the same relationship as the capitalized words. Each relationship is used no more than once in each numbered item.

1. ARCHITECT : BLUEPRINT :: _____
   (A) idle : busy _____
   (B) house : building _____
   (C) composer : symphony _____
   (D) staples : join _____
   (E) build : construct _____

2. BETRAY : DECEIVE :: _____
   (A) tight : loose _____
   (B) work : labor _____
   (C) autumn : season _____
   (D) dock : lake _____
   (E) sculptor : statue _____

3. CEREMONY : WEDDING :: _____
   (A) jog : run _____
   (B) beat : defeat _____
   (C) tug : push _____
   (D) state : Utah _____
   (E) honey : sweet _____

4. DISTRICT : SECTION :: _____
   (A) boring : dull _____
   (B) triangle : shape _____
   (C) cut : bleeding _____
   (D) hockey player : puck _____
   (E) elephants : India _____

5. ETERNAL : TEMPORARY :: _____
   (A) powerful : strong _____
   (B) raw : cooked _____
   (C) gills : fish _____
   (D) quartz : rock _____
   (E) pepper : hot _____

6. FRAGRANT : ROSE :: _____
   (A) pirate : steal _____
   (B) fragile : china _____
   (C) lumber : sawmill _____
   (D) petal : flower _____
   (E) lumberjack : timber _____

7. IGNITE : PUT OUT :: _____
   (A) rest : activity _____
   (B) persuade : advertisement _____
   (C) dusk : darkness _____
   (D) carelessness : accident _____
   (E) eat : food _____

8. QUARANTINE : ISOLATION :: _____
   (A) wash : clothes _____
   (B) halt : continue _____
   (C) command : order _____
   (D) liar : dishonest _____
   (E) crime : punishment _____

9. SCHEME : PLOT :: _____
   (A) maps : direct _____
   (B) private : public _____
   (C) sand : beach _____
   (D) order : arrange _____
   (E) brush : hair _____

10. VICTIM : SUFFER :: _____
   (A) folktale : story _____
   (B) monster : scary _____
   (C) arrive : leave _____
   (D) victor : win _____
   (E) lawyer : courtroom _____

CONNECTING NEW WORDS AND PATTERNS

Lesson 8   ANALOGIES

Directions. On each line, write the letter or letters that describe the type of relationship the words have to each other. Choose from the following types:

S synonym	A antonym	PW part and whole	PA performer and action
F function	L location	CE cause and effect	PO performer and object
D degree	C classification	CQ characteristic quality	AO action and object

Circle the letter of the pair of words that has the same relationship as the capitalized words. Each relationship is used no more than once in each numbered item.

1. ABUNDANT : PLENTIFUL :: _____
   (A) sour : lemon _____
   (B) rich : wealthy _____
   (C) sharp : blunt _____
   (D) chicken : poultry _____
   (E) mail carrier : letter _____

2. DESCRIPTIVE : DETAILED :: _____
   (A) helpful : hurtful _____
   (B) still : motionless _____
   (C) destructive : war _____
   (D) bumper : car _____
   (E) teacher : chalk _____

3. DESIRABLE : DISGUSTING :: _____
   (A) bright : faded _____
   (B) clean : tidy _____
   (C) pane : window _____
   (D) wash : hair _____
   (E) dirty : filthy _____

4. DRAMATIC : DULL :: _____
   (A) comical : gloomy _____
   (B) magical : enchanting _____
   (C) grass : green _____
   (D) trial : courthouse _____
   (E) song : words _____

5. EXTRAORDINARY : UNUSUAL :: _____
   (A) baby : innocent _____
   (B) feet : walk _____
   (C) awful : bad _____
   (D) buy : sell _____
   (E) children : nursery _____

6. GEOLOGY : SCIENCE :: _____
   (A) waltz : dance _____
   (B) vulture : fly _____
   (C) accept : deny _____
   (D) rain : flood _____
   (E) stem : apple _____

7. POSSESS : HAVE :: _____
   (A) lift : raise _____
   (B) steal : thief _____
   (C) give : receive _____
   (D) load : camera _____
   (E) book : library _____

8. PREHISTORIC : ANCIENT :: _____
   (A) fishing pole : cast _____
   (B) explorer : travel _____
   (C) poison ivy : itch _____
   (D) key : typewriter _____
   (E) yell : shout _____

9. SATISFY : DISAPPOINT :: _____
   (A) mapmaker : draw _____
   (B) laces : shoe _____
   (C) gift : pleasure _____
   (D) approve : reject _____
   (E) reduce : lessen _____

10. TERRAIN : GROUND :: _____
   (A) earth : plant _____
   (B) answer : ask _____
   (C) ask : request _____
   (D) iron : hard _____
   (E) seed : sprout _____

CONNECTING NEW WORDS AND PATTERNS

Lesson 9 | ANALOGIES

Directions. On each line, write the letter or letters that describe the type of relationship the words have to each other. Choose from the following types:

S synonym	A antonym	PW part and whole	PA performer and action
F function	L location	CE cause and effect	PO performer and object
D degree	C classification	CQ characteristic quality	AO action and object

Circle the letter of the pair of words that has the same relationship as the capitalized words. Each relationship is used no more than once in each numbered item.

1. AMBITIOUS : CONTENT :: _____
   (A) quick : rapid _____
   (B) Earth : planet _____
   (C) large : small _____
   (D) furnace : heat _____
   (E) leaf : green _____

2. COUNTERFEIT : FAKE :: _____
   (A) plain : fancy _____
   (B) rain : flood _____
   (C) money : buy _____
   (D) banana : sweet _____
   (E) difficult : hard _____

3. ENVY : JEALOUSY :: _____
   (A) hospital : medicine _____
   (B) roof : building _____
   (C) desire : want _____
   (D) chef : pot _____
   (E) artificial : natural _____

4. EXCLAIM : SAY :: _____
   (A) rent : apartment _____
   (B) inspect : glance _____
   (C) poet : imaginative _____
   (D) inner : outer _____
   (E) spark : fire _____

5. GALAXY : STAR :: _____
   (A) slice : knife _____
   (B) hoofed : horse _____
   (C) nightmare : terror _____
   (D) jockey : ride _____
   (E) tree : bark _____

6. ORNAMENTAL : SHRUB :: _____
   (A) igloo : home _____
   (B) write : typewriter _____
   (C) money : bank _____
   (D) useful : tool _____
   (E) leave : arrive _____

7. REIGN : KING :: _____
   (A) flower : carnation _____
   (B) door : knob _____
   (C) pasture : cattle _____
   (D) serve : waiter _____
   (E) seedling : tree _____

8. SOLITARY : LONER :: _____
   (A) Boston : city _____
   (B) fussy : agreeable _____
   (C) similar : alike _____
   (D) burner : stove _____
   (E) graceful : ballerina _____

9. TRANSPARENT : GLASS :: _____
   (A) breakable : window _____
   (B) foggy : clear _____
   (C) carve : kachina doll _____
   (D) strings : guitar _____
   (E) cold : shiver _____

10. WARDROBE : OUTFIT :: _____
    (A) rider : saddle _____
    (B) refrigerator : chill _____
    (C) tool set : wrench _____
    (D) water : wet _____
    (E) tiny : huge _____

CONNECTING NEW WORDS AND PATTERNS

Lesson 10 | ANALOGIES

Directions. On each line, write the letter or letters that describe the type of relationship the words have to each other. Choose from the following types:

S synonym	A antonym	PW part and whole	PA performer and action
F function	L location	CE cause and effect	PO performer and object
D degree	C classification	CQ characteristic quality	AO action and object

Circle the letter of the pair of words that has the same relationship as the capitalized words. Each relationship is used no more than once in each numbered item.

1. APPROPRIATE : UNSUITABLE :: _____
   (A) disappearance : search _____
   (B) valuable : gem _____
   (C) fresh : stale _____
   (D) helpful : useful _____
   (E) teeth : comb _____

2. BOAST : BRAG :: _____
   (A) try : attempt _____
   (B) accept : refuse _____
   (C) giggle : joke _____
   (D) bubble : fragile _____
   (E) beat : drum _____

3. CULTIVATE : GARDEN :: _____
   (A) shock : scream _____
   (B) feed : starve _____
   (C) food : refrigerator _____
   (D) harvest : crop _____
   (E) clown : amuse _____

4. ELIMINATE : INCLUDE :: _____
   (A) start : finish _____
   (B) pear : fruit _____
   (C) copy : duplicate _____
   (D) eat : banana _____
   (E) swings : playground _____

5. EXPORT : GOODS :: _____
   (A) make : create _____
   (B) squeeze : hold _____
   (C) wildflowers : field _____
   (D) write : letter _____
   (E) traveler : map _____

6. INVITING : ATTRACTIVE :: _____
   (A) funny : serious _____
   (B) orange : juicy _____
   (C) librarian : book _____
   (D) gossip : embarrassment _____
   (E) incorrect : wrong _____

7. OCCASION : BIRTHDAY :: _____
   (A) quantity : amount _____
   (B) kingdom : ruler _____
   (C) quilt : bed _____
   (D) athlete : compete _____
   (E) book : dictionary _____

8. ORDINARILY : USUALLY :: _____
   (A) carton : contain _____
   (B) quickly : fast _____
   (C) newspaper : column _____
   (D) accident : injury _____
   (E) car : garage _____

9. PRECIPITATION : SNOW :: _____
   (A) doll : toyshop _____
   (B) marry : wed _____
   (C) sport : golf _____
   (D) hire : fire _____
   (E) strum : guitar _____

10. TRADITION : CUSTOM :: _____
    (A) clock : hands _____
    (B) filth : dirt _____
    (C) summer : warm _____
    (D) egg : hatch _____
    (E) gasoline : gas station _____

CONNECTING NEW WORDS AND PATTERNS

Lesson 11 | ANALOGIES

Directions. On each line, write the letter or letters that describe the type of relationship the words have to each other. Choose from the following types:

S synonym A antonym PW part and whole PA performer and action
F function L location CE cause and effect PO performer and object
D degree C classification CQ characteristic quality AO action and object

Circle the letter of the pair of words that has the same relationship as the capitalized words. Each relationship is used no more than once in each numbered item.

1. APPRECIATE : DESPISE :: _____
   (A) dog : fetch _____
   (B) interest : bore _____
   (C) question : response _____
   (D) whole : entire _____
   (E) monkey : animal _____

2. BRAILLE : READ :: _____
   (A) valley : hill _____
   (B) tiny : small _____
   (C) bracelet : jewelry _____
   (D) cackle : hen _____
   (E) essay : write _____

3. CAMPAIGN : POLITICIAN :: _____
   (A) dime : shiny _____
   (B) board : chess set _____
   (C) swamp : desert _____
   (D) compete : athlete _____
   (E) cab : taxi _____

4. CONSCIENCE : GUIDE :: _____
   (A) brain : think _____
   (B) hunger : eat _____
   (C) bedroom : apartment _____
   (D) mail carrier : pouch _____
   (E) ice : cold _____

5. ENTERTAIN : PERFORMER :: _____
   (A) needy : independent _____
   (B) oven : bake _____
   (C) write : author _____
   (D) strap : backpack _____
   (E) scene : view _____

6. FURIOUS : ANNOYED :: _____
   (A) head : scalp _____
   (B) delighted : glad _____
   (C) break : repair _____
   (D) wear : hat _____
   (E) desert : oasis _____

7. GENUINE : REAL :: _____
   (A) push : grab _____
   (B) magician : perform _____
   (C) rake : leaves _____
   (D) solo : alone _____
   (E) space : rocket _____

8. JUVENILE : MATURE :: _____
   (A) combined : separate _____
   (B) ill : dying _____
   (C) varied : different _____
   (D) infant : crib _____
   (E) close : gate _____

9. THEME : SUBJECT :: _____
   (A) open : close _____
   (B) feather : bird _____
   (C) habit : custom _____
   (D) climb : ladder _____
   (E) chair : furniture _____

10. URGE : SUGGEST :: _____
    (A) mix : blender _____
    (B) slip : fall _____
    (C) crash : bump _____
    (D) mail : letter _____
    (E) hold : drop _____

CONNECTING NEW WORDS AND PATTERNS

Lesson 12 **ANALOGIES**

Directions. On each line, write the letter or letters that describe the type of relationship the words have to each other. Choose from the following types:

S synonym   A antonym   PW part and whole   PA performer and action
F function   L location   CE cause and effect   PO performer and object
D degree   C classification   CQ characteristic quality   AO action and object

Circle the letter of the pair of words that has the same relationship as the capitalized words. Each relationship is used no more than once in each numbered item.

1. BALLOT : VOTER :: _____
   (A) cottage : door _____
   (B) kangaroo : Australia _____
   (C) newspaper : throw _____
   (D) order form : customer _____
   (E) tight : stretched _____

2. DISSOLVE : MELT :: _____
   (A) student : read _____
   (B) wash : cleanse _____
   (C) penny : coin _____
   (D) barber : razor _____
   (E) bee : busy _____

3. GUIDANCE : ADVICE :: _____
   (A) penalty : punishment _____
   (B) teacher : exam _____
   (C) freeze : boil _____
   (D) violin : string _____
   (E) piano : play _____

4. HAZARD : DANGER :: _____
   (A) chance : opportunity _____
   (B) animal : rabbit _____
   (C) drama : perform _____
   (D) shouting : attention _____
   (E) warm : cool _____

5. INEXPENSIVE : COSTLY :: _____
   (A) lawyer : professional _____
   (B) wild : untamed _____
   (C) dressy : casual _____
   (D) ice cream : cold _____
   (E) room : straighten _____

6. MERCHANDISE : MALL :: _____
   (A) grocer : fruit _____
   (B) bread : baked _____
   (C) snout : bear _____
   (D) groceries : supermarket _____
   (E) drama : literature _____

7. PROTEST : AGREE :: _____
   (A) raise : lower _____
   (B) skyscraper : building _____
   (C) memorize : speech _____
   (D) street : paved _____
   (E) wound : pain _____

8. REMEDY : CURE :: _____
   (A) scorching : freezing _____
   (B) memory : recollection _____
   (C) race : exciting _____
   (D) tower : castle _____
   (E) planet : Saturn _____

9. REVOLUTION : REVOLT :: _____
   (A) author : revise _____
   (B) limousine : driver _____
   (C) election : select _____
   (D) street : avenue _____
   (E) contest : enter _____

10. TEMPORARY : PERMANENT :: _____
   (A) calm : upset _____
   (B) test : final exam _____
   (C) fur : soft _____
   (D) mountain : hill _____
   (E) first : earliest _____

CONNECTING NEW WORDS AND PATTERNS

Lesson 13 | ANALOGIES

Directions. On each line, write the letter or letters that describe the type of relationship the words have to each other. Choose from the following types:

S	synonym	A antonym	PW	part and whole	PA performer and action
F	function	L location	CE	cause and effect	PO performer and object
D	degree	C classification	CQ	characteristic quality	AO action and object

Circle the letter of the pair of words that has the same relationship as the capitalized words. Each relationship is used no more than once in each numbered item.

1. AMATEUR : PROFESSIONAL :: ____
   (A) healthy : fit ____
   (B) mechanic : wrench ____
   (C) plum : fruit ____
   (D) loud : bagpipe ____
   (E) neat : disorderly ____

2. COMPLAINT : PROBLEM :: ____
   (A) milk : nourishing ____
   (B) umbrella : protect ____
   (C) praise : success ____
   (D) coffee : brew ____
   (E) sport : hockey ____

3. DEBT : PAY OFF :: ____
   (A) jeweler : gem ____
   (B) sky : cloud ____
   (C) rocks : stones ____
   (D) April : month ____
   (E) law : obey ____

4. DUPLICATE : COPY :: ____
   (A) ax : chop ____
   (B) baker : pie ____
   (C) position : location ____
   (D) question : test ____
   (E) polar bear : white ____

5. MOURNING : DEATH :: ____
   (A) celebration : victory ____
   (B) bear : den ____
   (C) sip : milk ____
   (D) summer : season ____
   (E) hummingbird : fly ____

6. OMIT : INCLUDE :: ____
   (A) statesman : lead ____
   (B) recover : improve ____
   (C) trunk : tree ____
   (D) collect : taxes ____
   (E) pay : earn ____

7. REBEL : OBEY :: ____
   (A) scare : frighten ____
   (B) bore : entertain ____
   (C) sheriff : protect ____
   (D) wing : airplane ____
   (E) president : Lincoln ____

8. REGRET : FEELING :: ____
   (A) refrigerator : kitchen ____
   (B) bubble : pop ____
   (C) pleasantness : attitude ____
   (D) bear : growl ____
   (E) oil : slippery ____

9. SELF-RESPECT : SELF-ESTEEM :: ____
   (A) France : nation ____
   (B) faith : belief ____
   (C) word : sentence ____
   (D) reward : punish ____
   (E) magazine : read ____

10. SYMPATHY : PITY :: ____
    (A) entrance : exit ____
    (B) springtime : breezy ____
    (C) cards : shuffle ____
    (D) robbery : theft ____
    (E) dog : pet ____

CONNECTING NEW WORDS AND PATTERNS

Lesson 14 | ANALOGIES

Directions. On each line, write the letter or letters that describe the type of relationship the words have to each other. Choose from the following types:

S synonym   A antonym   PW part and whole   PA performer and action
F function   L location   CE cause and effect   PO performer and object
D degree   C classification   CQ characteristic quality   AO action and object

Circle the letter of the pair of words that has the same relationship as the capitalized words. Each relationship is used no more than once in each numbered item.

1. OBVIOUS : HIDDEN :: ____
   (A) scarce : rare ____
   (B) tired : exhausted ____
   (C) soap : clean ____
   (D) completed : unfinished ____
   (E) candle : burn ____

2. PREY : HUNTED :: ____
   (A) eyes : see ____
   (B) door : slam ____
   (C) tornado : damage ____
   (D) nail : hardware ____
   (E) inspired : artist ____

3. PROHIBIT : ALLOW :: ____
   (A) teacher : chalk ____
   (B) water : liquid ____
   (C) throw : toss ____
   (D) defend : attack ____
   (E) gardener : trim ____

4. RECKLESS : CAREFUL :: ____
   (A) clumsy : graceful ____
   (B) sister : relative ____
   (C) fish : aquarium ____
   (D) overdue : late ____
   (E) damage : destroy ____

5. RESEMBLE : MATCH :: ____
   (A) flowers : garden ____
   (B) motorcycle : seat ____
   (C) globe : round ____
   (D) suggest : demand ____
   (E) load : film ____

6. RESPONSIBILITY : DUTY : ____
   (A) robin : bird ____
   (B) firefighter : ladder ____
   (C) job : occupation ____
   (D) life : death ____
   (E) smoke : hazy ____

7. SUBURBS : OUTSKIRTS :: ____
   (A) speed : danger ____
   (B) areas : sections ____
   (C) coin : quarter ____
   (D) menu : restaurant ____
   (E) wagon : carry ____

8. TRAGEDY : SUFFERING :: ____
   (A) lens : camera ____
   (B) glance : stare ____
   (C) necklace : jewelry ____
   (D) delay : tardiness ____
   (E) ride : bike ____

9. UNITE : DIVIDE :: ____
   (A) work : loaf ____
   (B) collie : dog ____
   (C) cowboy : stirrup ____
   (D) squirrel : tree ____
   (E) flowers : arrange ____

10. VOCAL : PARROT :: ____
    (A) teeth : bite ____
    (B) dangerous : hazardous ____
    (C) quiet : library ____
    (D) green : color ____
    (E) cave : bats ____

CONNECTING NEW WORDS AND PATTERNS

Lesson 15   ANALOGIES

Directions. On each line, write the letter or letters that describe the type of relationship the words have to each other. Choose from the following types:

S synonym   A antonym   PW part and whole   PA performer and action
F function   L location   CE cause and effect   PO performer and object
D degree   C classification   CQ characteristic quality AO action and object

Circle the letter of the pair of words that has the same relationship as the capitalized words. Each relationship is used no more than once in each numbered item.

1. BALLAD : SONG :: ____
 (A) laugh : cry ____
 (B) praise : flatter ____
 (C) contest : rules ____
 (D) explanation : understanding ____
 (E) portrait : painting ____

2. COMPLIMENT : INSULT :: ____
 (A) critic : movie review ____
 (B) singer : perform ____
 (C) eagle : bird ____
 (D) hate : detest ____
 (E) disappoint : please ____

3. COURTEOUS : IMPOLITE :: ____
 (A) swimmer : swim ____
 (B) quick : rabbit ____
 (C) expensive : cheap ____
 (D) lawful : legal ____
 (E) biology : science ____

4. FRANTIC : UPSET :: ____
 (A) wild : lively ____
 (B) scoreboard : gym ____
 (C) jazz : music ____
 (D) push : pull ____
 (E) poet : write ____

5. GALLANT : PRINCE :: ____
 (A) shark : fin ____
 (B) clever : tricky ____
 (C) round : ball ____
 (D) difficult : easy ____
 (E) bicyclist : helmet ____

6. HESITATE : PAUSE :: ____
 (A) walk : stroll ____
 (B) wax : candle ____
 (C) shark : ocean ____
 (D) tree : oak ____
 (E) pass : fail ____

7. IMPATIENCE : DELAYS :: ____
 (A) take : grab ____
 (B) athlete : train ____
 (C) thirst : dryness ____
 (D) path : trail ____
 (E) ship : mast ____

8. REHEARSAL : DRILL :: ____
 (A) horrible : wonderful ____
 (B) tune : melody ____
 (C) doorbell : push ____
 (D) towel : dry ____
 (E) attic : house ____

9. RESERVOIR : STORE :: ____
 (A) point : direct ____
 (B) flexible : stubborn ____
 (C) guest : arrive ____
 (D) worship : admire ____
 (E) paper clip : join ____

10. SUPERIOR : AVERAGE :: ____
 (A) strike : match ____
 (B) parent : nurture ____
 (C) pumpkin : orange ____
 (D) dog : pet ____
 (E) love : like ____

READING NEW WORDS IN CONTEXT

Why We Read Strategically

Reading is active. As you read, you step into the writer's world. When you come across a new idea, you usually look for a clue to help you determine the writer's meaning. You move ahead to see if the idea is explained, or you retrace your steps to look for any signs you missed.

You can use these same strategies to build your vocabulary. If you don't know the meaning of a word, you should look in the passage surrounding the word for hints. These hints are called context clues. The more you practice hunting for context clues, the better you become at reading new words, and the larger your vocabulary will grow.

The following reading selection shows the kinds of context clues you will find in the Reading New Words in Context lessons.

Strategic Reading: An Example

Long, long ago, long before there were humans on earth—much less humans who could record history—dinosaurs walked the earth. During these **prehistoric** times, strange and wonderful creatures ruled the entire earth. All in all, *this* **reign** lasted 135 million years.

The **forefathers** and foremothers of the dinosaurs were the thecodonts, mighty reptiles who were *also the ancestors* of many other reptiles as well as all of today's birds. One of their descendants was a huge flying reptile. Another was a creature with a body like that of a turtle but with a 25-foot-long neck. Like the dinosaurs, these unusual *and* **extraordinary** creatures became extinct. Any of these creatures has the power to *stun,* **astonish,** *and amaze* us, but it is the dinosaurs that most people find especially fascinating.

Some dinosaurs were **mammoth** creatures. *The euhelopus, for example, was 60 feet tall and weighed 50,000 pounds.* In contrast, the 20-foot, 7,000-pound stegosaurus seems almost small. Although enormous size *was* a **characteristic** of many dinosaurs, others were much, much smaller, no bigger than a chicken or a duck. Some of these smaller ones looked much like either the iguana or the komodo dragon, two reptiles that inhabit earth today.

Note that a *summary* indicates the meaning of **prehistoric**.

A *pronoun* (*this*) refers us to the meaning of **reign**.
The meaning of **forefathers** is made clear through *restatement*, that is, through saying the same thing in a different way.

A *coordinating conjunction* (*and*) provides a clue to the meaning of **extraordinary**. The words *but, or,* and *nor* are other coordinating conjuctions.
Note that a clue to the meaning of **astonish** is provided by using the word in a *series* of words that have similar meanings.
An *example* provides the key to understanding **mammoth**.

A form of the verb *to be* (*was*) links an example of a characteristic to the word **characteristic**.

Some of the dinosaurs were fierce, meat-eating creatures. Often, other *milder and gentler dinosaurs were unable to defend themselves from the more savage ones and thus became their* **victims**. Even the vegetarian dinosaurs who roamed about peacefully snacking on plants could be quite frightening to other species that shared the planet. A 55-ton brachiosaurus lumbering across the countryside would have presented a real **threat,** *a clear danger,* to any unsuspecting creature who got in its way. The huge Triceratops had frightening horns on its nose and over both of its eyes. The sight of this 10-ton animal bounding along at 30 miles per hour certainly scared the newly emerging mammals that had to scurry out of its way. Nevertheless, it was also a threat to any other dinosaur that tried to attack it.

Although groups of dinosaurs might be in **competition** with each other, *cooperation within a group was also common.* Members of a species might travel in a herd, eat and nest together, share responsibility for the young, and present a united defense against enemies.

Scientists are still debating about why the dinosaurs disappeared. We do not know for sure. All we know is that **twilight** *arrived for these creatures at the same time all across the earth. Then, in a twinkling, it was night,* and the dinosaurs were gone.

In a *cause-and-effect* relationship, one thing causes another thing to happen. The meaning of **victims** is established through a cause-and-effect relationship.

An *appositive phrase* contains a noun or pronoun that explains the noun or pronoun beside it. An appositive phrase indicates the meaning of **threat**.

Note that the meaning of **competition** is established through *contrast,* the placement of opposites near each other to point out their difference.

The meaning of **twilight** is established through *figurative language.* Figurative language is language that imaginatively describes one thing through something else.

A Final Note

How can you learn strategic reading? Practice is a great way to improve your skill. The following lessons will help you learn the different context clues a writer uses. As you complete each lesson, you will become a more effective reader.

READING NEW WORDS IN CONTEXT

Lesson 1 | CONTEXT: Amazing Nature

Introduction. What do you and your friends think about such creatures as Bigfoot and the Loch Ness monster? Are they just products of people's imagination, or do they really exist?

In the following article, a student writes for the school newspaper about some of the most famous mysterious creatures. The article gives you an opportunity to expand your vocabulary. Below are twenty vocabulary words that are used in the passage and in the exercise that follows it.

astonish	descendant	journalism	quote	symbol
conference	doubtful	legend	reliable	twilight
definite	innumerable	majority	session	unexpectedly
deny	interview	navigator	summarize	vivid

In Search of Bigfoot

The **conference** (1) here Saturday on the world's little-known, mysterious creatures was fascinating. This meeting made it clear to me that many people truly believe that some of these creatures exist but that others remain **doubtful** (2). Some of the information may **astonish** (3) you; it certainly amazed me!

Take Bigfoot, the large, ape-like creature reportedly seen throughout the United States for years. Is Bigfoot a **legend** (4), a myth, a fanciful story? Or is Bigfoot a real creature? Bigfoot, who walks on two feet, has been sighted by more than two thousand people. A man from California said that in 1967 a female Bigfoot **unexpectedly** (5) appeared in a clearing and then just as suddenly disappeared into the forest. The man took pictures of the creature. Experts have said the film could not have been faked. Thus many people trust the pictures as **reliable** (6) evidence. Some people think Bigfoot is a **descendant** (7) of or related across many generations to a prehistoric ape.

The Creature of Loch Ness
Because I study **journalism** (8), I collect and write about the news. What I heard during the conference about Scotland's Loch Ness monster certainly was news to me! I was able to **interview** (9) some interesting people about "Nessie." For example, I had a face-to-face discussion with a Scotsman who claims he has seen the Loch Ness monster six times. He gave me a **vivid** (10) description of the monster: a dark creature, forty feet long, with one hump, a long neck, and a small head. He saw the creature rising out of the water shortly after sunset, during a foggy **twilight** (11). I wish I could **quote** (12) him, but he was so interesting to listen to that I forgot about writing down his exact words. He thinks there are many of these big creatures, perhaps giant mammals or reptiles, in Loch Ness. Scientists have tried to find the creatures with sonar, but they have found nothing certain, or **definite** (13), so far.

There also was a group meeting on sea monsters. During this **session** (14), a man who was a **navigator** (15) of a ship in the Bahamas said he once almost steered right into some sort of giant sea creature. He then told stories about the Lusca, a creature said to be part dragon and part octopus.

Not all scientists reject, or **deny** (16), the existence of the giant octopus.

Dinosaurs Live?

More than half of the people at the conference, a **majority** (17), attended my favorite **session**. It was about dinosaurs that still are seen in the tropics of central Africa. These dinosaurs are similar to sauropods, plant-eaters with long necks and small heads. The people in the Congo call the creatures Mokele-Mbembe. There have been **innumerable** (18) sightings, more than anyone can count. In 1983, a zoologist claimed to have seen one. Some scientists say it's not out of the question that dinosaurs still live there because the land was not covered with ice during the Ice Age.

To end, I'll **summarize** (19) the main reason that many scientists think creatures like Bigfoot and the Mokele-Mbembe may exist. In brief, they point out that previously unknown animals continue to be discovered. For example, the Komodo dragon was discovered in 1912 and a new species of shark was discovered in 1976. The International Society of Cryptozoology (the study of mysterious animals) has a fitting **symbol** (20). The society is represented by a giraffe relative discovered by scientists in the late 1800s.

EXERCISE *Reading Strategically* ✍

Directions. Answer each of the following items by circling the letter of the correct answer. You may need to refer to the selection as you answer the items. The numbers of the items are the same as the numbers of the boldface vocabulary words in the selection.

1. The writer of this article gives a clue to the meaning of **conference**. What is the clue?
 (A) The writer says that it was held here.
 (B) The writer refers to it in the next sentence as a meeting.
 (C) The writer says it was about little-known, mysterious creatures.
 (D) The writer refers to it as fascinating.

2. You can tell from the article that people who are **doubtful** are
 (A) convinced
 (B) at the conference
 (C) unknown
 (D) not sure

3. In the first paragraph of the essay, **astonish** means
 (A) to amaze
 (B) to inform
 (C) to report
 (D) to interest

4. All of the following are good definitions of **legend** *except*
 (A) a myth
 (B) a fanciful tale
 (C) a popular story passed down through the ages
 (D) a story based heavily on factual events

5. How does the writer let us know that when something happens **unexpectedly**, it happens without warning?
 (A) The writer says the event took place in a clearing in 1967.
 (B) The writer tells us that Bigfoot appeared and disappeared.
 (C) The writer connects **unexpectedly** with the word suddenly.
 (D) The writer hints that Bigfoot is real.

6. In the second paragraph, **reliable** means
  (A) fake
  (B) trustworthy
  (C) on film
  (D) not dependable

7. The writer explains that Bigfoot may be a **descendant** of a prehistoric ape. Here, **descendant** means
  (A) something that has fallen from a great height
  (B) someone or something related across generations
  (C) something that rises to great heights
  (D) someone or something related to a prehistoric ape

8. In the article we learn that the writer's field is **journalism**. Here, **journalism** means
  (A) writing books
  (B) collecting and writing news
  (C) attending conferences and panels
  (D) reading about ideas

9. Which of the following is an example of an **interview** described by the writer of the article?
  A) There was a group meeting that included the navigator's story about Lusca.
  (B) The author learned about the Loch Ness monster.
  (C) The author met interesting people.
  (D) The author had a face-to-face discussion with a Scotsman.

10. Which of the following is an example of a **vivid** description?
  (A) I was able to interview some interesting people about "Nessie."
  (B) I had a face-to-face discussion with a Scotsman who claims he has seen the Loch Ness monster.
  (C) The dark creature was forty feet long, with one hump, a long neck, and a small head.
  (D) His accent made it difficult for me to write down his exact words.

11. The author writes, "He saw the creature rising out of the water shortly after sunset, during a foggy **twilight**." Here, **twilight** means
  (A) after sunset but before dark
  (B) early in the morning
  (C) at noon
  (D) when it is foggy

12. Which of the following is the reason that the writer is not able to **quote** the Scotsman?
  (A) The writer could not understand the Scotsman because of his heavy Scottish accent.
  (B) The writer preferred to make up the information.
  (C) The Scotsman had absolutely nothing new or interesting to say about the Loch Ness monster.
  (D) The man was so interesting that the writer forgot to write down the exact words.

13. The writer says that scientists have not yet been able to discover anything **definite** about the Loch Ness monster. Here, **definite** means
   (A) sonar
   (B) certain
   (C) so far
   (D) giant

14. The writer's favorite **session** was about dinosaur sightings in Central Africa. Here, **session** means
   (A) a group
   (B) a heated debate
   (C) a group meeting
   (D) a sea monster

15. The writer of this article gives a clue to the meaning of **navigator**. What is the clue?
   (A) The **navigator** steered the ship.
   (B) The **navigator** saw a giant sea creature.
   (C) The **navigator** captured Lusca.
   (D) The **navigator** told stories.

16. The writer tells us that not all scientists **deny** the existence of a giant octopus named Lusca. Here, **deny** means
   (A) to like
   (B) to publicize
   (C) to reject
   (D) to create

17. The author writes, "More than half of the people at the conference, a **majority**, attended my favorite **session**." Here, **majority** means
   (A) a lot
   (B) a few
   (C) more than half
   (D) a group of oddballs

18. The author writes that there have been **innumerable** sightings of the creature called Mokele-Mbembe. Here, **innumerable** means
   (A) too few to count
   (B) too many to be counted
   (C) any number over one hundred
   (D) sightings by zoologists

19. In the last paragraph of the article, **summarize** means
   (A) to maintain
   (B) to discover suddenly
   (C) to continue
   (D) to state briefly

20. You can tell from the article that a **symbol** is
   (A) something that represents something else
   (B) a relative of the giraffe
   (C) a stunning scientific discovery
   (D) something that is fitting

READING NEW WORDS IN CONTEXT

Lesson 2 | CONTEXT: Amazing Nature

Introduction. Tornadoes are the most violent of the world's winds. A tornado can have wind speeds of more than three hundred miles per hour. Many people also regard tornadoes as the most amazing or curious of the world's natural forces. What is it about tornadoes that causes amazement?

The following article gives you an opportunity to expand your vocabulary. Below are twenty vocabulary words that are used in the article and in the exercise that follows it.

aviation	declare	disastrous	foundation	miraculous
bombard	demonstration	disturb	ignore	mischievous
collapse	departure	exception	incident	nuisance
collide	detect	fatal	locally	predict

Beyond Oz: The Truth about Tornadoes

Dorothy and Toto landed in Oz before the days of **aviation** (1). They didn't need to fly in an airplane. They had a natural form of travel—a tornado.

If you saw the movie *The Wizard of Oz,* you may recall the **miraculous** (2) landing of the girl and her dog (right on top of a wicked witch). The miracle of their incredible fall to earth is described in a work of fiction. However, real-life tornadoes also produce wonderful tales that sound like miracles.

Truth Stranger Than Fiction

Many fascinating stories are told of tornadoes picking up animals or objects and carrying them away. During one true **incident** (3) in 1966 in Kansas, a tornado picked up a homemade cake and deposited it, completely undamaged, in a field in Missouri. Another occurrence involves the strange **departure** (4) of two women and a boy from a Missouri town in 1899. They went away quite suddenly when a tornado swept them up and carried them, unharmed, a quarter of a

mile. One of the women later told about being in the tornado. She said she didn't crash into anything. She had been worried, though, that she would **collide** (5) with a wild horse that was also in the tornado.

In her book *These Happy Golden Years,* which is about prairie life in the late 1800s, Laura Ingalls Wilder includes a story about a tornado. The story provides a good **demonstration** (6) of a tornado's unusual abilities. It shows us how powerful a tornado can be as Laura describes one carrying away a small house. Later, after the storm has passed, the door of the house, undamaged, falls to the ground exactly where the house had been.

According to another tale, a tornado carried a house right off the **foundation** (7), the base on which it was built. The tornado had removed all the contents of the house except for two items. These **exceptions** (8) were a table and the gold-fish bowl on top of it. They remained quite unbothered. Who can say why the tornado did not **disturb** (9) the table and the goldfish bowl?

Raining Frogs and Fish

Some of their tricks make tornadoes seem like **mischievous** (10) children. Tornadoes, for example, have been known to pull the water right out of a river and then drop the water on unsuspecting people. When this happens, sometimes the tornadoes also **bombard** (11) people with frogs and fish from the rivers. These repeated assaults from the sky can be more than an annoyance, an inconvenience, or a **nuisance** (12). They can cause injury, too.

Many reliable people **declare** (13) that stories such as these are true. However, many other people make it clearly known that they think some of these stories are hogwash. You may want to ask some people within your community whether tornadoes have done unusual things **locally** (14).

Although **miraculous** tornado stories are interesting, we should not **ignore** (15) the fact that tornadoes can be **disastrous** (16). We should pay attention to the possible dangers from tornadoes. Tornadoes can cause much damage to property, and their force can cause a building to **collapse** (17)—just completely fall apart. They also can be **fatal** (18) to people. Most deaths from tornadoes result from flying debris.

Because they use scientific instruments to discover tornado formations, experts now often can **detect** (19) when tornadoes will occur. However, no one can tell beforehand exactly what will happen during a tornado. As you can imagine, it would be impossible to **predict** (20) the strange things tornadoes do.

EXERCISE *Reading Strategically* ✍

Directions. Answer each of the following items by circling the letter of the correct answer. You may need to refer to the selection as you answer the items. The numbers of the items are the same as the numbers of the boldface vocabulary words in the selection.

1. The writer of this article about tornadoes gives a clue to the meaning of **aviation**. What is the clue?
   (A) The writer tells about Dorothy and Toto.
   (B) The writer mentions a natural form of travel.
   (C) The writer says the girl and her dog landed in Oz.
   (D) The writer relates the word to flying in an airplane.

2. In the second paragraph of the article, **miraculous** means
   (A) related to stories
   (B) related to tornadoes
   (C) recalling
   (D) related to miracles

3. In the third paragraph of the article, **incident** means
   (A) occurrence
   (B) tornado
   (C) homemade cake
   (D) deposit

4. Which of the following is an example of a **departure** that occurs in the article?
   (A) A homemade cake was dropped undamaged in a field.
   (B) Two women and a boy were swept away by a tornado.
   (C) Two women and a boy lived in Missouri in 1899.
   (D) Tornadoes can lift up very heavy items.

5. The writer says that although the woman did not crash into anything in the tornado, she did worry that she would **collide** with a wild horse. Here, **collide** means
(A) to disagree
(B) to harness
(C) to crash
(D) to sweep

6. According to the article, why is Laura Ingalls Wilder's story of the tornado a good **demonstration** of a tornado's abilities?
(A) It happened in the late 1800s.
(B) It is a true story about her youth.
(C) It shows how powerful a tornado can be.
(D) It is printed in a book that has been read by millions.

7. The writer says that a tornado carried a house off of its **foundation**. Here, **foundation** means
(A) on the roof
(B) the base on which the house was built
(C) the size of the house
(D) all the contents of the house

8. The article says that a tornado re-moved all the contents of a house with the **exception** of a table and a goldfish bowl. You can tell from the article that
(A) the table and the goldfish bowl were the last things to disappear
(B) the table, and the goldfish bowl were the first things to disappear
(C) only the table and the goldfish bowl were not removed from the house
(D) the tornado was not very powerful

9. The writer asks, "Who can say why the tornado did not **disturb** the table and the goldfish bowl?" Here, **disturb** means to
(A) bother
(B) please
(C) make
(D) display

10. The author says that tornadoes can seem as **mischievous** as
(A) rivers
(B) goldfish in a bowl
(C) children playing tricks
(D) fish and frogs

11. The writer says that a tornado has been known to **bombard** people with frogs and fish. Here, **bombard** means
(A) to drop frogs and fish
(B) to pull water from rivers
(C) to annoy someone
(D) to assault repeatedly from above

12. The writer of the article gives a clue to the meaning of **nuisance**. What is the clue?
(A) The writer contrasts **nuisance** with the word injury.
(B) The writer links **nuisance** to the words annoyance and incon-venience.
(C) The writer says that a **nuisance** is a repeated assault.
(D) The writer links **nuisance** to the word sky.

13. All of these are good definitions for **declare** *except*
(A) to make clearly known
(B) to say openly
(C) to state firmly
(D) to deny privately

14. In the article, the author writes that you may want to ask people about the unusual things that tornadoes have done **locally**. Here, the word **locally** means
   (A) within a community
   (B) in a foreign country
   (C) recently
   (D) worldwide

15. The author writes, "We should not **ignore** the fact that tornadoes can be **disastrous**." Here, **ignore** means
   (A) to believe without doubt
   (B) to be interested in
   (C) to pay no attention to
   (D) to prove

16. Which of these is a reason that tornadoes may be **disastrous**?
   (A) People should take them seriously.
   (B) They can be very damaging to people and property.
   (C) Most deaths from tornadoes occur from flying debris.
   (D) Tornado stories can be very interesting.

17. In the article, **collapse** most nearly means to
   (A) be stronger
   (B) sway
   (C) be built
   (D) fall apart

18. The author writes that tornadoes can be **fatal** to people. Here, **fatal** means
   (A) lively
   (B) deadly
   (C) exciting
   (D) depressing

19. In the last paragraph of the article, **detect** means to
   (A) to occur
   (B) to escape
   (C) to imagine
   (D) to discover

20. How does the writer let you know that to **predict** an event is to say ahead of time what will happen?
   (A) The writer says that it is impossible to tell beforehand what a tornado will do.
   (B) They writer says that tornadoes always do strange things.
   (C) The writer says that scientific instruments can discover tornado information.
   (D) The writer says that no one can prevent a tornado.

READING NEW WORDS IN CONTEXT

Lesson 3 | CONTEXT: Amazing Nature

Introduction. There are spiders, spiders everywhere. No matter what you think about spiders, they're difficult to avoid. How long have spiders existed? How many different kinds of spiders are there? What are some spider myths? How does a spider use its web? Is a spider an insect?

The following essay answers these questions and gives you an opportunity to expand your vocabulary. Below are twenty vocabulary words that are used in the essay and in the exercise that follows it.

abdomen	congratulate	flexible	heroic	mobile
caution	dread	foe	hoist	paralysis
commotion	error	generation	involve	previous
competition	escort	gratitude	maximum	separation

The Wide and Wonderful World of Spiders

Whenever they see a spider, some of my friends make a big **commotion** (1), rushing around and yelling. "Ooh, a spider!" they shout. "Get it away." Sure, they should be watchful and use **caution** (2) when near a few kinds of spiders, such as black widows. Most spiders, however, are harmless to humans. People should learn to overcome their fear of spiders and appreciate how helpful they really are.

For one thing, we should **congratulate** (3), or praise, the spider for its ability to survive. Did you know that spiders have been around for at least 300 million years? Fossils of spiders that old have been found.

There are at least 30,000 different kinds of spiders in the world. Some scientists think the **maximum** (4) may be more than 100,000 kinds. Of course, even that greatest possible number of spiders is a long way from the more than 700,000 different species of known insects!

Spiders versus Insects

You are mistaken if you think spiders are insects. Many people make such an **error** (5), though. How do you tell them apart? One way is to look at the **separation** (6) of each animal's body parts. A spider's body is divided into two sections: a head and thorax combination and an **abdomen** (7). The **abdomen** is the belly. An insect's body, on the other hand, has three parts. Also, a spider has eight legs, and an insect has six. And while an insect has feelers and often has wings, a spider does not.

Because most people give thanks to anything that gets rid of pests, we owe spiders some **gratitude** (8). They eat insects that are dangerous to plants and animals. Spiders are much more friend than **foe** (9) to humans.

Spiders vary greatly in size. People who are afraid of tiny house or garden spiders would **dread** (10) seeing a South American tarantula, which eats small birds. When walking in South America, people who are afraid of spiders probably would want an **escort** (11), someone to go with them.

The lowly spider may not seem like a brave or noble creature, but it has been a **heroic** (12) figure in many cultures for thousands of years. In an Achomawi Indian myth, for example, two brave spider brothers created the rainbow. A spider called Ananse is the hero of many African tales. For many years, parents have told these stories to their children. In this way, the stories have been handed down from one **generation** (13) to the next.

Spiders of Legend

Most myths about spiders **involve** (14) their ability to spin webs. One famous example comes from a Greek legend. According to this legend, a young girl named Arachne, who was a marvelous spinner and weaver, challenged the goddess Athena

to a weaving **competition** (15). As a result of the contest, Athena became jealous and turned Arachne into a spider. Today, spiders are members of the class of animals called arachnids.

A spider's silk threads are strong but **flexible** (16). The thread bends without breaking to suit the spider's needs. A spider spins a lifeline thread as it moves from one place to another and as a result is easily **mobile** (17) in the air. The spider can **hoist** (18), or lift, itself by using its lifeline. Many spiders spin sticky webs in which to catch insects. The spider injects its victim with poison that causes a quick **paralysis** (19). The victim, which can no longer function on its own, is trapped. Did you know that a spider can make a brand new web or use a **previous** (20) one that it has swallowed? Like humans, spiders know the value of recycling!

EXERCISE *Reading Strategically* ✍️

Directions. Answer each of the following items by circling the letter of the correct answer. You may need to refer to the selection as you answer the items. The numbers of the items are the same as the numbers of the boldface vocabulary words in the selection.

1. How does the writer let us know that **commotion** may mean noisy confusion?
   (A) The writer describes **commotion** as a peaceful time.
   (B) The writer describes **commotion** as rushing around and yelling.
   (C) The writer describes **commotion** as being friendly.
   (D) The writer describes **commotion** as a time of observation.

2. You can tell from the essay that to use **caution** means
   (A) to be afraid
   (B) to be excited
   (C) to be watchful
   (D) to be foolish

3. What is the best meaning of **congratulate** as used in the second paragraph in this essay?
   (A) It means to praise.
   (B) It means to find.
   (C) It means to survive.
   (D) It means to be able.

4. In the third paragraph of the essay, **maximum** means
   (A) the greatest possible number
   (B) the least possible number
   (C) less than enough
   (D) more than enough

5. The author says that people who think spiders are insects are in **error**. Here, **error** means

(A) a correction
(B) a difference
(C) a decision
(D) a mistake

6. Which of the following is an example of the **separation** of body parts of a spider?

(A) A spider does not have feelers or wings.
(B) A spider's body is divided into two sections.
(C) An insect's body has three parts.
(D) A spider has eight legs while an insect has six.

7. Another good word for **abdomen** is

(A) head and thorax
(B) feelers
(C) belly
(D) legs

8. Why does the writer believe that we owe spiders **gratitude**?

(A) There are up to 100,000 types of spiders.
(B) Spiders eat insects that can harm plants and animals.
(C) Spiders should not be confused with insects.
(D) We must be careful around some kinds of spiders.

9. The author writes, "Spiders are much more friend than **foe** to humans." Here, **foe** means

(A) a fake
(B) a mystery
(C) an ally
(D) an enemy

10. All of these are good definitions of **dread** *except*

(A) to look forward to with fright
(B) to fear something in the future
(C) to be sad about something
(D) to be afraid of

11. The author uses **escort** when talking about walking in South America. Here, **escort** means

(A) a tarantula or other poisonous spider
(B) a person who walks very quickly
(C) a person who goes with another person
(D) a person who is afraid of spiders

12. The author writes that the spider has been a **heroic** figure in many cultures for thousands of years. Here, **heroic** means

(A) lowly
(B) brave and noble
(C) cultured and worldly
(D) spiderlike

13. Passing tales from one **generation** to the next is most like

(A) a sister giving a birthday present to a brother
(B) parents handing down the family quilt to their children
(C) a child giving a grandparent a picture
(D) a brother baby-sitting his little sister

14. The writer notes that most myths about spiders **involve** spiders' ability to spin webs. Here, **involve** means

(A) to include
(B) to turn
(C) to disagree
(D) to reveal

15. In the essay, the author mentions a **competition** between the Greek goddess Athena and the weaver Arachne. Here, **competition** means
(A) a result
(B) a legend
(C) a contest
(D) a weaver

16. The phrase _____ is the best meaning of **flexible** as it is used in the last paragraph of the essay.
(A) made from silk
(B) bends without breaking
(C) strange and marvelous
(D) rigid and unbending

17. Why does the author say that a spider is **mobile** in the air?
(A) A spider's threads allow it to move from place to place.
(B) A spider's sticky web allows it to catch insects.
(C) A spider's thread bends without breaking.
(D) A spider injects its victim with poison.

18. In the last paragraph of the essay, **hoist** means
(A) to use
(B) to injure
(C) to spin
(D) to lift

19. The writer of this essay gives a clue to the meaning of **paralysis**. What is the clue?
(A) The writer mentions poison.
(B) The writer uses the word inject in the same sentence with **paralysis**.
(C) The writer says the victim can no longer function.
(D) The writer says that poison causes quick **paralysis**.

20. How does the writer let us know that **previous** may mean happening earlier than something else?
(A) The writer contrasts a **previous** web with a new web.
(B) The writer contrasts a web that one spider makes with a web that another spider makes.
(C) The writer hints that the spider will not make a web in the future.
(D) The writer indicates that **previous** is related to recycling.

READING NEW WORDS IN CONTEXT

Lesson 4 | CONTEXT: Amazing Nature

Introduction. Do you ever watch the *Nature* series on public television? If so, you know that there are thousands of kinds of animals with all kinds of abilities. The animals and their abilities are pretty amazing.

The following article tells about some amazing animal abilities. The article gives you an opportunity to expand your vocabulary. Below are twenty vocabulary words that are used in the article and in the exercise that follows it.

assault	discourage	hibernate	linger	requirement
conceal	disguise	imitate	portion	terminal
dainty	earnest	impostor	reference	vacuum
discomfort	gasp	inhale	regulate	vault

The Wild, Wonderful World of Animals

The animal kingdom is quite a place! If you take an **earnest** (1) look at it, you will gain a sincere respect for the remarkable abilities of animals. A serious study of the behaviors and abilities of various animals should be a **requirement** (2) for all students. Let's look at a few animals and their abilities and see if you agree that we all need to know something about the animal kingdom.

Hummingbirds are delicate and pretty, but these **dainty** (3) birds are also amazing flyers. They can stay in one place in the air while beating their wings more than fifty times a second. The common swift, however, certainly doesn't **linger** (4). It can fly for two to three hours at a time. A chimney swift may fly more than 100,000 miles in a year.

Animals Undercover

Many animals **disguise** (5) themselves for protection. For example, chameleons are lizards that can actually change color from green to brown to blend in with their surroundings. Some butterflies

can look like the leaves they rest on. To protect themselves during an **assault** (6) from another animal, hedgehogs roll themselves into a ball shape. Armadillos also try to avoid attacks in the same way. Many animals, such as moths and grasshoppers, can **conceal** (7) themselves by hiding near objects that are the same color or shape they are.

Other animals can **imitate** (8) the animals for which they are hunting. Some spiders, for example, act and move like the ants they are tracking. You could think of this kind of spider as an **impostor** (9), someone who deceives others by pretending to be something he or she isn't.

Some animals spend the winter in an inactive, sleeplike state. Animals such as bears **hibernate** (10) in their dens so they can survive the cold winter season. During hibernation, these animals are able to adjust or **regulate** (11) their body temperatures. Their body temperatures go down for the winter to reduce the animals' need for food. The dormouse is another animal that avoids the **discomfort** (12) of hunger by hibernating.

With its "thermostat" turned down, the dormouse sleeps comfortably in its nest. Some hibernating animals, such as bats, spend only a **portion** (13) of the winter, rather than the whole winter, asleep.

Have you ever wondered how some fish, frogs, and toads survive when their water supplies dry up? They survive by digging under the mud. They **inhale** (14), or breathe in air, through an opening to the surface.

Four-footed Animals in Flight

You may **gasp** (15)—or catch your breath suddenly in surprise—when you learn how far some animals can jump. The gray kangaroo can jump forty-four feet in one bound. Some animals, such as deer and large cats, can jump over high

obstacles, too. Would you believe that a mountain lion has been known to **vault** (16) a nine-foot fence? That height would **discourage** (17) most other animals, but large cats are always sure of their abilities.

Many studies of interesting animal abilities include **references** (18) to the anglerfish. It's no wonder that this fish is mentioned. It comes equipped with its own fishing lure. This lure begins at the fish's mouth. The end, or **terminal** (19), part of the lure is lighted. The anglerfish actually "fishes" for other fish. Attracted by the lure, small fish swim toward the anglerfish. When they arrive, the **vacuum** (20) of the anglerfish's open mouth greets them like a bottomless canyon.

EXERCISE *Reading Strategically*

Directions. Answer each of the following items by circling the letter of the correct answer. You may need to refer to the selection as you answer the items. The numbers of the items are the same as the numbers of the boldface vocabulary words in the selection.

1. The writer gives us a clue to the meaning of **earnest.** What is the clue?
  (A) The writer says animals have remarkable abilities.
  (B) The writer links **earnest** to the word serious.
  (C) The writer says **earnest** is something you gain.
  (D) The writer implies **earnest** is something you get by looking.

2. In the first paragraph of the article, **requirement** means
  (A) important study
  (B) bad behavior
  (C) something needed
  (D) natural ability

3. You can tell from the second paragraph of the article that **dainty** means
  (A) delicate and pretty
  (B) large and clumsy
  (C) short and sweet
  (D) square

4. Which of the following is an example of how a bird can **linger**?
  (A) The hummingbird stays in one place in the air by beating its wings rapidly.
  (B) The hummingbird is a delicate and pretty animal.
  (C) The common swift can fly for two to three hours at a time.
  (D) A chimney swift can fly over 100,000 miles per year.

5. Which of the following is an example of a way in which an animal can **disguise** itself?
   (A) A hedgehog can roll up like a ball.
   (B) Lizards live in trees.
   (C) An armadillo can sometimes avoid attack.
   (D) A butterfly can make itself look like a leaf.

6. The author writes that hedgehogs roll themselves into a ball shape "to protect themselves during an **assault**." Here, **assault** means
   (A) protection
   (B) attack
   (C) defeat
   (D) weapon

7. In the third paragraph of the article, **conceal** means
   (A) lose
   (B) sell
   (C) hide
   (D) display

8. How does the writer let you know that to **imitate** may mean to copy the actions of?
   (A) The writer says some animals hunt other animals.
   (B) The writer uses the words spiders and ants.
   (C) The writer explains tracking.
   (D) The writer uses the words act and move like.

9. The author says that you can think of a spider that acts like its prey in order to capture it as an **impostor**. Here, **impostor** means
   (A) someone who looks like a spider
   (B) something real
   (C) someone who asks for money
   (D) someone who pretends to be someone else

10. The author writes, "Animals such as bears **hibernate** in their dens so they can survive the cold winter season." Here, **hibernate** means
    (A) to be very active
    (B) to live in a sleeplike state
    (C) to migrate to a warmer climate
    (D) to pace back and forth

11. The writer gives us a clue to the meaning of **regulate**. What is the clue?
    (A) The writer links **regulate** with adjust.
    (B) The writer refers to regular activities.
    (C) The writer asks the reader to recall.
    (D) The writer links **regulate** to winter.

12. The author writes, "The dormouse is another animal that avoids the **discomfort** of hunger by **hibernating**." Here, **discomfort** means
    (A) too much comfort
    (B) lack of comfort
    (C) cold weather
    (D) low body temperature

13. You can tell from the article that a **portion** of the winter is less than the whole winter because the author uses the words
    (A) "With its 'thermostat' turned down"
    (B) "**hibernating** animals, such as bats"
    (C) "the dormouse sleeps comfortably in its nest"
    (D) "rather than the whole winter"

14. In this article, **inhale** means
    (A) to breathe under water
    (B) to breathe out
    (C) to exhale
    (D) to breathe in

15. Which of the following is the most likely reason that you would **gasp** when you learned how far some animals can jump?

(A) You were bored.
(B) You did not understand.
(C) You were surprised.
(D) You were sad.

16. The author asks, "Would you believe that a mountain lion has been known to **vault** a nine-foot fence?" Here, **vault** means

(A) to jump over
(B) to open a bank
(C) to crawl under
(D) to defeat an enemy

17. The author writes that a nine-foot fence would **discourage** most animals, but that a mountain lion is always sure of its ability. Here, **discourage** means

(A) to cause to be unsure about
(B) to make confident about one's abilities
(C) to display amazing courage and daring
(D) to make brave

18. The writer gives a clue to the meaning of **reference**. What is the clue?

(A) The writer refers to the anglerfish.
(B) The writer uses the word interesting.
(C) The writer uses the word mentioned.
(D) The writer says the word is used in examinations.

19. How does the writer let us know that **terminal** means end?

(A) The writer says that the anglerfish "fishes" for other fish.
(B) The writer says most studies of animals' abilities mention the anglerfish.
(C) The writer says that the anglerfish's lure is lighted at the end, or **terminal**, part.
(D) The writer says that **terminal** is another word for lighted.

20. How is the **vacuum** of the anglerfish's mouth most like a bottomless canyon?

(A) Both are places where animals live.
(B) Both are safe places to be.
(C) Both are full of water.
(D) Both are empty spaces.

READING NEW WORDS IN CONTEXT

Lesson 5 | CONTEXT: Amazing Nature

Introduction. Science kits or chemistry sets for young people have been popular for many years. Sometimes careers in science begin with these sets. Sometimes, too, young scientists startle and worry people with their experiments.

The following selection tells about a daring young scientist. The selection gives you an opportunity to expand your vocabulary. Below are twenty vocabulary words that are used in the selection and in the exercise that follows it.

automation	license	pharmacy	receipt	surgery
bureau	lunar	pierce	resign	suspicion
flammable	nephew	pry	static	toll
gossip	particle	ransom	stray	unmanned

The Adventures of Curious Jorge

Help! The natural world is in danger from my **nephew** (1), Jorge. He's the son of my sister, Pepita. People are beginning to **gossip** (2) about him. The rumors concern Jorge's crazy science experiments. I'm afraid most of these rumors are true, too.

Jorge's first experiment was with **static** (3) electricity, electricity produced by rubbing one object against another. I'm not sure what Jorge did, but he and his father had to **pry** (4) Pepita's pancakes off the wall. It took a lot of force to remove the pancakes, too. After that, Jorge's father told him that he could not work with electricity without a **license** (5), or permit. Whether or not this is true, Jorge's electrical experiments have stopped for the time being.

Tides in the Bathtub

Lunar (6) cycles and tides caught his interest next. He thought that maybe the cycles of the moon affect the splashing of water in the bathtub as they affect the ocean tides. I'm not sure, but I have a **suspicion** (7) that Jorge is now paying for a new bathroom carpet.

For a time, Jorge wanted to be a chemist. He mixed together chemicals in the science kit. He thought he had found cures for various illnesses. Jorge went to the drugstore to try to sell these chemical mixtures. At the **pharmacy** (8), the druggist was so bothered that I thought he was going to **resign** (9)—just give up his position on the spot. Jorge even went to the local Medical Information Bureau. A **bureau** (10) is an agency that collects or gives information. Of course, Jorge's so-called medicines interested no one at the medical agency.

One day a wandering dog came to my sister's house. Noticing that the **stray** (11) dog was hurt, Jorge offered to perform an operation. "You can't perform **surgery** (12). You're just a young science experimenter. You're not a doctor," my sister told him.

And then there was the time Jorge wanted to find out how a fire extinguisher works. He poured vinegar and sodium bicarbonate together to form carbon dioxide. The mixture blew out a candle.

Pepita made him do the experiment with the candle outside because there were too many **flammable** (13) items in the house. The linen curtains, for example, could easily be set on fire.

For a few weeks Jorge forgot about chemicals and became interested in machines. Designing little self-operating machines especially interested him. That's why he became interested in **automation** (14).

"I'd like to design a city bus that is completely automatic," Jorge told me one day. "You know, **unmanned** (15). In other words, no one would control it. There'd be no **toll** (16) for riding it, either—it would be free."

Jorge soon forgot about this idea, though, and went back to his science kit. Bus designing must have been too big a project for him.

His next experiment, however, wasn't very popular. He tested the effects of light waves on earthworms. For some reason, he had to conduct the experiment in the kitchen. I think he needed a

knife to **pierce** (17) holes in the shoeboxes in which he kept the worms. Making the holes was easy for him; listening to Pepita wasn't.

"Don't leave any worms in here," my sister said, "and I don't want a **particle** (18) of dirt left, not even if it's as small as the head of a pin!."

I'm partly to blame for Jorge's experiments. Last year, for his thirteenth birthday, I bought Jorge a science kit and two books of science experiments. But I kept the written proof of my purchase, the **receipt** (19), from the store. Maybe I could return the kit and books. I guess it's too late for that, though. Anyway, all of Jorge's experimenting has led to something good. He's been accepted at a special school for gifted young scientists.

I just hope a mad scientist doesn't kidnap Jorge to get his secrets. I'm not sure my sister would pay the **ransom** (20), no matter how little money was demanded.

EXERCISE   *Reading Strategically* ✍

Directions. Answer each of the following items by circling the letter of the correct answer. You may need to refer to the selection as you answer the items. The numbers of the items are the same as the numbers of the boldface vocabulary words in the selection.

1. All of the following are good definitions of **nephew** *except*
(A) the male offspring of your brother or sister
(B) your brother's or sister's parent
(C) your brother's or sister's son
(D) your child's male cousin

2. The writer of this selection gives us a clue to the meaning of **gossip**. What is the clue?
(A) The writer relates the word to rumors.
(B) The writer links the word to "crazy science experiments."
(C) The writer links the word to fear.
(D) The writer relates the word to danger.

3. **Static** electricity, according to scientific jargon, apparently means electricity
(A) that flows through most ordinary power lines
(B) that is used to power eggbeaters and most other small machines
(C) that is created by cats
(D) that is produced by rubbing one object against another object

4. In the second paragraph of the selection, **pry** means
(A) to force off with difficulty
(B) to snoop around
(C) to pray urgently and silently
(D) to paste with glue

5. What is the best meaning of **license** as used in the second paragraph of the selection?

   (A) a safe place
   (B) a book
   (C) a permit
   (D) a careful driver

6. Which of the following is the reason that **lunar** cycles caught Jorge's interest?

   (A) He thought that the moon's cycles affected the movement of bath water.
   (B) He thought he could keep bath water from splashing out of the tub.
   (C) He found the mechanics of bikes and other cycles interesting.
   (D) He thought that lunar cycles made people act **suspiciously**.

7. You can tell from the selection that to have a **suspicion** means to think something is true without being

   (A) worried
   (B) angry
   (C) sure
   (D) sincere

8. The author says that Jorge went to the **pharmacy** to sell his chemical mixtures to the druggist. Here, **pharmacy** means

   (A) a supermarket
   (B) a drugstore
   (C) a clinic
   (D) a science kit

9. The author writes, "The druggist was so bothered that I thought he was going to **resign**—just give up his position on the spot." Here, **resign** means

   (A) to enjoy work
   (B) to become angry
   (C) to make a sign
   (D) to give up a position

10. The author says that Jorge took his chemical mixtures to the Medical Information Bureau. Here, **bureau** means

    (A) the medical information in a science kit
    (B) a chest of drawers
    (C) a local drugstore
    (D) an agency that collects or gives information

11. Taking in a **stray** dog is most similar to

    (A) giving advice to a wandering musician
    (B) giving shelter to a homeless cat
    (C) going to see a traveling circus
    (D) operating on a person who is ill

12. Pepita told Jorge, "'You can't perform **surgery**. You're just a young science experimenter. You're not a doctor.'" Here, **surgery** means

    (A) an operation
    (B) a doctor
    (C) a science project
    (D) an experiment

13. Why didn't Pepita allow Jorge to do his experiment with the candles inside, near **flammable** items?

    (A) Such items burn easily.
    (B) Such items are everywhere.
    (C) Such items are expensive.
    (D) Such items are waterproof.

14. Which of the following is the reason that Jorge became interested in **automation**?

    (A) He wanted to design a bus that collected money automatically.
    (B) He was interested in animation.
    (C) He enjoyed designing self-operating machinery.
    (D) He was interested in chemicals.

15. The writer of the selection gives us a clue to the meaning of **unmanned**. What is the clue?

(A) The writer says that no one would pay a fare.

(B) The writer implies that someone would control the bus.

(C) The writer says no one would control the bus.

(D) The writer says no one would be allowed on the bus.

16. Jorge told the author that there would be no **toll** for riding his automatic bus. Here, **toll** means

(A) a door

(B) a fare

(C) a driver

(D) a bus

17. The author writes that Jorge "needed a knife to **pierce** holes in the shoeboxes in which he kept the worms." Here, **pierce** means

(A) to cut into many pieces

(B) to make a shoebox

(C) to make holes in

(D) to slice into strips

18. How could a **particle** of dirt left over from Jorge's experiment be like the head of a pin?

(A) Both are dirty.

(B) Both are very small.

(C) Both are sharp.

(D) Both were involved in Jorge's earthworm experiment.

19. Which of these is the most likely reason that the author would save the **receipt** for the science kit?

(A) The science kit costs a lot of money.

(B) The **receipt** shows proof of purchase.

(C) The **receipt** tells how to cook something.

(D) The **receipt** gives instructions for the science kit.

20. In the last paragraph of the selection, **ransom** means

(A) the kidnapping of someone to keep them from conducting scientific experiments

(B) secrets stolen from a scientist

(C) money that is paid to someone who has been kidnapped

(D) money that is demanded for the return of someone who has been kidnapped

READING NEW WORDS IN CONTEXT

Lesson 6 | CONTEXT: People and Places

Introduction. An anthropologist is a person who studies people and their cultures. People, of course, are part of the natural world, and their behavior is always interesting to examine. Margaret Mead (1901–1978) was a famous anthropologist. How did she become interested in this field, and what people did she study?

The following article answers these questions and gives you an opportunity to expand your vocabulary. Below are twenty vocabulary words that are used in the article and in the exercise that follows it.

analyze	destination	generous	profession	routine
biography	determination	identical	publicity	scholar
career	document	notion	reaction	self-confidence
debate	essential	offspring	respectable	thorough

The Life of an Anthropologist

Margaret Mead: The World Was Her Family is the title of one **biography** (1) of the anthropologist. The title of that book about Mead's life and **career** (2), or lifelong work, certainly is accurate. Mead's studies, writings, and ideas always got the public's attention because they received much **publicity** (3) through newspapers, magazines, and other popular media.

An Anthropologist Is Born

Mead was born in Philadelphia, and was the first child of Edward and Emily Mead. Both parents were involved in academics—he as an economics professor and she as a teacher and sociologist. They had four more **offspring** (4) in addition to Margaret. Mrs. Mead liked to **document** (5) her children's behavior, and the young Margaret also picked up the **routine** (6) of writing down her observations of her two young sisters. This regular procedure of observation and writing foretold Margaret's future.

At Barnard College in New York City, Mead was a good student. But she was a **scholar** (7) without a clear direction until she took an anthropology course her senior year. Anthropology excited her because studying people was an **essential** (8) activity in her life. It was as basic and necessary to her life as eating and sleeping. How wonderful to think that doing what she loved could be her occupation, her **profession** (9)!

Travels in the Pacific

As a professional, Mead took her first field trip in 1925 to the Samoan islands in the Pacific Ocean. Because she felt sure of her abilities, Mead had **self-confidence** (10). Her goal was to make a complete, or **thorough** (11), study of the behavior of teenage girls there. Specifically, she investigated the **notion** (12) that teenagers are the same the world over. Her conclusion after a year with the Samoan girls was that the idea that teenager everywhere are **identical** (13) was false. Her book *Coming of Age in Samoa* created **debate** (14) on the subject: Some critics supported her findings and others argued against them.

Mead's next **destination** (15) for field work was another place in the Pacific, Papua New Guinea. Here, she wanted to **analyze** (16) the native children's thoughts. The result of her detailed examination was her second book, *Growing Up in New Guinea*. This book also received ample, or **generous** (17), attention from the press and the public. Her response was a typical Mead **reaction** (18): She returned to the Pacific to study other cultures.

Mead's **determination** (19) to succeed in her own way guided her life, and this firm purpose took her far. Mead's accomplishments are highly **respectable** (20). For example, she was the author of thirty-nine books and many articles. She also made records and tapes. She was associated for years with the American Museum of Natural History and Columbia University, and she received many awards. In fact, by the time she died at the age of 77, Mead had headed so many organizations, made so many public lectures, and produced so many publications that she was a national celebrity.

EXERCISE   *Reading Strategically* ✍

Directions. Answer each of the following items by circling the letter of the correct answer. You may need to refer to the selection as you answer the items. The numbers of the items are the same as the numbers of the boldface vocabulary words in the selection.

1. The writer provides a clue to the meaning of **biography**. What is the clue?
  (A) The writer tells us that Margaret Mead was an anthropologist.
  (B) The writer tells us that the biography is about Mead's life.
  (C) The writer tells us that the title is accurate.
  (D) The writer tells us that the book is one biography.

2. In the first paragraph of the article, **career** means
  (A) a vacation
  (B) a life
  (C) a lifelong work
  (D) a book

3. You can tell from the article that **publicity** is
  (A) information that makes something known to the public
  (B) studies, writings, and ideas about the lives of well-known biographers
  (C) money
  (D) scholarly writing read by only a few anthropology experts

4. You can tell from the article that **offspring** are
  (A) jobs
  (B) careers
  (C) ideas
  (D) children

5. How does the writer let us know that **document** may mean to write down or record something?

(A) The writer says that Mrs. Mead was an observant parent.

(B) The writer says that Mrs. Mead disapproved of Margaret's observations.

(C) The writer notes that both Mrs. Mead and Margaret wrote down their observations.

(D) The writer considers writing a regular procedure.

6. What does **routine** mean as it is used in the second paragraph of the article?

(A) writing

(B) observing

(C) a regular procedure

(D) having sisters

7. In the third paragraph of the article, **scholar** means

(A) a person without direction

(B) a good student

(C) an area of anthropology

(D) a school

8. Which of the following is the most likely reason that the author believes studying people was an **essential** activity in Mead's life?

(A) It was basic and necessary to her life, just like eating and sleeping.

(B) It was an extravagant and wasteful use of her college education.

(C) Mead had no direction as a student.

(D) Mead was overjoyed to discover she could make a career of anthropology.

9. The author writes, "How wonderful to think that doing what she loved could be her occupation, her **profession**!" Here, **profession** means

(A) an occupation

(B) an obligation

(C) character

(D) a direction

10. Which of the following is the most likely reason that the author believes Margaret Mead had **self-confidence**?

(A) Mead was a scholar.

(B) Mead was an anthropologist.

(C) Mead felt sure of her abilities.

(D) Mead traveled around the world.

11. The author says that in Samoa, Mead made a **thorough** study of the behavior of the islands' teenage girls. Here, **thorough** means

(A) considerate

(B) regular

(C) about other cultures

(D) complete

12. The author writes that Mead "investigated the **notion** that teenagers are the same the world over." Here, **notion** means

(A) an idea

(B) a country

(C) an argument

(D) an agreement

13. The author says that Mead concluded that teenagers are not **identical** the world over. Here, **identical** means

(A) specific

(B) the same

(C) young

(D) worldly

14. Which of the following is the most likely reason that Margaret Mead's book about Samoan teenagers caused **debate**?

(A) Everyone agreed with her conclusions.

(B) No one thought she was correct.

(C) Everyone was critical.

(D) Some critics agreed with her and some disagreed.

15. Which of the following is an example of a **destination**?

(A) A **destination** is ample attention from the press.

(B) A **destination** is a detailed examination.

(C) A **destination** is Papua New Guinea.

(D) A **destination** is thoughts of native children.

16. Mead, says the writer, went to New Guinea "to **analyze** the native children's thoughts." Here, **analyze** means

(A) to study

(B) to receive

(C) to respond

(D) to return

17. All of the following are good definitions of **generous** as used in this article *except*

(A) intelligent

(B) ample

(C) more than enough

(D) plenty

18. The author writes that Mead's response to the publication of her second book was a typical **reaction**. Here, **reaction** means

(A) the future

(B) the public

(C) a response

(D) a study

19. In the last paragraph of the article, **determination** means

(A) guidance

(B) Mead's life

(C) success

(D) firm purpose

20. Which of the following is an example of one of Mead's **respectable** accomplishments?

(A) "Mead's **determination** to succeed in her own way guided her life."

(B) "This firm purpose took her far."

(C) "Some critics supported her findings and others argued against them."

(D) "She was the author of thirty-nine books and many articles."

READING NEW WORDS IN CONTEXT

Lesson 7   CONTEXT: People and Places

Introduction. One of the greatest empires of the past belonged to the Aztecs in Mexico. The Aztecs were wandering warriors before settling around A.D. 1200 in the area that is now Mexico City. They eventually dominated the region, but they first had to conquer the land. What natural difficulties did the Aztecs have to overcome? What was their capital city like? Who governed the empire? What were some of the Aztecs' beliefs?

The following selection gives you an opportunity to expand your vocabulary. Below are twenty vocabulary words that are used in the selection and in the exercise that follows it.

architect	consent	fragrant	management	sacrifice
betray	desperate	glimpse	plead	scheme
ceremony	district	ignite	quarantine	victim
conduct	eternal	interrupt	realm	victorious

Mexico's Aztec Heritage

If we could **glimpse** (1) Mexico's history during the 1400s, our quick look would find the Aztecs at the height of their power. The Aztec kingdom, or **realm** (2), was central Mexico. There they created a remarkable civilization.

The Floating Empire
Forming an empire in this area was not easy. The Aztecs began building their capital city, Tenochtitlan (tay-nawch-tee-TLAHN), on one of two islands in Lake Texcoco. The Aztecs soon expanded to the other island. To do so, they completed many canals, dams, and other engineering projects. The Aztecs didn't have room to farm on the islands so they developed a clever **scheme** (3). This plan, which became highly successful, led to the creation of floating gardens in the lake.

The city's huge temple-pyramids and many buildings were just as impressive as the floating gardens. Clearly, the person responsible for designing the buildings, the **architect** (4), was extremely creative. Nearly two hundred thousand

people are thought to have lived in the city at one time. The city was divided into four major areas. One **district** (5) included the marketplace.

The Aztec empire was ruled by an emperor who had almost total power. The emperor had four chief advisers. He put a close relative in charge of the **management** (6) of internal affairs. With the control of internal affairs taken care of, the emperor was free to direct, or **conduct** (7), foreign matters. He lived in an enormous palace. Many gardens filled with sweet-smelling flowers surrounded the buildings in the palace area. As a result, the palace area was **fragrant** (8).

Aztec Religious Practices
For the Aztecs, military might and religion went together. The Aztecs usually were **victorious** (9) in battle. Because of their successes, they were known as Warriors of the Sun. To celebrate their victories, the Aztecs killed thousands of captives as a **sacrifice** (10) to their sun god and their god of war. Each **sacrifice** was offered to the gods in a

ritual, or a **ceremony** (11). Some of the persons chosen to be killed and **sacrificed** considered the act an honor. Such persons would **consent** (12) to be sacrificed. Others who were chosen, however, considered themselves **victims** (13), helpless sufferers. Losing hope, these **desperate** (14) persons might **plead** (15) to be turned loose. However, their begging would fall on deaf ears because the priests would not **betray** (16) the gods. To turn against the gods would bring grief to the whole community.

The Aztecs used two calendar cycles. One calendar was a solar calendar that contained 365 days. The other was a 260-day religious calendar. The beginnings of these two cycles overlapped once every fifty-two years. The Aztecs believed that this period of overlap was a bad time. Normally, there would always be fires burning somewhere in the Aztec community. But during this period, which was called Binding Up of the Years, the Aztecs thought it was necessary to **interrupt** (17) all fires. When the danger was past, priests started the fires burning again. They would **ignite** (18) all the fires in the temples. The Aztecs also believed they should protect pregnant women during this time. As a result, they would **quarantine** (19) pregnant women just as today we put some diseased persons in a seperate place.

Since most powerful nations tend to think they will last forever, the Aztecs, too, probably thought their empire was **eternal** (20). However, it eventually fell to neighboring peoples and Spanish explorers of the 1500s.

EXERCISE *Reading Strategically* ✍️☞

Directions. Answer each of the following items by circling the letter of the correct answer. You may need to refer to the selection as you answer the items. The numbers of the items are the same as the numbers of the boldface vocabulary words in the selection.

1. The author writes, "If we could **glimpse** Mexico's history during the 1400s, our quick look would find the Aztecs at the height of their power." Here, **glimpse** means
   (A) to read quickly
   (B) to look quickly
   (C) to find again
   (D) to gain time

2. In the first paragraph of the selection, **realm** means
   (A) a kingdom
   (B) a reality
   (C) central Mexico
   (D) a civilization

3. The author says that the Aztecs developed a clever **scheme** to make up for the lack of farm land on the islands. Here, **scheme** means
   (A) a room
   (B) an empire
   (C) a school
   (D) a plan

4. The writer gives a clue to the meaning of **architect**. What is the clue?
   (A) The writer says that the **architect** lives in a city.
   (B) The writer links **architect** to the emperor's advisors.
   (C) The writer says that the **architect** must have been creative.
   (D) The writer says that an **architect** designs buildings.

5. In the third paragraph of the selection, **district** means
(A) an area
(B) a shopping center
(C) a city
(D) a design

6. The **management** of internal affairs as described in the selection is most similar to
(A) the direction of family matters
(B) the fighting of a war
(C) the construction of a temple-pyramid
(D) the harvest of crops

7. How does the writer let us know that **conduct** may mean to lead or direct?
(A) The writer mentions an orchestra.
(B) The writer gives **conduct** as another word for direct.
(C) The writer links **conduct** to foreign matters.
(D) The writer uses the word enormous.

8. Which of the following is the most likely reason that the palace area was **fragrant**?
(A) The palace was surrounded with sweet-smelling flowers.
(B) A creative **architect** designed the palace and grounds.
(C) The Aztec religion required the emperor's palace to be **fragrant**.
(D) Both internal and foreign affairs were discussed in the palace grounds.

9. You can tell from the selection that when the Aztecs were **victorious** in battle they
(A) refused to fight
(B) won
(C) declared a tie
(D) lost

10. The writer gives us a clue to the meaning of **sacrifice**. What is the clue?
(A) The writer says that military might and religion went hand in hand.
(B) The writer says that captives were always willing to be sacrificed.
(C) The writer says a **sacrifice** is military victory.
(D) The writer says that each **sacrifice** was offered to a god.

11. The author writes, "Each **sacrifice** was offered to the gods in a ritual, or a **ceremony**." Here, **ceremony** means
(A) a wedding
(B) a serious matter
(C) a ritual
(D) a celebration

12. Which of the following is the most likely reason that a captive would **consent** to being offered to the gods?
(A) The captive felt that it was an unfair practice.
(B) The captive believed that to be offered to the gods was an honor.
(C) The captive was captured by the Aztecs in battle.
(D) The captive begged to be set free rather than be offered to the gods.

13. The writer says that some of the captives who were chosen to be offered to the gods considered themselves **victims**. Here, **victim** means
(A) one who suffers
(B) one who is willing
(C) a hopeless person
(D) an honorable person

14. The author says that **desperate** prisoners begged to be set free. Here, **desperate** means
(A) different
(B) without hope
(C) lonesome
(D) diseased

15. The word **plead** in this selection means

(A) to refuse
(B) to hope
(C) to beg
(D) to ignore

16. Which of the following is the most likely reason that the priests would not **betray** the gods?

(A) The priests would not pray to the gods on behalf of the captives.
(B) The priests were deaf and could not hear the gods.
(C) The priests believed that it was wrong to make offerings to the gods.
(D) The priests believed that to turn against the gods would bring suffering upon the community.

17. All of the following are good definitions of **interrupt** *except*

(A) to damage
(B) to cause a break in
(C) to stop
(D) to discontinue

18. The author writes that after the period called Binding Up of the Years had ended, the Aztec priests would **ignite** all the fires in the temples. Here, **ignite** means

(A) to start a fire burning
(B) to be in a temple
(C) to extinguish
(D) to cover

19. How were pregnant Aztec women under **quarantine** during the Binding Up of the Years and people with certain sicknesses treated similarly?

(A) They were both highly honored by Aztec priests.
(B) They were both thought to be the disastrous results of the Binding Up of the Years.
(C) They were both placed apart from the rest of the community.
(D) They were both forbidden to put out fires during the Binding Up of the Years.

20. In the last paragraph of the selection, **eternal** means

(A) doomed
(B) unlikely to succeed
(C) lasting forever
(D) temporary

READING NEW WORDS IN CONTEXT

Lesson 8 | CONTEXT: People and Places

Introduction. The dominant mountain range on the North American continent is the Rocky Mountains. Many people just call them The Rockies. Map makers may tell you that the Rocky Mountains are officially part of the western mountain system known as the North American Cordillera. Where exactly are the Rocky Mountains? Where are the highest peaks in the range? How old is the range? Who were some early explorers?

The following article answers these questions and gives you an opportunity to expand your vocabulary. Below are twenty vocabulary words that are used in the article and in the exercise that follows it.

abundant	dramatic	geology	marvel	satisfy
barrier	establish	irregular	numerous	survey
descriptive	extraordinary	leisure	possess	terrain
desirable	feat	lieutenant	prehistoric	vicinity

The Backbone of North America

Think of the Rocky Mountains as the continent's backbone. This comparison is **descriptive** (1) because it creates a picture of a lengthy, solid spine. In fact, the chain stretches for about 3,000 miles from New Mexico, north through the continental United States and Canada, and into northern Alaska. The peaks of the Rocky Mountains form the Continental Divide, which separates the continent's river systems. The Rockies have an **irregular** (2) width. For example, the range in Utah and Colorado is as wide as 300 miles across, but the mountains are less than 100 miles wide at the Canadian border.

The Rockies in the United States
The Rocky Mountains in the United States may be divided into four groups. The Southern Rockies range from New Mexico to central Wyoming. Colorado contains the highest and most striking, or **dramatic** (3), peaks in the Rocky Mountains, with 46 peaks over 14,000 feet high. Mount Elbert (14,433 ft.) near Aspen, Colorado, is the highest peak in the Rockies. The Middle Rockies run from northwestern Colorado and northern Utah to the upper Yellowstone River in Montana, and they include the Teton range. The Northern Rockies begin in southern Idaho and continue to the Canadian border. They contain many glaciers, including the **numerous** (4) ones in the **vicinity** (5) of Glacier National Park in Montana. This area even has glaciers that can be reached easily on foot. Finally, the Brooks Range lies across northern Alaska. This range begins where the Canadian Rockies leave off.

For a mountain range, the Rocky Mountains are not old, although they were formed many years before recorded history. They date from the end of the Mesozoic era, about 60 to 70 million years ago. During that **prehistoric** (6) time, a large upheaval of the earth's crust created the Rocky Mountains. Someday you may want to take a **geology** (7) course to study such upheavals and other facts about the origin, history, and structure of the earth.

Early Inhabitants and Explorers

Many Native American peoples have lived in the Rocky Mountains, including the Navajo, the Shoshone, and the Ute. Europeans first started exploring the Rocky Mountains during the sixteenth century. That's when Francisco Vásquez de Coronado (1510–1554) of Spain led an expedition in the Southern Rockies. American explorers Meriwether Lewis (1774–1809) and William Clark (1770–1838) traveled the Northern Rockies in 1805 and 1806. Beaver trappers came to the Rockies in the 1820s. In 1830, some of these trappers joined together to **establish** (8) the Rocky Mountain Fur Company. Setting up this company was an important step in opening the Rockies to settlement. Noted American explorer John Charles Frémont (1813–1890) also explored the Rocky Mountains. In Wyoming in 1842, Frémont succeeded in the **feat** (9) of climbing a 13,745-foot peak. As a result of his accomplishment, the mountain was named Frémont Peak. Frémont held the ranks of **lieutenant** (10), major, and finally general in the army. One of his duties was to inspect carefully the lands he explored. Because of Frémont's **survey** (11), the first scientific maps of the American West could be created.

As you can imagine, the Rockies at first created a **barrier** (12), like a wall of rock, for explorers and settlers going to the Pacific Coast from the east. Over time, however, explorers created trails that cut through the often rugged **terrain** (13), or ground. Some of these trails became highway and railroad routes.

The Rocky Mountains are a valuable source of precious metals. The Rockies have yielded much gold, silver, copper, and other minerals that are in high demand. Thus, the mountains have been a **desirable** (14) destination to fortune seekers. They have been equally attractive to tourists. The mountains **satisfy** (15) tourists by answering their needs for mountain climbing, skiing, hiking, and other **leisure** (16) activities. Many people come to the Rockies simply to **marvel** (17) at the scenery. Their amazement is understandable because the Rockies **possess** (18) some of the most **extraordinary** (19), memorable, and spectacular scenery in North America. They also have plenty of wilderness areas—public parks in the Rockies are **abundant** (20).

EXERCISE *Reading Strategically* ☞

Directions. Answer each of the following items by circling the letter of the correct answer. You may need to refer to the selection as you answer the items. The numbers of the items are the same as the numbers of the boldface vocabulary words in the selection.

1. In the first paragraph of the article, **descriptive** refers to something that
   (A) paints a picture
   (B) is lengthy and solid
   (C) is in the Rocky Mountains
   (D) is a backbone

2. Which of the following is an example of the **irregular** width of the Rocky Mountains?
   (A) The Rocky Mountains are three hundred miles wide at points in Utah and Colorado.
   (B) The Rockies are higher in some places than others.
   (C) The peaks of the Rocky Mountains form the Continental Divide.
   (D) The width of the Rocky Mountains changes greatly between Utah and the Canadian Border.

3. The author says that Colorado contains the most **dramatic** peaks in the Rocky Mountains. Here, **dramatic** means
   (A) mountainous
   (B) striking
   (C) populated
   (D) coldest

4. What is the best meaning of **numerous** as used in the second paragraph of the article?
   (A) few
   (B) icy
   (C) many
   (D) some

5. The writer of this article gives a clue to the meaning of **vicinity**. What is the clue?
   (A) The writer relates **vicinity** to Glacier National Park.
   (B) The writer uses the preposition of.
   (C) A reference to area follows **vicinity**.
   (D) Information about glaciers follows **vicinity**.

6. You can tell from the article that **prehistoric** means
   (A) before recorded history
   (B) old-fashioned
   (C) something about mountain ranges
   (D) something more than 70 million years old

7. Which of these is the most likely reason that a student would take a course in **geology**?
   (A) The student wants to study the origin, history, and structure of the earth.
   (B) The student wants to study geodes.
   (C) The student wants to learn about all the planets.
   (D) The student wants to learn about the people who have explored the Rocky Mountains.

8. How does the author let you know that to **establish** a business means to set up a business?
   (A) The author defines **establish**.
   (B) The author says that the Rocky Mountain Fur Company was an important step in settling the Rockies.
   (C) The words **establish** and setting up are all used to refer to the beginning of the Rocky Mountain Fur Company.
   (D) Both **establish** and set up sound businesslike.

9. All of the following are good definitions for **feat** except
   (A) outstanding accomplishment
   (B) activity
   (C) daring act
   (D) admirable deed

10. You can tell from the article that **lieutenant** is
    (A) a foreign word
    (B) an explorer
    (C) a rank in the army
    (D) a rancher

11. John Charles Frémont was assigned to make a **survey** of unexplored lands in order to prepare a map. Making a **survey** of unmapped lands is most similar to
    (A) washing a car before it rains
    (B) looking at a map when lost
    (C) farming in a harsh environment
    (D) doing research before writing a research report

12. The author says that the Rocky Mountains created a **barrier** for explorers and settlers headed to the Pacific Coast. To make this point more strongly, the author says the **barrier** was like
    (A) the Rocky Mountains
    (B) the Pacific Ocean
    (C) rugged ground
    (D) a wall of rock

13. The author says that explorers cut
    trails through the rugged **terrain** of
    the Rockies. Here, **terrain** means
    (A) ground
    (B) railroad line
    (C) highway
    (D) mountain

14. The author writes that the Rockies
    "always have seemed **desirable** to for-
    tune seekers." Here, **desirable** means
    (A) lucky
    (B) attractive
    (C) frightening
    (D) metallic

15. The author writes, "The mountains
    satisfy tourists by answering their
    needs for mountain climbing, skiing,
    hiking, and other **leisure** activities."
    Here, **satisfy** means
    (A) to mountain climb
    (B) to attract
    (C) to answer needs
    (D) to offer leisure activities

16. Which of the following is an example
    of a **leisure** activity that is mentioned
    in the article?
    (A) satisfaction
    (B) surveying
    (C) skiing
    (D) fortune hunting

17. The writer of the article provides a
    clue to the meaning of **marvel**. What is
    the clue?
    (A) The writer lists **marvel** as a leisure
        activity.
    (B) The writer links the words **marvel**
        and simply.
    (C) The writer says that it is under-
        standable that people **marvel**.
    (D) The writer links the words **marvel**
        and amazement.

18. What is the best meaning of **possess** as
    it is used in the article?
    (A) attract
    (B) have
    (C) answer
    (D) need

19. All of the following are good defini-
    tions of **extraordinary** *except*
    (A) out of the ordinary
    (B) spectacular and unusual
    (C) exceptional
    (D) natural

20. In the last paragraph of the article,
    abundant means
    (A) spectacular
    (B) memorable
    (C) plentiful
    (D) little

READING NEW WORDS IN CONTEXT

Lesson 9 | CONTEXT: People and Places

Introduction. Sparkling and colorful gemstones are sure attention-getters. Rings, earrings, necklaces, bracelets, and crowns frequently glow with gems. People have worked gems such as diamonds and emeralds into jewelry for thousands of years. When looking at cut and polished gemstones, a person may find it hard to believe that they came out of chunks of rock within the earth.

In the following story, an old jeweler tells an unusual story about his introduction to gems and to his life's work. The story gives you an opportunity to expand your vocabulary. Below are twenty vocabulary words that are used in the story and in the exercise that follows it.

ambitious	galaxy	knapsack	portrait	solitary
counterfeit	heir	luxurious	reign	transparent
envy	honorable	oath	relate	wardrobe
exclaim	investment	ornamental	request	yacht

The Prince's Jewels

Believe it or not, you are the first to **request** (1) that I **relate** (2) the story of how I became an expert on gems, nature's most beautiful and prized minerals. Since you have asked politely, I will be happy to tell you the story.

Strangely enough, my interest began many years ago aboard a pleasure boat, a **yacht** (3), in the Mediterranean Sea. The boat was **luxurious** (4). Of course, anyone would expect it to be fancy and comfortable, because it belonged to a prince. He was **heir** (5) to a great fortune upon the death of his father, the king.

I had just been hired as a cabin boy and was not much younger than the prince. All I owned was either on me or in my **knapsack** (6), a kind of backpack. But I was an **ambitious** (7) youth. When the prince realized I was eager to better myself, he offered to help me.

Opportunity Knocks
One day the prince, sunning himself alone aboard

the **yacht,** started talking out loud about his latest **investment** (8), a rare diamond that he had bought in hopes of selling later for more money. As I listened to the prince, I became jealous. Fortunately, the prince was not aware of my **envy** (9).

The prince held up the diamond. "Why, I can see right through it. It is absolutely **transparent** (10)," the prince said. "This is the real thing. It's not **counterfeit** (11)," he continued.

Then to my complete surprise, I heard myself **exclaim** (12), like a child who cries out upon opening a marvelous present, "Sir, it's the most beautiful stone in the heavens, in the **galaxy** (13), among the stars!"

The prince, who had paid little attention to me before, just looked at me thoughtfully for several minutes. It seemed like hours to me.

"Yes," he said, as if answering himself. "I can see that you admire gems as much as I do. Would you like to learn about them with me?"

"Oh, yes," I replied.

"Very well," the prince said, "but you must take an **oath** (14) promising that you will never use the knowledge of gems for the purpose of creating false jewels. You and I will study diamonds, emeralds, rubies, sapphires, opals, turquoise, agate, jade, topaz, and other gems."

"With pleasure, sir," I replied.

A Student of Gems

From that day on, he taught me about gems. He showed me his valuable collection as well as pictures of famous gems.

"The **solitary** (15) stone in this necklace is a pink sapphire," he said. "It looks so splendid alone that it doesn't need any other stones with it. Remember that the sapphire is a type of mineral called corundum."

He pointed to a picture of the British Imperial State Crown with its famous black ruby. "This ruby would improve any clothes collection, not just the **wardrobe** (16) of the Queen of England."

"Such gems may be purely decorative, or **ornamental** (17), but the world can't have too much beauty," the prince added.

The prince showed me a **portrait** (18) of a beautiful woman. In the picture the woman was wearing the Hope Diamond, which is the largest blue diamond in the world.

Eventually the prince ruled the kingdom, and during this **reign** (19) I was his personal jeweler. When he died, I opened my own shop.

"I like gems," the prince once told me, "because they have such natural beauty and strength."

The prince was a good friend and an **honorable** (20) man. To show that I felt he was worthy of being greatly respected, I named my jewelry store The Prince's Gems.

EXERCISE Reading Strategically

Directions. Answer each of the following items by circling the letter of the correct answer. You may need to refer to the selection as you answer the items. The numbers of the items are the same as the numbers of the boldface vocabulary words in the selection.

1. In this story, **request** means
   (A) to write formally
   (B) to tell a story
   (C) to ask politely
   (D) to discuss briefly

2. In the story, the writer agrees to **relate** his tale. Here, **relate** means
   (A) to tell a story
   (B) to ask for something
   (C) to be happy
   (D) to prize minerals

3. You can tell from the story that a **yacht** is
   (A) a board
   (B) a huge ocean liner
   (C) a canoe
   (D) a pleasure boat

4. All of these are good definitions of **luxurious** *except*
   (A) shabby and poor
   (B) fancy and comfortable
   (C) splendid and fine
   (D) rich and refined

5. According to the second paragraph of the story, an **heir** is someone who
   (A) gives money away
   (B) works for a prince
   (C) owns a yacht
   (D) inherits something

6. The writer says that all he owned was either on him or in his **knapsack.** Here **knapsack** means
   (A) a yacht
   (B) a cabin boy
   (C) a backpack
   (D) a shirt

7. How does the writer of the story let you know that **ambitious** means eager or desirous?
   (A) The writer was eager to clean cabins.
   (B) The writer remembers that he was poor.
   (C) The writer notes that he was younger than the prince.
   (D) The writer states that he was eager to better himself.

8. According to the story, the rare diamond was an **investment** because the prince planned to
   (A) resell the diamond at a higher price
   (B) keep the diamond
   (C) give the diamond to the cabin boy
   (D) leave the diamond on the deck in the sun

9. Which of the following is an example of **envy** in the story?
   (A) The writer was eager to learn all that he could about gems.
   (B) The writer had a jealous reaction to hearing the prince's plan.
   (C) The prince offered to help the writer to better himself.
   (D) The prince intended to sell the gem.

10. In the story, the writer notes that the diamond is **transparent.** Here, **transparent** means
    (A) valuable
    (B) clear
    (C) absolute
    (D) real

11. How does the writer give you a clue to the meaning of **counterfeit?**
    (A) The writer can see right through the diamond.
    (B) The writer says the prince called the gem the real thing, not **counterfeit.**
    (C) The writer describes his complete surprise at the sight of such a beautiful gem.
    (D) The writer talks about the prince's money.

12. When the writer heard himself **exclaim** in surprise, he was like
    (A) a child who cries out
    (B) a king being crowned
    (C) a person who becomes faint from shock
    (D) a beautiful stone

13. How does the writer give a clue to the meaning of **galaxy?**
    (A) The writer compares the **galaxy** to a beautiful stone.
    (B) The writer links **galaxy** to the words heavens and stars.
    (C) The writer believes diamonds are a marvelous present.
    (D) The writer calls the **galaxy** a marvelous present.

14. In the story, the prince says, "You must take an **oath** promising that you will never use the knowledge of gems for the purpose of creating false jewels." Here, to take an **oath** means
    (A) to devote your life
    (B) to promise
    (C) to study
    (D) to learn about gems

15. You can tell from the story that **solitary** means
    (A) alone
    (B) favorite
    (C) splendid
    (D) clustered

16. In the story, **wardrobe** means
(A) a crown
(B) a clothes collection
(C) a picture
(D) a gem collection

17. The writer uses **ornamental** when talking about jewels. Here, **ornamental** means
(A) useful
(B) mechanical
(C) practical
(D) decorative

18. A **portrait** is the same thing as
(A) a beautiful woman wearing jewels
(B) a blue diamond
(C) a picture of someone
(D) a wealthy prince

19. The writer says, "The prince ruled the kingdom, and during this **reign**, I was his personal jeweler." Here, **reign** means
(A) a kingdom
(B) the childhood of a prince
(C) the period of time a ruler is in power
(D) a king's personal jewelry

20. In the last paragraph of the story, **honorable** means
(A) beautiful, strong, and intelligent
(B) worthy of being respected
(C) like a gem
(D) certain

READING NEW WORDS IN CONTEXT

| Lesson 10 | **CONTEXT: People and Places**

Introduction. Japan is a small country composed of four main islands and approximately four thousand smaller islands in the Pacific Ocean. However, it is one of the world's most important countries. It is highly industrialized and has a large population. What is the Japanese land like? What are Japan's natural resources?

The following article gives you an opportunity to expand your vocabulary. Below are twenty vocabulary words that are used in the article and the in exercise that follows it.

appropriate	contribute	export	import	ordinarily
assume	cultivate	forefathers	inaccurate	precipitation
boast	disadvantage	gorgeous	inviting	quantity
contrast	eliminate	hearty	occasion	tradition

The Pride of the Japanese

With good reason, the Japanese are proud of their land. One of the things they **boast** (1) of is the striking variety of Japan's geographical features. This variety is expressed in the **contrast** (2) between the snowcapped peak of Mount Fuji and the lowland plains. Mountains, agricultural fields, forests, and a rugged coastline **contribute** (3) to Japan's natural beauty. You could say that each adds to the wonder of the Japanese landscape. If you've seen pictures of the country's magnificent landscape, you have an idea of how **gorgeous** (4) it is.

Don't **assume** (5) that the Japanese islands are flat just because they contain millions of people and several large cities. To suppose so would be **inaccurate** (6). The truth is that more than three fourths of Japan is hilly and mountainous. After all, the islands were formed by volcanoes. There are 196 volcanoes in Japan, of which about 30 are active. **Ordinarily** (7), the volcanoes aren't a problem, as significant eruptions are unusual. Japan's most famous peak, Mount Fuji, looks

threatening to some inexperienced hikers. However, it remains **inviting** (8) to mountain climbers who are enthusiastic, strong, and **hearty** (9).

Unique Farming Methods

The hills might be considered a **disadvantage** (10) for farmers. But actually, Japanese farmers have been able to make the land an asset rather than a drawback. Today's farmers still **cultivate** (11) the hillsides for growing crops in the same way that their **forefathers** (12), or ancestors, prepared the land. They create terraces, or level surfaces, along the hillsides to hold the soil. The terraces also help hold water that runs down the hills. In the mountains, there is a great deal of rain and snow. This **precipitation** (13) enables rice, one of Japan's major crops, to grow. The annual rice festival is a big **occasion** (14) in rice-farming communities. This special event takes place in June or July.

Another of Japan's striking natural features is its forests. About half of Japan is covered with trees. Japan has a good timber industry. But the Japanese are careful not to **eliminate** (15) all of their forests. To keep their forests from disappearing, they limit the cutting of trees.

Japanese Trade

Although it has many natural resources above ground, Japan doesn't have a large **quantity** (16) of mineral deposits below ground. For example, the amount of iron ore in Japan is small. As a result, Japan must rely on other countries and **import** (17) from them quite a few natural resources, such as iron ore. Many of these resources are necessary for Japan's huge **export** (18) trade.

Japan sells such products as motor vehicles, steel, and electronics to other countries.

In a discussion of Japan's natural treasures, it is suitable, or **appropriate** (19), to mention the country's coastline. The eastern shore is especially rugged and beautiful. In the picturesque coastal villages, people carry on a noble, vital **tradition** (20) of fishing the ocean around Japan. However, many of the people improve upon the custom of fishing by using modern techniques to catch the fish. In general, by balancing the time-honored with the new and improved, Japan as a nation has become one of the world's success stories.

EXERCISE   *Reading Strategically*

Directions. Answer each of the following items by circling the letter of the correct answer. You may need to refer to the selection as you answer the items. The numbers of the items are the same as the numbers of the boldface vocabulary words in the selection.

1. Which of the following is an example of something that the Japanese **boast** of?
   (A) They **boast** of the false notions foreigners have about Japan.
   (B) They **boast** of the pride that the Japanese take in their land.
   (C) They **boast** of the lack of flat land to farm.
   (D) They **boast** of the striking variety of Japan's natural features.

2. The writer gives us a clue to the meaning of **contrast.** What is the clue?
   (A) The writer uses a high mountain and a low plain as an example of **contrast.**
   (B) The writer links **contrast** to the word snowcapped.
   (C) The writer says that anyone who has seen a picture of a Japanese landscape knows how gorgeous Japan is.
   (D) The writer says that the Japanese are proud of their land.

3. In the first paragraph of the article, **contribute** means
   (A) to take from
   (B) to add to
   (C) to say to
   (D) to see clearly

4. You can tell from the article that **gorgeous** means
   (A) flat
   (B) hilly
   (C) magnificent
   (D) rugged

5. What is the best meaning of **assume** as used in the second paragraph of the article?
   (A) It means to be surprised.
   (B) It means to deny.
   (C) It means to hope.
   (D) It means to suppose.

6. Which of the following is a reason that it would be **inaccurate** to call the Japanese islands flat?
   (A) Japan is home to several large cities.
   (B) Japan is actually hilly and mountainous.
   (C) Millions of people live in Japan.
   (D) Japan is quite flat.

7. How does the writer let us know that **ordinarily** means usually?
   (A) The writer says that 30 of Japan's 196 volcanoes are active.
   (B) The writer implies there is a problem with the number of volcanic eruptions in Japan.
   (C) The writer predicts an eruption.
   (D) The writer says that significant eruptions of Japan's active volcanoes are not usual.

8. All of the following are good definitions of **inviting** *except*
   (A) threatening
   (B) highly attractive
   (C) tempting
   (D) interesting

9. The writer gives a clue to the meaning of **hearty.** What is the clue?
   (A) The writer says Mt. Fuji can be threatening to some hikers.
   (B) The writer says that Japan's mountains are a **disadvantage** to farmers.
   (C) The writer links **hearty** to the words enthusiastic and strong.
   (D) The writer relates **hearty** to the word famous.

10. Which of the following is a reason that Japan's hills have not been a **disadvantage** to Japanese farmers?
    (A) The farmers have put down their hoes and started a thriving tourist industry on the mountainsides.
    (B) The farmers have stopped farming the land the way that their ancestors did.
    (C) The farmers have realized that the mountains are a drawback and now farm only on the lowland plains.
    (D) The farmers have been able to keep the land from being a drawback through creative farming techniques.

11. To **cultivate** land for growing crops as described in the selection is most similar to
    (A) hiking in the mountains
    (B) harvesting a field of wheat
    (C) putting the icing on a cake
    (D) preparing a canvas before painting

12. In the third paragraph of the article, **forefathers** means
    (A) offspring
    (B) ancestors
    (C) farmers
    (D) hillside dwellers

13. The author says that **precipitation** allows rice to grow in the mountains. Here, **precipitation** means
    (A) crops
    (B) mountains
    (C) rain and snow
    (D) dry land

14. The author writes, "The annual rice festival is a big **occasion** in rice-farming communities." Here, **occasion** means

(A) a special event
(B) a major crop
(C) people looking forward
(D) something solemn

15. How are the Japanese careful not to **eliminate** the trees of their forests?

(A) They do not allow a timber industry to exist.
(B) They keep the forests looking strikingly beautiful.
(C) They cut down more trees than they need.
(D) They do not overcut the trees.

16. The author writes, "Japan doesn't have a large **quantity** of mineral deposits below ground." Here, **quantity** means

(A) a mineral
(B) an amount
(C) a resource
(D) iron ore

17. The author says that Japan relies on other countries and **imports** many natural resources. Here, **import** means

(A) to send to other countries
(B) to have no natural resources
(C) to bring in from other countries
(D) to buy only iron ore

18. You can tell from the article that to **export** something is

(A) to produce it
(B) to bring it in from abroad
(C) to send it abroad
(D) to produce steel from iron ore

19. In the last paragraph of the article, **appropriate** means

(A) suitable
(B) lucky
(C) beautiful
(D) special

20. The author writes that the Japanese "carry on a noble, vital **tradition** of fishing the ocean around Japan." Here, **tradition** means

(A) ocean fishing
(B) custom
(C) treasure
(D) improvement

READING NEW WORDS IN CONTEXT

Lesson 11 | CONTEXT: Ecology and Environment

Introduction. Where did you first hear about environmental issues? It may have been from your parents or a teacher, or from newspapers or television news reports. You also may have been exposed to environmental concerns from the picture books you read or had read to you as a child.

The following essay gives you an opportunity to expand your vocabulary. Below are twenty vocabulary words that are used in the essay and in the exercise that follows it.

appreciate	conscience	genuine	mammoth	theme
braille	doubtless	inform	plot	urge
campaign	entertain	inspiration	reduction	visual
characteristic	furious	juvenile	text	widespread

Environmental Literature for Kids

A sense of right and wrong about the environment may not begin in the cradle. But it can begin to grow shortly afterward. Such a sense is called a **conscience** (1). For many years, publishers of **juvenile** (2) literature have done their share to spread the save-the-environment message to their young readers. The best of these books **inform** (3), or tell, about specific problems and **entertain** (4) by amusing and interesting their readers.

Bill Peet, a former artist for the Disney Studios, wrote and illustrated *Farewell to Shady Glade* in 1966. The book has become an environmental classic for young readers. The story line, or **plot** (5) of the story, is built around various animals that are forced to leave their beloved Shady Glade because it is being destroyed by huge, **mammoth** (6), monsterlike machines.

Another early environmental spokesperson for young readers was Theodor Seuss Geisel, also known as Dr. Seuss (1904–1991). In 1971, Dr. Seuss gave us *The Lorax*. In this book, an unusual creature called the Lorax begins a **campaign** (7) against environmental pollution. As part of its plan, the Lorax says that the trees can't speak for themselves, so he must speak for them. He stands on a tree stump and shouts angrily and loudly. He is **furious** (8) about the effects of pollution on the Truffula Trees, the Humming Fish, the Swomee Swans, and the Brown Bar-ba Loots. Young readers **appreciate** (9) the Lorax's colorful world, and they also value his message.

Twenty years later, author-illustrator Lynne Cherry also speaks for the trees in her book *The Great Kapok Tree*. Her written **text** (10) and the paintings that go with it focus on the preservation of the Amazon rain forest. Cherry went to the rain forest of Brazil to research her illustrations of plants, animals, and insects. The book features maps showing the original area covered by the world's rain forests and the much smaller area that the rain forests cover today. This **reduction** (11) of trees alarms environmentalists.

The Great Kapok Tree is a **visual** (12) treat. However, it is more than just pleasing to look at. Its message is timely and important. The book features various animals that try to **urge** (13) a man not to chop down a great kapok tree. Each of their attempts to convince the man tells the reader something about the relationships among the plants and animals of the rain forest.

One of today's foremost authors and illustrators of picture books, Chris Van Allsburg (b. 1941), also tackles the environmental problem. His book *Just a Dream* (1990), deals with environmental concerns in a mysterious manner **characteristic** (14), or typical, of Van Allsburg's style. In Van Allsburg's story, a young boy named Walter litters, doesn't believe in sorting trash to recycle, and makes fun of planting trees for future generations. One night, though, Walter has a dream about a future time when the earth is ruined by **widespread** (15) pollution. The thought of pollution covering a large area of the planet sincerely concerns Walter. As a result, he wakes up with a **genuine** (16) feeling of responsibility toward the environment. The idea of taking responsibility for the environment is central to the book. It is a **theme** (17) that is timely and that deserves our attention.

It is **doubtless** (18) that these books and others about the environment have reached thousands of young readers. The number of these books that have been sold proves that their audience is large. The books certainly have been an **inspiration** (19) for many readers by influencing their lives and pushing them towards new ideas. In addition to regular English editions, some juvenile books also are available in foreign language editions and in special editions such as **braille** (20), a system of writing for the visually impaired.

EXERCISE *Reading Strategically*

Directions. Answer each of the following items by circling the letter of the correct answer. You may need to refer to the selection as you answer the items. The numbers of the items are the same as the numbers of the boldface vocabulary words in the selection.

1. The writer provides a clue to the meaning of **conscience**. What is the clue?
   (A) The writer tells us that many books for young readers deal with the environment.
   (B) The writer tells us that a **conscience** is a sense of right and wrong.
   (C) The writer tells us that a **conscience** develops early in a child's life.
   (D) The writer tells us that a **conscience** is damaging to the environment.

2. How does the writer let us know that **juvenile** may mean suitable for young people?
   (A) The writer links **juvenile** to literature.
   (B) The writer links **juvenile** to birth and the cradle.
   (C) The writer links **juvenile** literature to young readers.
   (D) The writer links **juvenile** to books about the environment.

3. In the first paragraph of the essay, **inform** means
(A) to amuse
(B) to entertain
(C) to tell
(D) to worry

4. You can tell from the essay that **entertain** means
(A) to **inform**
(B) to amuse and interest
(C) to have a conscience
(D) to publish

5. What is the best meaning of **plot** as used in the second paragraph of the essay?
(A) literature
(B) building
(C) animal
(D) story line

6. In the second paragraph of the essay, **mammoth** means
(A) huge
(B) destructive
(C) noisy
(D) green

7. The writer provides a clue to the meaning of **campaign.** What is the clue?
(A) The writer identifies it as personal.
(B) The writer relates it to the environment.
(C) The writer refers to it as a plan.
(D) The writer is against it.

8. The author writes that the Lorax "is **furious** about the effects of pollution on the Truffula Trees, the Humming Fish, the Swomee Swans, and the Brown Bar-ba Loots." Here, **furious** means
(A) loud
(B) standing on a tree stump
(C) very angry
(D) interested in pollution

9. The author says that young readers **appreciate** the Lorax's message as well as his colorful world. Here, **appreciate** means
(A) readers
(B) message
(C) dislike
(D) value

10. The author writes, "Her written **text** and the paintings that go with it focus on the preservation of the Amazon rain forest." Here, **text** means
(A) written part of book
(B) preservation
(C) illustrations and drawings
(D) book cover

11. How does the writer let us know that **reduction** means the amount by which something is made smaller?
(A) The writer hints that the rain forests are near extinction.
(B) The writer links the **reduction** of trees and land to the shrinking area of the rain forest.
(C) The writer says that the **reduction** of trees is due to environmentalists.
(D) The writer says that Lynne Cherry's book features maps.

12. You can tell from the essay that **visual** means
(A) timely and important
(B) foremost
(C) connected with sight
(D) having to do with

13. All of the following are good definitions of **urge** *except*
(A) convince
(B) persuade
(C) ask earnestly
(D) force

14. The author uses **characteristic** to describe Chris Van Allsburg's mysterious manner of writing because
   (A) a mysterious manner is typical of his writing
   (B) everyone's manner is mysterious
   (C) no one understands his books because they are very mysterious
   (D) his manner is usually never mysterious

15. Walter, the hero of Chris Van Allsburg's *Just a Dream,* dreams of **widespread** pollution that poisons the planet. Here, **widespread** means
   (A) a map of a large area
   (B) covering a large area
   (C) separated from a large area
   (D) devastated

16. Which of the following is the most likely reason that Walter's feeling of responsibility toward the environment is **genuine**?
   (A) He didn't believe that **widespread** pollution was a real concern.
   (B) He woke from a troubled sleep.
   (C) His dream made him sincerely concerned about it.
   (D) He did not remember why his dream worried him.

17. The author says that taking responsibility for the environment is a **theme** of Van Allsburg's *Just a Dream.* Here, **theme** means
   (A) commitment
   (B) haunting vision
   (C) timely
   (D) main idea

18. According to the selection, why is it **doubtless** that books about the environment have reached many readers?
   (A) Only foreign language editions have sold well.
   (B) Book sales prove that the books have a large audience.
   (C) Book sales show that not many people are interested in the books.
   (D) Many people are **doubtful** that books can help save the environment.

19. In the last paragraph of the essay, **inspiration** means
   (A) a timely vision
   (B) a lifelong depression
   (C) a positive influence
   (D) books

20. What is the best meaning of **braille** as used in the last paragraph of the essay?
   (A) **Braille** is writing for the visually impaired.
   (B) **Braille** is writing for young readers.
   (C) **Braille** is writing for non-English-speaking people.
   (D) **Braille** is writing for all students.

READING NEW WORDS IN CONTEXT

Lesson 12 CONTEXT: Ecology and Environment

Introduction. Sarah Cynthia Sylvia Stout, a character in a poem by Shel Silverstein, ran into problems because she wouldn't take the garbage out. Today, the whole planet is running into problems because there is too much garbage to take out. How much garbage is there? What can be done?

The following article gives you an opportunity to expand your vocabulary. Below are twenty vocabulary words that are used in the selection and in the exercise that follows it.

adjust	corporation	foul	issue	remedy
applaud	disgust	guidance	merchandise	revolution
ballot	dissolve	hazard	persuade	temporary
candidate	employer	inexpensive	protest	villain

The Garbage Glut

Have you ever walked past a trash can on the street and noticed a **foul** (1), dirty, or rotten smell? The awful smell came from garbage.

Does the sight of litter and trash in the streets, along highways, and in public parks **disgust** (2) you? It sickens most people.

Garbage, Garbage, Everywhere

Do you worry about what eventually will happen to all the **merchandise** (3) in the stores? Much of the goods bought and sold in stores will end up as garbage.

We all produce garbage. It won't go away. Garbage lasts a long time; it's not a **temporary** (4) problem.

The **issue** (5) of garbage is part of a broader question that has to do with people's attitudes toward the environment. This question is finally being addressed. Recently, a **revolution** (6) is taking place in the way people think about garbage. In the last few years, many people have completely changed their lifestyles in order to create less garbage. Many of these people have

also tried to **persuade** (7) others to do the same. Have you been talked into reducing your garbage output?

Some eye-opening statistics may help convince you. It is estimated that each person in the United States discards an average of about four pounds of garbage every day. Such activity is not criminal, but it makes every person a **villain** (8) in the fight against garbage. An average family may throw away more than two tons of garbage a year. Most of this trash goes to overcrowded landfills where much of it will not break up for many years. For example, nonrecyclable plastics will take almost forever to **dissolve** (9). Some of the garbage is toxic. There is a risk that a toxic material will get into the soil and water and create dangers for humans. Therefore, toxic garbage can become a **hazard** (10) to the environment and public health.

What You Can Do

What can you do? There are many ways you can help **remedy** (11) or relieve the garbage problem:
• First, change your own habits so that you

produce less garbage. Recycle all that you can, including paper, cardboard, glass, cans, and aluminum. You can also recycle clothes, food, and many other items around your home. Get used to reusing what you can. If you **adjust** (12) in this way, your changes can make a big difference.

• Talk to people about the need to recycle and not throw away so much garbage. Most people want to help. They just need advice, or **guidance** (13).

• Urge people to support a **candidate** (14) running for public office who has a concern about the environment and will work for improved recycling programs. When a person votes, his or her **ballot** (15) should count for the environment.

• Ask each adult you know if his or her place of employment has a recycling program. If not, urge

the adult to talk to his or her **employer** (16) about beginning one. If the boss is worried that such a program may cost too much, explain that the program can be **inexpensive** (17) and easily organized. Check with a local or state recycling program for details.

• If a local company is a big garbage producer, petition that **corporation** (18) to recycle. The people that own and work for a company usually will listen to concerned citizens.

• Write letters of **protest** (19) if you object to a company's overuse of packaging or the packaging of products in nonrecyclable containers.

• Be sure to let individuals or companies that do a good job with garbage know that you **applaud** (20) and approve of their efforts.

EXERCISE *Reading Strategically* ☞

Directions. Answer each of the following items by circling the letter of the correct answer. You may need to refer to the selection as you answer the items. The numbers of the items are the same as the numbers of the boldface vocabulary words in the selection.

1. The writer of the article wonders if you have ever walked past a trash can and noticed a **foul** smell. Here, **foul** means
(A) pleasant and cheery
(B) silly
(C) rotten or awful
(D) delicious

2. All of the following are good definitions of **disgust** *except*
(A) to cause a feeling of excitement
(B) to sicken
(C) to produce a feeling of distaste
(D) to make ill or repulse

3. The writer of this article gives a clue to the meaning of **merchandise**. What is the clue?
(A) The writer links **merchandise** to goods bought and sold.
(B) The writer uses the synonym garbage.
(C) The writer disapproves of **merchandise**.
(D) The writer notes that people throw away **merchandise**.

4. The writer reminds us that the gar-
bage problem is not **temporary**. Here,
temporary means
(A) lasts a long time
(B) does not last a long time
(C) gigantic
(D) will never go away

5. The writer explains that the **issue** of
garbage is part of a broader question.
Here, **issue** means
(A) garbage
(B) a publication
(C) an attitude
(D) a question

6. You can tell from the article that
revolution means
(A) a complete change
(B) the environment
(C) many people
(D) time when no change takes place

7. The writer of the article gives a clue to
the meaning of **persuade**. What is the
clue?
(A) The writer hints that to **persuade**
is to bring about revolution.
(B) The writer links **persuade** to our
throwaway society.
(C) The writer connects **persuade** to
creating less garbage.
(D) The writer asks if you have
been talked into producing less
garbage.

8. The writer uses **villain** to describe
people who throw away too much
trash. Here, **villain** means
(A) hero
(B) fighter
(C) do-gooder
(D) wrongdoer

9. How does the writer of the article let
you know that **dissolve** means to
break up or melt?
(A) The writer notes that the trash in
landfills takes a long time to break
up.
(B) The writer hints that plastics are
filling up landfills.
(C) The writer thinks that our system
of recycling is breaking down.
(D) The writer explains that melting
plastic is the best way to recycle it.

10. Which of the following is an example
of a way that toxic garbage can be a
hazard?
(A) Toxic garbage is easy to store.
(B) People are learning to produce
less toxic garbage.
(C) Toxic garbage can get into the
water supply.
(D) Toxic garbage can be recycled.

11. You can tell from the article that
remedy means
(A) to make the problem worse
(B) to relieve
(C) to ignore
(D) to emphasize

12. How does the writer let us know that
adjust may mean to change in order to
correct?
(A) The writer lists several ways
people can make a difference by
changing their habits.
(B) The writer tells what can and cannot be recycled.
(C) The writer wants to make a
difference.
(D) The writer says people should
throw away everything now
before the landfills are closed.

13. In the article, another word for
guidance is
(A) need
(B) hope
(C) advice
(D) more people

14. In the article, a person who is a
candidate is
(A) elected
(B) running for public office
(C) concerned about the environment
(D) not interested in what people say

15. The author writes, "When a person
votes, his or her **ballot** should count
for the environment." Here, **ballot**
means
(A) opinion
(B) experience
(C) vote
(D) dislike

16. The writer uses **employer** when talk-
ing about the place one works. Here,
employer means
(A) place
(B) recycler
(C) friend
(D) boss

17. In the article, a program that is
inexpensive
(A) is too expensive
(B) is not easily organized
(C) is not possible
(D) does not cost a lot

18. You can tell from the article that
corporation means
(A) a garbage producer
(B) the people that own and work for
a company
(C) a group of concerned citizens who
organize to make changes in a
company's policies
(D) people who listen to citizens'
comments

19. Which of the following is the most
likely reason that you would write a
letter of **protest** to a company?
(A) You agree with the company's
policies and want to encourage it
to continue on the same track.
(B) You want to know more about the
company's policies.
(C) You object to the company's
policies.
(D) You want to apply for a job with
the company.

20. In the last paragraph, **applaud** means
(A) to approve
(B) to dislike
(C) to distrust
(D) to envy

READING NEW WORDS IN CONTEXT

Lesson 13 CONTEXT: Ecology and Environment

Introduction. You don't have to leave the city to appreciate and defend nature. Some people do, however. Some people move to the country or to the woods so they can experience more of nature firsthand. They also want to be where they can help protect nature from pollution and destruction.

The following selection tells about a remarkable woman who decided to move to the woods. The selection allows you an opportunity to expand your vocabulary. Below are twenty vocabulary words that are used in the selection and in the exercise that follows it.

absorb	debt	mourning	rebel	self-respect
amateur	duplicate	offense	regret	simplify
complaint	intrusion	omit	resident	sympathy
cooperate	keen	privacy	security	tension

Goodbye to the City

Anne LaBastille needed to get away. She wanted to escape the strain of city life and the **tension** (1) caused by the demands people made on her. She felt the need to **rebel** (2) against the control of the city. She also wanted to resist the control that other people had over her life. In other words, she wanted a less complicated way of living. To **simplify** (3) her life, she decided to go to the woods to live. This may seem like an extreme response, but it made sense for LaBastille, a wildlife ecologist. (An ecologist is a biologist who studies the relationship between living things and their environment.) She built a cabin by Black Bear Lake and another one by Lilypad Lake in the Adirondack Mountains of northern New York.

Walden Revisited

Her popular books, including *Woodswoman* and *Beyond Black Bear Lake,* reveal no troubled feeling, or **regret** (4), about her lifestyle. She clearly is in **sympathy** (5) with Henry David Thoreau, the American writer and naturalist who went to live alone with nature at Walden Pond in the 1800s. This shared understanding is clear to anyone who has read Thoreau's classic work, *Walden.*

LaBastille built her first log cabin at Black Bear Lake in the mid-1970s. She named the cabin West of the Wind. She enjoyed exploring the woods and lakes, day and night. She felt that she was a **resident** (6) not only of her cabin but also of the woods. She considered the woods her home. LaBastille also enjoyed serving as a guide to visitors. She especially liked helping women gain a sense of personal worth, of **self-respect** (7), through camping and backpacking experiences.

Because she lived and worked in nature, nature came to **absorb** (8) all of LaBastille's time. It took up her attention completely both in relaxing and in working. She soon began sharing her sharp, enthusiastic, **keen** (9) insight into nature by writing books and articles for such magazines as *National Geographic.* Readers could tell that she was a professional, not an **amateur** (10), ecologist.

Trouble in Paradise

However, advancing civilization started interrupting LaBastille's peaceful life at Black Bear Lake. One type of **intrusion** (11) was the people who kept making demands on her personal life. As a result, it became increasingly difficult for LaBastille to keep her **privacy** (12). She found that **security** (13), even in the woods, became a concern. For example, she had to lock the cabin doors at night.

Another **intrusion** into LaBastille's peaceful life came from the sky. The ecologist became extremely concerned about acid rain in the Adirondacks and **complained** (14), or protested, through her writings. Because she knew that people everywhere must work together to prevent acid rain, she urged all nations to **cooperate** (15) to stop acid rain. She also considered spraying by airplanes an **offense** (16) against nature and joined with other Black Bear Lake **residents** to stop the harmful practice.

Perhaps to escape the creeping advance of civilization, LaBastille decided to build a cabin deeper in the woods in 1984. LaBastille recognized that she owed Thoreau thanks for his inspiration. So she paid her **debt** (17) by naming her new cabin, which was on Lilypad Lake, Thoreau II. However, the new cabin was not a copy or a **duplicate** (18) of Thoreau's cabin. LaBastille's cabin was smaller than Thoreau's. To his cabin, Thoreau had added a root cellar in which to store food. LaBastille, however, didn't want a root cellar; she chose to **omit** (19) it from her design.

Unlike Thoreau, LaBastille did not live completely alone. She had the companionship of her devoted Pitzi, a German shepherd. German shepherds are great companions for women living alone in the woods, LaBastille writes. Pitzi lived with LaBastille during her first years at Black Bear Lake. LaBastille grieved when Pitzi died. However, following a period of **mourning** (20) for Pitzi, she got two other German shepherds, Condor and Chekika.

EXERCISE *Reading Strategically*

Directions. Answer each of the following items by circling the letter of the correct answer. You may need to refer to the selection as you answer the items. The numbers of the items are the same as the numbers of the boldface vocabulary words in the selection.

1. The writer gives us a clue to the meaning of **tension**. What is the clue?
   (A) The writer compares it to modern life.
   (B) The writer says it is caused by wildlife.
   (C) The writer links it to strain.
   (D) The writer says that ecology is the study of **tension** in modern life.

2. In the first paragraph of the selection, **rebel** means
   (A) to agree
   (B) to resist
   (C) to control
   (D) to escape

3. Which of the following is a reason that Anne LaBastille wanted to **simplify** her life?

(A) She had always wanted to live in the woods.

(B) Her life had become too complicated.

(C) She was a wildlife ecologist.

(D) Her life was no longer difficult enough.

4. What is the best meaning of **regret** as used in the second paragraph of the selection?

(A) **Regret** means a happy feeling.

(B) **Regret** means a change in lifestyle.

(C) **Regret** means a troubled feeling.

(D) **Regret** means looking forward hopefully.

5. You can tell from the selection that **sympathy** means

(A) shared feeling and understanding

(B) resentment toward naturalists

(C) disagreement

(D) partnership

6. Which of the following is a reason that LaBastille felt that she was a **resident** of the woods?

(A) She was a hermit.

(B) She owned the woods.

(C) She never felt as safe in the woods as she did inside her cabin.

(D) She felt that the woods were her home.

7. In the third paragraph of the selection, **self-respect** means

(A) selfishness

(B) a sense of personal worth

(C) a sense of loneliness

(D) the ability to survive in the wilderness

8. Which of the following is an example of the way that nature came to **absorb** LaBastille's time?

(A) LaBastille tried to get away from nature in her free time.

(B) LaBastille could not relax even when she was not working.

(C) It was clear that LaBastille was a professional ecologist.

(D) Nature took up all of LaBastille's attention, both off work and on.

9. All of the following are good definitions of **keen** *except*

(A) leisurely

(B) enthusiastic

(C) piercing

(D) sharp

10. The author writes, "Readers could tell that she was a professional, not an **amateur,** ecologist." Here, **amateur** means

(A) not professional

(B) professional

(C) young

(D) old

11. Which of the following is an example of an **intrusion** that bothered LaBastille?

(A) People made demands on her personal life.

(B) LaBastille never had any visitors and became lonely.

(C) LaBastille found that she could not control her temper around visitors.

(D) The people of Black Bear Lake wished that LaBastille would keep to herself.

12. Which of the following is the most likely reason that LaBastille could not keep her **privacy**?
(A) She became lonely.
(B) She did not like living in the public eye.
(C) People frequently came to visit her.
(D) Someone stole it when she left her door unlocked.

13. How does the writer let you know that **security** may mean protection or safety?
(A) The writer compares the word to a secret.
(B) The writer says **security** was a concern.
(C) The writer talks about Thoreau.
(D) The writer points out the need to lock cabin doors.

14. The author says that LaBastille **complained** about acid rain through her writing. Here, **complained** means
(A) praised
(B) concerned
(C) protested
(D) committed a crime

15. You can tell from the selection that **cooperate** means
(A) to protest
(B) to work together
(C) to complain
(D) to fight

16. The author writes that LaBastille "considered spraying by airplanes an **offense** against nature." Here, **offense** means
(A) protective measure
(B) harmful action
(C) natural purpose
(D) agreement

17. The author says that LaBastille paid her **debt** to Thoreau by naming her second cabin after him. Here, **debt** means
(A) a mortgage payment
(B) a copy of an original
(C) a rent payment
(D) something that is owed

18. Thoreau II, says the author, "was not a copy, or **duplicate**, of Thoreau's cabin." Here, **duplicate** means
(A) a payment for a debt
(B) something that is larger
(C) a copy
(D) something that is smaller

19. Choosing to **omit** a root cellar from the design of a house is most similar to
(A) choosing to put a paragraph back in an essay
(B) choosing to leave a paragraph out of an essay
(C) choosing to rewrite a paragraph of an essay
(D) choosing to publish an essay in a school newspaper

20. In the last paragraph of the selection, **mourning** means
(A) grieving
(B) peace
(C) before noon
(D) looking for

READING NEW WORDS IN CONTEXT

Lesson 14   CONTEXT: Ecology and Environment

Introduction. The world's largest land animals—elephants—are in trouble. Both the African elephant and its slightly smaller relative the Indian elephant, are on the endangered species list. Why are they in trouble? What is being done to help the elephants?

The following essay gives you an opportunity to expand your vocabulary. Below are twenty vocabulary words that are used in the essay and in the exercise that follows it.

benefit	massacre	prohibit	severe	tragedy
captivity	migrate	reckless	suburbs	unfortunate
decrease	obvious	resemble	survival	unite
eavesdrop	prey	responsibility	threat	vocal

Elephants In Danger

Elephants are big (an African elephant can stand thirteen feet tall), but a little tender, loving care still can **benefit** (1), or help, them. In recent years, many people and governments have realized what a **tragedy** (2) it would be to lose all of the world's elephants. This disaster probably will not occur. New laws and plans are helping to keep elephants alive. As a result, the species' chances of **survival** (3) may be improving.

The Ivory Trade

Perhaps you have seen pictures of a killing of a herd of elephants. Such a brutal and large-scale killing is known as a **massacre** (4). Irresponsible, uncaring, and **reckless** (5) people have wiped out whole elephant herds because they wanted ivory tusks to sell. The ivory trade was a major reason for the **decrease** (6) in the numbers of elephants in both Africa and Asia. For example, the estimated population of African elephants went from 1,300,000 in 1979 to 600,000 in 1989. Now laws in most countries **prohibit** (7) killing elephants for their tusks. These laws forbidding

the wasteful killing are a positive development. But it is **unfortunate** (8) that elephants still are hunted as **prey** (9) by illegal hunters. The unlucky elephant is still a victim of hunters who disobey the law.

A new and harsher **threat** (10) to the elephants is from increasing human populations in Africa and Asia. This possible danger is, in fact, the most **severe** (11) one facing elephants. People are taking more and more of the elephants' grazing lands for new developments. The elephants' homes are being destroyed to make room for **suburbs** (12), towns on the edges of cities. Some countries have recognized their **responsibility** (13), or obligation, to the elephants. These countries have made it their duty to create protected wildlife parks. Elephants, like humans, need enough land to maintain their societies and families. Elephants need plenty of land because they **migrate** (14), moving from place to place in search of food.

Zoos also help to save the elephants, but their role is small. Many animals don't act the same in confined areas as they do in the wild. The Indian elephant, for example, rarely reproduces in **captivity** (15). Even the most modern zoo isn't an adequate substitute for the elephant's natural environment.

Speaking Out to Help the Elephant

Increased public awareness about the nature of elephants also is important. The more people know and care about the elephant, the more **vocal** (16) they should become. Speaking out is an important step in the efforts to save the elephants. We already know that elephants **resemble** (17) humans in some ways. They may be even more similar to us than we know. It is **obvious** (18) that elephants are intelligent and sensitive. It is also clear that they have a strong sense of family. They seem to feel many emotions. Some people have seen elephants cry. Just imagine what we might discover if we could listen in, or **eavesdrop** (19), on a conversation among elephants. Don't you think people should **unite** (20) and, by working together, save these creatures?

EXERCISE Reading Strategically

Directions. Answer each of the following items by circling the letter of the correct answer. You may need to refer to the selection as you answer the items. The numbers of the items are the same as the numbers of the boldface vocabulary words in the selection.

1. You can tell from the essay that if we **benefit** the elephants, we ____ them.
   (A) like
   (B) adjust
   (C) help
   (D) stand by

2. The author writes, "Many people and governments have realized what a **tragedy** it would be to lose all of the world's elephants." Here, **tragedy** means
   (A) relief
   (B) comedy
   (C) plan
   (D) disaster

3. How does the writer provide a clue to the meaning of **survival**?
   (A) The writer speaks of having a plan.
   (B) The writer refers to keeping the elephant species alive.
   (C) The writer refers to having a disaster.
   (D) The writer tells about governments making new laws.

4. In the essay, **massacre** means
   (A) herd of African or Indian elephants
   (B) killing something
   (C) killing many animals or people
   (D) a picture of animals

5. In the second paragraph, the writer gives a clue to the meaning of **reckless**. What is the clue?
   (A) The writer describes people and elephants.
   (B) The writer uses **reckless** in a sentence with wiped out.
   (C) The writer places **reckless** in a series with irresponsible and uncaring.
   (D) The writer refers to whole herds.

6. Which of the following is an example of a **decrease** that is mentioned in the essay?

(A) The elephant population dropped between 1979 and 1989.

(B) The writer mentions two different years.

(C) The amount of elephants' grazing land taken for development has risen.

(D) The writer includes the detail of the number of tons of ivory sold.

7. In the essay, **prohibit** means

(A) to be legal

(B) to forbid

(C) to allow at certain times

(D) to relate to elephants

8. All of these are good definitions of **unfortunate** *except*

(A) unfavorable

(B) not fortunate

(C) unlucky

(D) positive

9. What is the best meaning of **prey** as used in the second paragraph?

(A) **Prey** is someone who hunts illegally.

(B) **Prey** is someone who hunts elephants.

(C) **Prey** is something that is hunted.

(D) **Prey** is something against the law.

10. You can tell from the essay that **threat** means

(A) a possible danger

(B) a population

(C) an elephant

(D) a fact

11. Another word that means nearly the same thing as **severe** is

(A) kind

(B) threatening

(C) increasing

(D) harsh

12. The writer explains that the elephants' land is being destroyed to make room for **suburbs,** towns on the edges of cities. Here **suburbs** means

(A) towns built outside of cities

(B) underground

(C) homes for elephants

(D) built on elephants' grazing grounds

13. The writer uses **responsibility** when talking about some countries' obligations to elephants. Here, **responsibility** means

(A) emotion

(B) duty

(C) recognition

(D) laws

14. The writer gives a clue to the meaning of **migrate.** What is that clue?

(A) The writer describes in great detail the elephants' diet.

(B) The writer notes how elephants move from place to place.

(C) The writer explains that elephants need a lot of sleep.

(D) The writer describes the life of elephants that live in zoos.

15. In the essay, **captivity** means

(A) outside a zoo

(B) forced confinement

(C) the natural environment of free, wild animals

(D) behavior of zoo animals

16. The author writes, "The more people know and care about the elephant, the more **vocal** they should become." Here, **vocal** means

(A) outspoken

(B) worried

(C) publicly aware

(D) written

17. The writer uses **resemble** to explain how elephants are like humans. Here, **resemble** means

(A) to know
(B) to have more
(C) to be larger than
(D) to be similar to

18. What is the best meaning of **obvious** as used in the last paragraph of the essay?

(A) **Obvious** means difficult to see.
(B) **Obvious** means clear.
(C) **Obvious** means just like an elephant.
(D) **Obvious** means senseless.

19. Eavesdrop in this essay means

(A) to join in
(B) to sit in
(C) to listen in
(D) to talk like elephants

20. Which of the following is an example of how people can **unite** to save the elephant?

(A) People can listen in on elephants' conversations.
(B) People can work hard to save the elephant.
(C) People can work together to save the creatures.
(D) People can be similar to the elephant.

Name _____ Date _____ Class _____

Lesson 15 CONTEXT: Ecology and Environment

Introduction. You may have thought concerns about the environment and ecology started in this century. They didn't, however. Many early voices of warning came during the nineteenth century. Some of these were from Native Americans who loved the land.

The following letter gives you an opportunity to expand your vocabulary. Below are twenty vocabulary words that are used in the letter and in the exercise that follows it.

anthem	ballad	frantic	justify	rehearsal
apologize	compliment	gallant	nominate	reservoir
application	courteous	hesitate	promotion	specify
associate	engage	impatience	qualify	superior

Dear Cara,

I wish you could have been at my school's Earth Day celebration this year. Last year's event was good but ordinary. By contrast, this year's celebration was far **superior** (1). My teacher asked if she could **nominate** (2) me as chairperson of the celebration. Deep down, I was unsure whether I wanted to be named to the position. I didn't **hesitate** (3) in giving my answer, though. I agreed to accept the position without delay.

Why? It occurred to me that we could use Earth Day to honor one of my heroes, Chief Seattle (1790–1866). Have you heard of him? He was a chief of the Suquamish and the Dwamish nations in the Pacific Northwest in the 1800s. We can still find many **applications** (4) today for Chief Seattle's words about the environment, so my committee and I decided to put them to use during the Earth Day celebration. People were encouraged to think about the environment when they heard Chief Seattle's words. Everyone really responded well. Because it furthered our cause, I feel that the theme, Chief Seattle Talks About the Earth, was a successful **promotion** (5).

I think the following quotations will **justify** (6) my admiration of Chief Seattle. See if they aren't reason enough for you.

•"The air is precious. It shares its spirit with all the life it supports."

•"The earth is our mother. What befalls the earth befalls all the sons and daughters of the earth."

•"What is man without the beasts? . . . Whatever happens to the beasts also happens to the man."

Chief Seattle was a brave, noble, **gallant** (7) leader. He also was **courteous** (8). The quotations above show his politeness and grace. He spoke these gentle words to United States officials who wanted to buy the land of his defeated people.

For Earth Day, some students wrote a sentimental song, a **ballad** (9), about Chief Seattle. Others used the chief's words to compose an **anthem** (10) to his ideas. This song of devotion to Chief Seattle was very moving.

Another group wrote and performed a short play about Chief Seattle. The play wasn't going well until the final practice. At that **rehearsal** (11) the play finally began to work. The actors represented a variety of animals, such as eagles, wolves, deer, bears, and horses. In the play, each of these animals was an **associate** (12) of Chief Seattle's at his meetings in Washington, D.C. They joined with him to tell about the earth. Using the animals was a clever idea of the writer, a friend of mine. I gave her a **compliment** (13) after the play, and I truly meant the praise.

As portrayed in the play, Chief Seattle showed no **impatience** (14) with government officials. He was calm and didn't seem to mind the endless government delays and interruptions. As a result, no one ever viewed him as **frantic** (15). He had a large supply, a **reservoir** (16), of strength as he urged his listeners to respect the land of his ancestors.

Chief Seattle did not define, or **specify** (17), exactly what people should do to protect the environment. However, he asked people to love and preserve the land, water, and air "for your children's children."

His ideas definitely would **qualify** (18) him as one of the country's first and greatest environmental spokespersons. Don't you think he would be fit for such a position? If he were alive today, Chief Seattle surely would **engage** (19), or join, in Earth Day celebrations.

Well, I'm sorry my letter is so long! Therefore, I do **apologize** (20). I thought you would be interested in Chief Seattle, though. I hope to hear from you soon.

Sincerely,

Kevin

EXERCISE *Reading Strategically*

Directions. Answer each of the following items by circling the letter of the correct answer. You may need to refer to the selection as you answer the items. The numbers of the items are the same as the numbers of the boldface vocabulary words in the selection.

1. How does the writer let us know that **superior** does not mean ordinary?

(A) The writer contrasts **superior** with something ordinary.

(B) The writer says that **superior** means good.

(C) The writer compares an event to a celebration.

(D) The writer shows that **superior** means worse than ordinary.

2. In the letter, **nominate** means

(A) to reject

(B) to be chairperson

(C) to be unsure of oneself

(D) to name to a position

3. As used in the first paragraph, **hesitate** means

(A) to delay

(B) to hurry

(C) to agree to

(D) to honor

4. The writer explains that even today we can find **applications** for Chief Seattle's words. Here, **applications** means

(A) worthy causes

(B) uses

(C) personal information

(D) a variety of things

5. The writer says that the theme, "Chief Seattle Talks About the Earth" was a successful **promotion** because
   (A) it was spoken by Chief Seattle
   (B) it was a good cause
   (C) it furthered their cause
   (D) the writer found few uses for Chief Seattle's words

6. You can tell from the letter that **justify** means
   (A) to deny strongly
   (B) to give reasons for
   (C) to tell everyone
   (D) to admire strongly

7. How does the writer let us know the meaning of **gallant**?
   (A) The writer links **gallant** to leader.
   (B) The writer refers to Chief Seattle's **gallant** words.
   (C) The writer suggests that **gallant** means generous.
   (D) The writer includes **gallant** in a series with brave and noble.

8. Another good word for **courteous** is
   (A) rude
   (B) polite
   (C) aloof
   (D) dignified

9. The writer uses **ballad** when describing some music played on Earth Day. Here, **ballad** means
   (A) something that weights down a ship
   (B) a sentimental song
   (C) a religious ceremony
   (D) a piece of music played on drums

10. The writer mentions that some students "used the chief's words to compose an **anthem**." Here, **anthem** means
    (A) regional music
    (B) a song sung only on Earth Day
    (C) a song of devotion
    (D) any song written by students

11. Another good word for **rehearsal** is
    (A) practice
    (B) refusal
    (C) public performance
    (D) try-out

12. The writer tells about a play in which different animals acted as **associates** to Chief Seattle. Here, **associate** means
    (A) agent
    (B) representation of an animal
    (C) fellow representative
    (D) politician

13. Which of these is the most likely reason that the writer gave his friend a **compliment**?
    (A) The writer disliked the play she wrote.
    (B) The writer thought he could write a better play.
    (C) The writer had ideas about making the play she wrote better.
    (D) The writer thought the play she wrote deserved praise.

14. Which of the following is an example of how Chief Seattle showed no **impatience**?
    (A) Chief Seattle was calm and polite.
    (B) Chief Seattle had a large supply of strength.
    (C) Chief Seattle praised the writer's clever idea.
    (D) Chief Seattle did not know what to do.

15. How does the writer give a clue to the meaning of **frantic**?
    (A) The writer connects **frantic** to a view.
    (B) The writer contrasts **frantic** and the word calm.
    (C) The writer says **frantic** describes result.
    (D) The writer uses **frantic** as a synonym of calm.

16. In this letter, **reservoir** means
(A) a reservation
(B) reserved
(C) a large supply
(D) very little

17. The writer notes that Chief Seattle did not define or **specify** what people should do for the environment. Here, **specify** means
(A) to be special
(B) to define
(C) to speculate
(D) to protect

18. The writer explains that Chief Seattle's ideas "certainly would **qualify** him as one of the country's first . . . environmental spokespersons." Here, **qualify** means
(A) to make unsuited for a position
(B) to make too good for a position
(C) to make fit or suited for a position
(D) to improve the quality of something

19. In the last paragraph of the letter, **engage** in means
(A) to join in
(B) to marry
(C) to be lively
(D) to disapprove of

20. The writer feels a need to **apologize** because he _____ writing such a long letter.
(A) is happy about
(B) is proud of
(C) hopes he succeeded in
(D) is sorry about